The
MAINE
SPORTING CAMP
COOKBOOK

by
Alice Arlen

DOWN EAST BOOKS

Map on p. 256 by Ruth Ann Hill.
Art on pages 13, 77, 135, and 195 by Mandela Johnson
Cover art by Barbara Loken
Book design by Janet L. Patterson

Recipes marked with asterisks on pages 17, 20, 45, 72, 150, and 184 excerpted from
*Maine Sporting Camps: A Year-Round Guide to Vacationing at Traditional
Hunting & Fishing Lodges,* © 2003 by Alice Arlen.
Reprinted with permission of the publisher,
The Countryman Press/W.W. Norton & Company, Inc.

ISBN 0-89272-649-0
LCCN: 2003113883
Printed at Versa Press, E. Peoria, Ill.

5   4   3   2   1

Down East Books
A division of Down East Enterprise, Inc.,
Publisher of *Down East,* the Magazine of Maine

Book orders: 1-800-685-7962
www.downeastbooks.com

Contents

Other Books by Alice Arlen

Nonfiction

Maine Sporting Camps

She Took to the Woods:
A Biography and Selected Writings of Louise Dickinson Rich

Pine Cay

In the Maine Woods:
The Insider's Guide to Traditional Sporting Camps (2 editions)

A Taste of Hallowell

Half a Mind: Hashing, the Outrageous New Sport

Poetry

2096: Journal of Indian Literature

Excavation: America Sings Anthology

About Maine Sporting Camps

When people think of Maine, most picture lighthouses and a beautiful, rugged coast. True. But upland and inland, tucked in the woods beside fresh waters, stand classic rustic compounds known as "sporting camps." Unique to the state, they are structural landmarks of a traditional way of life. Some folks call them hunting and fishing lodges, but their name correctly refers to their purpose as destinations for many sporting pastimes, such as hiking, boating, cross-country skiing, snowshoeing, snowmobiling, dogsledding, and white-water rafting as well as hunting and fishing. Maine sporting camps have always been open to paying customers and are an entrepreneurial resource distinctive to the state and an important part of Maine's cultural heritage.

The typical camp compound looks like it has grown out of the woods from which it was built. It generally includes several log guest cabins, often with woodstoves and simple accommodations, and a log dining lodge. The camps are often accessible only by boat or plane, or hours of driving over backwoods dirt roads. The reverse of a desert oasis, sporting camps are little clearings carved out of a landscape of trees.

The rise of the Maine sporting camp, starting as early as the 1850s, was due to a series of interrelated factors at work in the Northeast. Entire Indian tribes were being shipped out to the Midwest, immigrants were flooding the country, and people were on the move. Some went west in pursuit of land or gold; others stayed in the East and found their way to the newly available tribal lands. By 1860, thanks to cheap and plentiful labor, urban industrialization was well under way, and thanks in part to British capital, the American railroad system was opening up previously inaccessible areas. Five years later, at the end of the Civil War, the Northeast was poised for a huge industrial, technological, and economic expansion.

At the same time, intellectuals and writers such as Henry David Thoreau mourned what they saw as America's increasingly mechanical and fabricated culture, and society's growing alienation from nature. Published in 1864, Thoreau's book *The Maine Woods* expressed the growing conviction among the newly created and substantial upper middle class that life in the polluted, industrialized eastern cities undermined the health and welfare of both individuals and the family. He extolled an alternative life in the clean air and waters of the Maine backwoods.

Conditions were ripe for sporting camps to enter the scene. People of the post–Civil War/Victorian era discovered that canoeing, hunting, fishing, and hiking could all be enjoyed as recreational, rather than merely functional, activities. Not only did people have aesthetic and health-related motives for escaping from cities, they also had the expendable income and leisure time to fund that escape. It is no coincidence that the apex of the sporting-camp industry in Maine—the late 1800s, when at least three hundred camps were thriving—was also the golden age of lumbering, the iron and steel industries, and railroading.

At a certain point, someone realized that the very rail lines bringing *down* trainloads of Maine timber to fuel factory burners could also carry *up* trainloads of "sports," as they were known in the business, to be housed in abandoned logging camps. Enterprising individuals quickly recognized a business opportunity. They built and advertised camps, and, as sporting-camp owners, welcomed guests arriving by rail from Boston to Philadelphia and beyond. (Ironically, many who "took the airs" were families of the magnates whose factories were causing the very pollution they sought to escape.)

World War I saw a slump in the sporting-camp industry, and by the end of World War II, Americans could no longer spend the time or money on the traditional month-or-two-long vacation at a Maine sporting camp. Automobiles and "motor coaches" (campers) were replacing railroads as the major source of transportation. The road system in Maine was poor in general, and practically nonexistent into most sporting camps. Motels and campgrounds accessible by car and trailers/campers became the rage. Finally, air transportation took travelers out of New England altogether. Over the years, camps burned, some became resorts, some sold as condominiums or individual cottages, and others were simply abandoned and quietly rotted away.

Fortunately, tucked away here and there were individuals who proudly struggled to maintain a tradition that has turned out to be a crucial stabilizing factor in the Maine woods. Over the years, their descendants or long-term owners have worked steadily with surrounding large landowners (timber companies) to help preserve the quality of the resources that bring guests from all over the world to their special spots. And they have bought and hired locally, helping the rural Maine economy. Happily, these few hardy souls are now witnessing a renewed interest in Maine sporting camps.

We have come full circle. People recognize their basic need for what sporting camps have to offer: fresh air and water, natural sights and sounds, bright stars, time for real conversations with loved ones, a place to unplug, slow down, and "hear the silence." People are realizing the importance of patronizing and protecting these precious places and the pristine land surrounding them. We are fortunate indeed that sporting camps still provide solace and a wilderness playground for us all. May it ever be so!

About This Book

Since 1992, I have traveled more than 25,000 miles of mostly backwoods Maine roads researching sporting camps, and at this point, as I turn into the camp at hand, I invariably feel a sense of coming home. The essence of the sporting-camp experience is a deep sense of permanence, continuity, and connectedness. Guests come into the dining room with ruddy cheeks and a glow of well-being from a day outdoors, strangers share stories over meals of delicious home-cooked food, generations of family and friends sing songs around a campfire or the lodge piano.

The Maine Sporting Camp Cookbook gives you a flavor, literally, of the special sporting-camp world for your reading and eating enjoyment. The book is organized by season and includes quotes from camp owners along with their recipes. I have also included a map and contact information for the camps featured.

In terms of food, sporting camps generally fall into two categories: American Plan, where all your meals are provided (Modified American Plan includes only breakfast and dinner), and Housekeeping Plan, where you bring and prepare your own food. The camps featured in this cookbook offer the American or Modified American Plan; in other words, they are the "cooking camps."

Guests return to "their" sporting camp year after year in large part because the owners have created a little backwoods community that feels right to them—and this definitely includes the food served. Getting good, home-cooked meals to the table, day after day, involves huge amounts of planning, care, and time. Most of the cooks are many miles from a grocery store and often must prepare meals without the benefit of modern conveniences. Because of their remoteness and the large number of people to feed, cooks rely on bulk supplies, canned goods, and other nonperishable foods. However, breads and pastries are generally made from scratch. Depending upon the owners' location, season, and inclination, the vegetables served may involve tending a garden (and keeping the woodland creatures at bay!).

A grocery/errand day can go like this: At breakfast, review the To Do list for any last-minute additions, walk down to the dock, boat across the lake to the landing, drive an hour or so out to the food pickup (sometimes a meat truck with the weekly order), then to a grocery store and/or dairy pickup, do any other errands (hardware, post office, banking), drive back to the landing, unpack everything from the truck and repack it into the boat, boat back to camp, unpack everything from the boat and carry or wheel the loads up to the kitchen/pantry, and unload it all yet again! And this procedure happens every single week (on top of maintenance, cleaning and laundry, guest registration/pickup, guiding, camp activities, guest questions, along with the continued preparation/service of meals, and the occasional emergency or two).

Just so you know, I have not tested all the recipes in this book. I figure, most of them have fed many people for many years, so they ought to work and be good. I hope these recipes serve and please you. (If you do find a dud, maybe you can take it on as a charity case and try to improve its character!) The recipes I have tried myself have been delicious. In a few instances, as you will see, I couldn't help adding my own two-cents' worth (not by way of improving them, necessarily, just sharing what happened along the way for me).

Which brings me to how I, and a majority of the sporting-camp cooks whom I have spoken with, actually cook. I see recipes as the result of a creative process between a person and the food at hand—whether from the cupboard, field, or garden. This is how I learned to cook. My mother was a working artist, landscape designer, and immensely creative person; my father was a businessman and a gifted organic gardener. They both loved to travel, and both enjoyed cooking. Consequently, we had fresh, interesting, artistically presented food. When my mother cooked, we were regularly presented with "experiments." A few were dismal, but a high percentage were wonderful and opened our culinary horizons. For her, measuring cups and spoons were not precision instruments but convenient containers for holding liquids or solids. It was always "a pinch" here, a "dollop" there, stir it up, taste it, take a risk; add some inspiration and play around with it until it's the best you can do with what you have on hand at the time. (Actually, a great metaphor for how to approach life . . .)

Recipes are living history: recorded generosity passed along from one friend, one generation, to another. Some of the recipes in this book are undoubtedly either straight from an old cookbook or long-forgotten magazine, or are adaptations twice or thrice removed. Many are culled from years of experience in the kitchen or with the type of food that is to be prepared. They appeal to a range of palates and are generally straightforward in their preparation.

So, happy reading and happy eating!

This book honors and celebrates a very special breed of people, the sporting-camp owner, as well as the sporting-camp industry, a living Maine tradition. Sporting-camp owners truly know the meaning of the word hospitality, *and I want to thank them for their help, generosity, and kindness over the years.*

A Few Specifics

Seasons

In this book, the term *season* refers to the typical patterns followed in a sporting-camp year: The spring season is from April to June; summer from July through August; autumn from September through November; and winter from December to March. Interestingly, there is no single "best" season for sporting camps. For some, spring fishing is their busiest time; for others, it is summer, when families arrive. Other camps earn their bread and butter during the fall hunting season, and a number rely on snowmobile and ski business. Each camp, however, does have a "downtime" or two; they either close for a certain interval or they keep their fingers crossed that their busy season(s) will tide them over through the rest of the year.

Seasonal

This term means different things, of course, depending upon where you happen to live. The state of Maine itself is so large (more than 30,000 square miles), so far north (bordering Canada on three sides), and has so many ecosystems (marine and inland) that it covers three planting zones. Additionally, some of the produce featured in this book actually falls within two seasons in Maine. For example, strawberry harvest comes at the end of spring/beginning of summer; the harvest of zucchini, tomatoes, carrots, and beets straddles summer and fall. For easy reference, I have generally grouped similar items together in one season, despite the fact that in the real world they may show up in more than one season. Thus, trout/salmon recipes are grouped together mostly in the spring section even though people fish for those species in the fall as well. Some placement is arbitrary—to round out a season in this book—but hopefully will make a bit of sense.

Recipes

The recipes featured run the gamut from single-serving portions to enough to feed a camp full of hungry guests. (Most of the large recipes are easily halved.)

Also, I have included some recipes from former camp owners. They kept their special corners of the industry alive and well, and I want to honor them for their years of commitment and hard work. (Plus, they have some great recipes!) A few owners gave me recipes that appeared, perhaps with slightly altered ingredients or name, in the now out-of-print *Maine Sporting Camp Association* cookbook. In addition, there are six recipes (noted with an asterisk) that also appear in my book *Maine Sporting Camps* (see copyright page for full details).

Many camp owners shared their favorite recipes for game and locally caught fish, which they prepare for personal consumption even though they are not allowed to offer these items on their menus. However, successful hunters and anglers *may* bring in their own fish or game and have the camp chef cook it up just for them.

Recipe Comments

My added comments (in italics) in no way indicate a special preference for particular recipes. I have tried and enjoyed many of the recipes that do not have any added comments.

Terminology

I have tried to stay clear of brand names whenever possible. "Vegetable shortening" means Crisco or a similar product. "Baking spray" means something like Pam, and "dairy whip" means something like Cool Whip. Some recipes *are* product-specific, and if the product is made in Maine, I have included ordering information in the Resources section on page 255. Unless stated otherwise "can" and "package" refer to the regular size found in supermarkets, not to super-sized containers.

Spring Season
April, May, June

Come spring, in remote and seemingly placid settings across the state of Maine, a frenzy of activity is under way. Many sporting camps close during the winter, so spring is the beginning of a new year for them, and April is the time for opening up camp. It is a huge undertaking. Although it may seem a romantic or tranquil way of life—and there *are* such moments, otherwise people wouldn't do it—sporting-camp ownership involves a lot of good old hard work.

A Maine winter usually leaves souvenirs of its presence, by way of fallen limbs, damaged roofs or leaky interiors, and droppings of the tiny critters that have managed to bite or burrow their way into cabins or sheds, or even kitchens. This all needs to be cleaned and fixed, the mechanical systems (boat motors, plumbing, generator, cabin and kitchen stoves) have to be in working order, beds and baths must be prepared, new staff may have to be trained, and large quantities of food need to be lugged in. And all of this happens while the weather is still "nippy" (around freezing) and roads are covered in slushy snow or slippery with mud. The tiny window of prep time closes rapidly.

Because there are four distinct seasons in Maine, people look forward to signs that spring has arrived. Ice begins to break up on the lakes and rivers (many folks stake small sums on ice-out date contests); male loons arrive on the newly opened waters; and the hillsides reverberate with shrill "come hither" calls for their mates. The warming earth sends forth cold-hardy, astringent eatables such as dandelion greens, fiddleheads, rhubarb, chives, and asparagus to cleanse our intestinal systems and build health for our bodies. The irony is that most sporting-camp owners are too swamped with chores and visitors to spend time in fields and marshes foraging and picking, and rely instead on local or regional suppliers for bulk produce.

May and June signal the arrival of "schools" of anglers eager to catch the cold-water trout and salmon that are surface feeding on newly hatched insects. Meanwhile, lettuce, radishes, spinach, herbs—"salad fixin's"—are poking their way up in camp gardens. In woods and fields, newborn animals rise up on wobbly legs, and everywhere the rush of life takes hold. Sporting camps are generally in full swing by this time, and many long-term fishing friendships pick up where they left off the year before. Since more people are practicing catch and release, the quality and quantity of the fish has been getting better and better. Naturally, a few freshly caught specimens do make their way into sporting-camp kitchens. This blissful, busy rite of spring continues until the end of June, when waters warm up and the school year is over.

Breakfast Fare

– Bear Spring Cinnamon Rolls for a Crowd –

Peg Churchill: "We have a standard menu that's been the same for decades: turkey on Wednesday, chicken on Sunday, ham on Tuesday. Thursday and Friday are surprise days where we feature what's in season or try new recipes. I do the ordering, and Ron and I will work on the job training for new staff. We have a high percentage of people who have been working with us for years. The prize definitely goes to our chef, Mr. Pearl, who has been here for over fifty years!"

Edward Pearl Sr.: "I use my basic bread dough for these rolls."

The Bear Spring Basic Bread Dough recipe on p. 22 will make 50 rolls. Halve or quarter the original recipe if you want a smaller yield. For a smaller batch of dough, 1 cup of confectioners' sugar will make enough glaze for a 9 x 13-inch pan.

Prepare desired amount of Bear Spring Basic Bread Dough (p. 22), and let it rise once, then punch down and shape the rolls. If you are making a full recipe, cut the prepared dough into fourths. If making half the dough recipe, divide it in two. Roll out each piece into a rectangle about 3/4 inch thick, and top with the following cinnamon-sugar mixture.

Cinnamon-Sugar Mixture (amount for each dough rectangle, about 12 rolls):

   3 tsp. cinnamon, 1/2 cup brown sugar

Sprinkle the mixture evenly over each rectangle and roll up the dough into long "sausages" approximately 2 1/2 inches in diameter at the ends. Slice into rounds about 1/2 inch thick and place in greased 9 x 13-inch pans. (I use 16 x 26-inch pans, which hold 6 rolls across and 9 down.) Let the rolls rise again for 1/2 hour.

Preheat the oven to 400°. Bake the cinnamon rolls for 20 minutes.

Glaze:

   Full batch—**3 cups confectioners' sugar, milk**
   Smaller batch—**1 cup confectioners' sugar, milk**

In a bowl, combine sugar with enough milk to get the consistency of heavy syrup. Dribble the glaze over the rolls while they are still hot. Remove from pan(s) and serve.

– Cobb's Maple Nut Crunch –

Betty Cobb: "It takes us three trips to open up for the season. The first trip (early to mid-April), we can generally make it to camp over the ice (on Pierce Pond). We bring a portable 'winter kitchen' and food supplies with us. We have as many people as we can find come in for the weekend, and we wash every log and clean out all the wood stoves and fix the major damage from winter. For the second trip, if we don't like the way the ice looks, we have to walk around the edge of the lake. That's when we take down all the curtains, do all the linens. This is by hand, using the old wringer washing machine on the 'wash porch.' We clean the rugs, the bedspreads, iron everything, make sure the generator works. By May 1, fishing season opens, if the ice is out.

"I remember one time I was at Lindsay Cove (the end of the road) with food for the camps. The ice hadn't gone out yet and we were in the third-trip phase. I got to camp and there were fishermen already there. A couple had walked around the lake—holding their cat in a cage and a bouquet of flowers—and here there's ice on the lake and the wind's blowing a gale! This is typical stuff. Anyway, the third trip we put it all together: We get the generator and kitchen up and running, wash all the dishes, wash all the windows, and do the rest of the yard work."

Gary Cobb: "We just keep doing stuff until it's done . . . which is never!"

2 cups whole flax seed, $1/2$ cup chopped walnuts, $2/3$ cup maple syrup

Combine ingredients in a bowl until well blended. Spread on a cookie sheet and bake at 350° for 5 minutes. Remove from the oven and stir. Return to the oven, and bake an additional 5 minutes.

· ·

MAPLE SYRUP

One of the annual spring activities around several sporting camps is tapping maple trees and boiling up maple syrup. You put on your snowshoes, go out with an auger, and drill into the sugar maples about two inches deep and about two to three feet from the ground (the lower you drill into—or "tap"—them, the faster the sap flows). They say the old-timers used to cut into the trees with an axe, which killed the tree after about five years!

Today, the process can be an elaborate operation, complete with miles of plastic tubing that feed into a "boiling-off" shack. The raw sap runs thin and clear and is not very sweet. See p. 74 for more information.

– Cobb's French Toast –

Betty Cobb: "Our neighbors at Abbe's Island gave me this recipe. I like making something the night before and just slipping it into the oven the next morning."

> **1 T butter, 1 loaf day-old white bread cubed, 1 (8-ounce)**
> **package cream cheese cubed, 12 large eggs, 1^1/$_2$ cups milk,**
> **^{1}/$_3$ cup pure maple syrup**

Butter a 9 x 13-inch baking pan. Spread half the bread in the pan. Sprinkle half the cream cheese cubes over the bread. Repeat with remaining bread and cheese. Whisk together the eggs, milk, and maple syrup and pour over the mixture in the pan. Cover and refrigerate overnight.

In the morning, preheat oven to 350°. Bake, uncovered, for 30 to 40 minutes or until a knife inserted in the center comes out clean. Let the French toast stand for 15 minutes. Serve warm with additional maple syrup and/or preserves or fruit compote.

– Deer Run Buckwheat Pancakes* –

Darlene Berry: "People love these. If you don't have buttermilk on hand, we've found you can use regular milk with two teaspoons cream of tartar and two tablespoons melted butter. Also, we use the best buckwheat we can find [see Resources section for information about Ployes Buckwheat], and only real Maine maple syrup. You can also sprinkle fresh fruit on top of the pancakes while on the griddle, then flip them to cook the other side."

> **1 cup white flour, 2 cups buckwheat flour, 1 tsp. baking soda,**
> **buttermilk to make a thin batter, 1 egg (optional)**

In a big bowl, combine all ingredients. If batter is sticky, add the egg. Ladle onto a preheated, greased griddle. Cook until brown on one side; flip and brown the other side.

• •

STRAWBERRIES

Depending upon where you live in Maine, strawberries can be available fresh at the end of June or at the beginning of July. The wild variety is small, about the size of a blueberry, and sweet. They hold their shape and flavor in baked goods.

• •

– Eagle Lake Strawberry Pancakes –

Ed Clark: "I like to think of our place as a 'new' 130-plus-year-old set of sporting camps. We've brought back the dining room and installed a new kitchen. The birch-bark wall lining in our guest log cabins is a unique thing here, and the lodge stone fireplace is billed as one of the largest in Maine.

"Eagle Lake is in the very northern part of Maine, only eighteen miles from Canada. Paula and I first saw the camps at the beginning of April, and we were able to drive across the lake in a truck a couple of times, the ice was still so thick. This is the time of year for making maple sugar—you want warmish days and cool nights.

"We make pancakes served with pure maple syrup made here in Eagle Lake Village by Lucien Dube, who will often deliver the syrup from his camp right across our thoroughfare. I've always gotten rave reviews by using Bisquick. I basically follow the directions on the box, but I never measure, and I go heavy on the eggs. Don't forget to have the berries at room temperature so the pancakes will cook thoroughly."

During the summer season, small, wild Maine blueberries or strawberries can be substituted for the sliced strawberries.

2 cups Bisquick, 2 eggs, 1 cup milk, 1 tsp. vanilla, 1 cup thin-sliced strawberries

The amounts above will make 14 pancakes. Estimate how many servings you'll need, and go from there.

I put the eggs in a bowl, determine how much Bisquick and milk I'll need, and then stir those ingredients together with a whisk to make a fairly thin batter. (You can tinker with it until it reaches the desired consistency.) My "secret ingredient" is the vanilla.

Slice the strawberries very thin. Get a greased pancake skillet hot, and pour out a batch of pancakes. Sprinkle strawberries on the top center of the pancakes, pushing them down into the batter with a fork or knife.

Don't forget to serve with real maple syrup!

– Harrison's Baked Eggs –

Tim Harrison: "We're about 170 miles from Mount Katahdin, the northern terminus of the Appalachian Trail, and hikers going from north to south come through here in the spring. There's a short side trail from a lean-to at the southern end of Pierce Pond that leads right to our camps. We offer the hikers our famous twelve-pancake breakfast. Fran and I both like to cook, and I do the breakfasts. I make the pancakes thin, put in different types of fruit, and sprinkle them with confectioners' sugar—because hikers *really* love sugar. Here's something else our guests love."

For each serving:
> 2 large eggs, 1/3 to 1/2 cup cooked ham and/or bacon cut into bite-sized pieces, 1/3 to 1/2 cup shredded mozzarella and ched-dar cheese, 5 or 6 low-salt Ritz crackers crumbled, chopped fresh chives (optional)

In a 4-inch-diameter baking dish, carefully drop in the eggs. Cover with the ham/bacon. Sprinkle on the cheeses and top with cracker crumbs. Bake at 400° for 15 to 20 minutes. Remove from the oven and sprinkle with chives (if desired). Serve immediately. (Remember to use an oven mitt!)

– Mount Chase Poached Eggs for a Crowd –

Sara Hill: "For this, I just use a muffin pan or two, put the pan(s) in water, and bake the eggs in the oven. I think they're called 'shirred eggs' when cooked this way."

Preheat the oven to 400°. Take your muffin pan(s) and spray each cup with cooking spray. Break an egg into each cup and sprinkle each with salt and pepper to taste. If you like, sprinkle a little cheese on top, too (I like Monterey Jack or cheddar). Place the muffin pan(s) in a slightly larger pan and fill larger pan with hot water to reach halfway up the muffin pan. Bake for 15 to 20 minutes or until the eggs are done the way you like them.

– Rideout's Brunch Lemon Landlocked Salmon –

Jami Lorigan: "It's busy here in the beginning of April, trying to get things ready. By mid-April, once we're open, it's even more frenzied. By May 1, it's crazy. Fortunately, we've had very steady help over the years. Some of our staff have been here since Larry Rideout opened the place in 1947. No matter who is staffing the kitchen, we still use our traditional old recipes. Most of our landlocked salmon is caught in the spring. People say this recipe is the best fish they've ever had."

Gut, scale, and rinse each salmon well in cold water. Do not cut off the head. Place fish on top of a square of heavy foil. Place 3 T butter inside the belly cavity along with 4 slices of lemon. Salt and pepper to taste. Place 3 or 4 more slices of lemon on top of each fish, then bring the foil around the fish and roll it down to seal, making a little packet.

Put the foil packet(s) in a baking dish and cook at 325° for 35 to 45 minutes, or until the fish is flaky and falls off the bone (you'll be able to easily lift all the bones right out). We serve the salmon (still in the foil packets) on individual plates, and guests enjoy the wonderful lemon aroma when they unwrap their fish. (My cooks check the fish before serving to make sure it is fully cooked, and if it doesn't look presentable, they simply put it on a plate with a little extra lemon for garnish.)

– West Branch Pond Breakfast Trout* –

Carol Kealiher: "West Branch Pond Camps have been in our family since 1910. My mother inherited the camps when I was two and a half years old, and I'm the second generation in the female line running it. In the spring of 1974, our little family of two adults (Andrew and me) and our two kids (two-year-old Jack and seven-month-old Nathan) took over the care and running of the camps.

"The pond is fly-fishing, with nice pan-sized brook trout. Although we encourage catch and release, we'll cook breakfast trout for people from time to time. People sure appreciate our home-cooked food here."

6 slices bacon, 6 (8- to10-ounce) trout (cleaned, with heads and tails still on), 1 1/4 cup yellow cornmeal, salt and lemon pepper to taste, 1/3 cup canola oil, 4 thinly sliced pieces of lemon or orange, parsley for garnish

Fry the bacon in a cast-iron pan until crisp and brown. Place on a paper towel and set aside. Reserve the bacon fat. Rinse the fish, then dredge it in cornmeal. Salt and pepper both sides to taste. Add the canola to the bacon fat. Heat the oil/fat until very hot, but not smoking. Fry the trout for 3 to 4 minutes per side. (Use spaghetti tongs or a wide pancake turner for turning.) Shake the pan frequently to avoid sticking. The trout should be golden and crisp on the outside, moist and tender on the inside. (If your pan is too small, cook the fish in batches and keep warm in a low oven.) Serve one trout per person. Garnish as you wish with the lemon/orange, some parsley, and the bacon (crumbled). Serves 6.

– Tim Pond Pancakes at a Glance –

Betty Calden: "Here is an easy reference for making pancakes. The amounts listed assume three large pancakes per serving. Add more milk if you like a thinner consistency. Chocolate chips or any kind of berry can be gently stirred into the batter at the end."

Ingredient	2 servings	5 servings	10 servings
flour	2 cups	5 cups	10 cups
baking powder	4 tsp.	10 tsp.	6 $2/3$ T
sugar	4 T	10 T	1 $1/4$ cups
salt	1 tsp.	2 $1/2$ tsp.	5 tsp.
cooking oil	4 T	10 T	1 $1/4$ cups
eggs	2	5	10
milk	2 cups (+)	4 cups (+)	8 cups (+)

Breads

– Bear Spring Basic Bread Dough –

This is a helpful backwoods recipe because none of the ingredients needs refrigeration. It makes 4 loaves, but can easily be halved.

Ron Churchill: "We have thirty-two cabins at Bear Spring Camps, so it's a lot to take care of. We put up posters locally, and the first week in April, over school break, we have kids raking and removing the blow-downs, dealing with repairs from winter damage. We also hire part-time help each Saturday to assist the cabin girls with the changeover. Many of our full-time staff people are re-hires. Then, the Monday after school break, I hook up all the water systems. By the second week after ice-out, we have a crew that comes in and puts in all the docks. It's basically the same crew we've had for twenty years. Two weeks before camp opens, we send out the kitchen orders and supplies start rolling in. Finally, ten days before Memorial Day, we open."

> 1 quart (4 cups) lukewarm water, 3 T yeast, 1 T salt, 1 cup
> sugar, 1 cup ($1/2$ pound) lard or shortening, 1 cup dry milk,
> 8 cups flour

Mix together all the ingredients except the flour in a large mixing bowl, and let it work for 15 minutes or so, or until bubbly. Add the flour gradually and mix in a mixer, using the dough hook. (It can also be kneaded by hand.) Add flour until the dough no longer sticks to the side of the bowl. Set bowl, covered, in a warm place to rise (about an hour).

Punch down dough and place onto a floured surface. Form into 4 loaves and place in greased loaf pans. Let rise again until loaf sized.

Bake at 350° for approximately 35 minutes, or until loaf is golden brown, and the top, when tapped, sounds hollow.

You can also form the dough into dinner rolls by shaping into balls, or placing chunks in greased muffin pans. Let rise and then bake for 20 minutes.

– Bowlin's Biscuits –

**3 cups flour, 5 tsp. baking powder, 1/2 tsp. salt, 1 stick butter,
1 cup whole milk**

In a bowl, sift together first three ingredients. Then add little slices of butter and incorporate (we use our fingers) until well mixed in. Using a fork,
stir in the milk until mixture holds together. Turn out onto a lightly floured
surface and pat—do not roll out—until dough is about 1/2-inch thick. Cut
with a large donut cutter (or glass). Bake at 425° for 5 to 7 minutes or
until golden brown. Serves 8 to 12 (depending on size of cutter).

– Bradford's Cream Biscuits –

Igor Sikorsky: "Bradford's was started in 1890. We're located at the headwaters of the
Aroostook River watershed, which empties into the St. John River, which then heads
north and east into New Brunswick. Most rivers everywhere else flow south, but the
waters in northern Maine all flow north."

Karen Sikorsky: "Igor and I have created a way to be sporting-camp owners together
without falling into the old wife-in-the-kitchen, husband-outdoors roles. Although we both
have very strong opinions, this job works for us because we're willing to be flexible and
we have a shared sense of humor."

**2 cups flour, 1 tsp. salt, 1 T baking powder, 2 tsp. sugar,
1 to 1 1/2 cups heavy cream, 1/2 cup melted butter**

Combine the dry ingredients. Slowly add the cream, mixing together
gently, until the mixture comes together as dough. Knead lightly for
1 minute on flour-dusted board. Pat the dough to 1/2 inch thick and cut
it into 12 biscuits. Dip each piece into the melted butter, coating on all
sides, and place 2 inches apart on a cookie sheet.

Preheat the oven to 425° and bake the biscuits for about 15 minutes,
or until they are golden.

– Cobb's Cloud Rolls –

Gary Cobb: "When we open up, we wash the insides of all the log cabins, sweep snow off the roofs, wash the windows—it goes on and on. There's no water then. You have to dig a hole in the ice, pump up the water, then lug it around. But it's a very beautiful time of year because you're here in total wilderness; there's not another person or human sound."

Betty Cobb: "This comes from Mrs. Judson's bread recipe. She and 'Pa' Judson ran the first motel at Sugarloaf [ski area] when it was just starting up. Many people in Maine work one job in the fall/winter and another in the spring/summer, so some of her people worked for us here at Pierce Pond during our season [May through mid-November]."

Betty lists this recipe just as "Mrs. Judson's Bread," but I call it "Cloud Rolls" because I've tasted them . . .

**1 1/2 quarts (6 cups) warm water, 1/2 cup sugar, 1 T salt,
3 packages dry yeast, 1/2 cup oil, 12 to 14 cups flour,
1 cup (plus) melted margarine/butter**

In a big bowl, or big mixer, combine water, sugar, salt, and yeast and let it sit for 10 minutes. Add oil and enough flour so that dough holds together and pulls away from sides of bowl. Let rise until double in bulk. Punch down and turn out onto a floured board.

Cut or pull into pieces about the size of an egg. Knead each piece in the palm of your hand. Dip each piece in the margarine/butter on sides and bottom (not the top) and place pieces right next to each other in a big baking pan (or two). Let rise again until nearly double.

Bake in a 350° oven for 30 to 35 minutes, or until tops are light golden brown.

– Enchanted Outfitter's Pita Bread –

Gloria Hewey: "There are about a dozen white-water rafting companies in the West Forks area, and in the spring hundreds of people are up here enjoying the rivers. In addition to the cabins, we have a restaurant that's open to the public. I'd never run a restaurant or bar before we came here in 2001, and I was trying to do everything myself. Talk about a quick learning curve! We were full every weekend. I remember the day I had a bar full of people waiting for drinks and twelve orders waiting to be cooked. One of the rafting guides tried to help me. My husband, Craig, came in and got going at the bar. Next day, a lady up the road called. She worked the whole season and wouldn't take a penny.

"I started making this recipe on a wood-burning cookstove when I was raising my daughter in a log cabin. I like to use it for sandwiches here at camp because it holds in whatever filling you're using. If you have a glass section on your oven door, look in and watch the pitas cooking. They puff right up like balls."

> **5 to 6 cups flour, 1 T sugar, 2 tsp. salt, 1 T dry yeast (1 package), 2 cups warm water (120° to 130° on candy thermometer)**

In a big bowl, add all the ingredients and mix thoroughly. Add enough flour to make a soft dough that pulls away from the side of the bowl, adding an additional 3/4 cup if necessary. Place in a greased bowl. Turn to expose greased top, cover with a clean kitchen towel, and let rise in a warm place until double in bulk (about 1 hour).

Preheat oven to 450°. Punch down the dough and divide it into 6 pieces. Roll out pieces to the size of a large pancake. Bake on lightly greased pan for about 5 minutes or until light brown.

– Maynard's Cinnamon Bread –

Gail Maynard: "We've been lucky that our place has been in the same family for generations. So much in Rockwood [on Moosehead Lake] depends on our type of business. There are no factories around. People in the area look forward to the start of the season each year. My crew works for four or five months, and then they have to look for work somewhere else.

"One of our guests gave this recipe to me years ago. I generally serve it for supper, but it also makes wonderful toast (or French toast) for breakfast."

> *Cinnamon Bread:*
> **1 cup sugar, 1/2 cup shortening, 2 eggs, 1 tsp. vanilla, 1 cup sour cream, 1/4 cup milk, 2 cups flour, 1 1/2 tsp. baking powder, 1 tsp. baking soda, 1/2 tsp. salt**

> *Sugar Mixture:*
> **1/4 cup granulated sugar, 2 tsp. ground cinnamon, 1 1/2 tsp. grated orange peel**

In a bowl, cream together the shortening and sugar. Add the eggs and vanilla and blend in the sour cream and milk. In another bowl, combine the dry ingredients, then mix with the creamed ingredients.

Spread a quarter of the batter in a greased bread loaf pan and sprinkle the sugar mixture over it. Add the remaining batter. Sprinkle the remaining sugar mixture on top. Take a knife and gently swirl the cinnamon-sugar mixture into the batter.

Bake in a 350° oven approximately one hour, or until toothpick inserted in the center of bread comes out clean. Remove from the pan and let bread cool on rack.

– Rideout's Biscuits –

Jami Lorigan: "We use these for our Turkey Pot Pie [page 163] or for strawberry shortcake, or they're delicious on their own."

(See the Resources section for information aboutBakewell Cream.)

**4 cups flour, 4 tsp. baking soda, 2 tsp. Bakewell Cream,
pinch of salt, 1/2 cup vegetable shortening, 2 cups milk**
Sift the first 4 ingredients into a big bowl. Cut in the shortening with a fork. Add milk and blend lightly with the fork. Dough should have a slightly sticky consistency. Sprinkle a countertop with some flour and spoon dough onto flour. Gently form a dough ball and pat all surfaces with flour. Flatten dough to a 1- to 1 1/2-inch thickness with palm, then roll out to about 1/2-inch thickness. Using round cutter (glass, can, or biscuit cutter), cut as many biscuits as possible. Gently compact the remaining dough, then flatten to proper thickness with palm. Repeat until dough is used up, handling it as little as possible. Place in a buttered rectangular baking pan, right next to each other. Bake at 425° for 10 minutes or until nicely browned.

Appetizers

– Bosebuck's Mainer Meatballs –

Diane Schyberg: "We're in a 500,000-acre wilderness area and have a thirteen-mile dirt access road which is basically unusable during spring thaw, so we have only a couple of weeks at the end of April to pull everything together. One of the things I notice this time of year is the number of moose along the roads. They're coming up to lick the salt left over from the winter plowing and sanding. We can't serve moose meat to the public, but these are very good if you happen to have some. You can use any other kind of ground meat."

Meatballs:
1 pound ground moose meat, 2 T olive oil, 1 egg, 1 tsp.
crushed garlic, 1/4 cup seasoned breadcrumbs, 1/4 tsp. salt,
1/8 tsp. pepper
Combine well. Form into 1 1/2-inch balls. Brown in large frying pan or Dutch oven, in 1/4 cup olive oil.

Sauce:
1 can mushroom soup, 1 can water, 8-ounce can sliced
mushrooms, 1/4 cup red wine
Combine and pour over meatballs. Simmer for half an hour. Serve on a small plate and garnish with parsley. These can also be served as an entrée over egg noodles.

– Eagle Lodge Bat Wings –

Here is the first of several Heritage Recipes that I have included to honor former long-term sporting-camp owners, who have all been very conscious of passing the helm along to able stewards of their properties and guest lists. Individually and collectively, the people noted (as well as others not included because of the format/criteria of the book) have made a lasting, positive impact on the sporting-camp industry and on the lives of the people they have touched, including mine. This Heritage Recipe is from Tami and John Rogers, who owned Eagle Lake Camps from 1994 to 2004.

John Rogers: "In May 1997, we started our first Maine Guide School session."

Tami Rogers: "And then we added our Sea School, for a captain's license, and our Wellness Retreats. For our spring retreat, people would come and fish, watch the moose and other wildlife, relax. One of the features of opening up cabins in the spring is bats. They are a welcomed and not-so-welcomed friend of sporting-camp owners. They are friends because they help eliminate some of the unwanted insects. They're not so welcomed when they show up in places where they shouldn't be. This can create sweaty palms, heart palpitations, shallow breathing, and lots of ducking out of the way. When this happens, the only good bat is a 'bat wing' bat."

> **1 (5-pound) bag "bat" (chicken) party wings, 1 tsp. dry mustard, 1/2 cup molasses, 1/2 cup soy sauce, 1/3 cup vegetable oil, 3 cloves minced garlic, 1 chopped onion, salt and pepper to taste**

Place the chicken wings in a large freezer bag or container. In a bowl, combine remaining ingredients and pour over the chicken. Refrigerate overnight, or at least 8 hours.

Place the chicken on a baking pan lined with tinfoil and bake at 350° for 1 hour. Yummy, and a great reward for surviving those bats!

– Indian Rock Frogs' Legs and Crawfish –

JoAnne Cannell: "Ken is a Micmac. There have been a number of intermarriages among the Passamaquoddys, whose reservation surrounds us in Grand Lake Stream, and the Micmacs and Penobscots, but they each still have a real sense of their history as individual tribes. Ken and I are both very interested in tradition, history, and nature, and we like to eat off the land when we can."

Ken Cannell: "At the end of June around here, the big bullfrogs come out of the marshes and don't mind being seen. You hear their mating calls at night. That's when I go into the small bogs, marshes, and ponds covered with lily pads and spear them with a four-pronged metal spear (on the end of a broomstick, so I can reach out far enough). I pass them to a friend in the back of the canoe, where we have a board across the gunwales. He chops off the legs, which drop into a little bucket below the board, and discards the frog body, which is then lunch for fox, blue herons, and eagles. We usually get about a bread bag full.

"I love frogs' legs with crawfish, which you can find at night with a flashlight in any body of water around the state. Raccoons and blue heron feed on crawfish, and if there are eels in a lake, they will come in close at night and eat them, too. Lake trout love them. They look a bit like tiny lobsters, and you cook them the same way."

Frogs' Legs:

Skin the frogs' legs by taking a fork and placing a prong on each side where you've cut them, and just pull down. Roll the legs in flour and Italian breadcrumbs.

Heat about 1 inch of cooking oil, along with 2 to 3 tsp. of butter, in a large, heavy skillet until it's hot enough to sear the meat immediately. Cook the legs until they are brown, about 1 1/2 minutes per side. Be careful not to overcook, because the meat is so tender. It tastes like a cross between chicken and sweet pork chops and just melts in your mouth.

Crawfish:

Pour one inch of water into a pot and add a little salt. Heat the water to boiling and pour in the crawfish. Cover the pot and steam/boil the crawfish 3 to 5 minutes, until they turn bright red. The frogs' legs and crawfish are so delicate and tasty, I don't dip them in anything.

– Katahdin Lake Sautéed Dandelion Blossoms –

Suzan Cooper: "Dandelion blossoms should be picked in the morning, when they are fully open. Since they close when they are washed, picking in a clean, unsprayed area is important. We are fortunate. Our camps have been here since 1885, and when Baxter Park was created in 1930, it gave us a 200,000-acre next-door neighbor. There are no other public camps within eleven miles of us in any direction, so we truly are in a wilderness area. This is a special spring dish and is wonderful with trout."

2 cups dandelion blossoms, 2 eggs beaten, 1/2 tsp. salt, 1/2 cup butter, 1/2 cup (approx.) flour, salt and pepper to taste

Cut any dandelion stems back to about 1/4 inch long. Beat the eggs and salt lightly in a small bowl. Melt the butter in a skillet. Place flour on a shallow bowl or plate and dip the blossoms individually first into the egg, then into the flour. Place into the skillet pom-pom side down (stem up) and sauté until lightly browned. Season with additional salt and pepper if desired. Serves 4.

– Katahdin Lake Trout Patties –

Al Cooper: "These are so good! They are a great way to use any cooked trout you may have left after a big feed."

> **2 cups cooked trout (bones and skin removed), 1 egg beaten,
> 2 T milk, 1/3 cup diced onion, 1/2 cup flour, 1 1/2 tsp. baking
> powder, 1/2 cup dry breadcrumbs, 1/2 cup oil**

In a bowl, combine all ingredients up to breadcrumbs and mix well. Form into half-inch-thick patties. Pour breadcrumbs into a shallow bowl or plate and coat the patties lightly on both sides (adding more breadcrumbs if needed). Heat oil in a skillet and fry the patties.

– McNally's/Nugent's Whitefish Nuggets –

John Richardson: "Ice-out doesn't happen here at Nugent's, along the ninety-two-mile Allagash Wilderness Waterway, until the middle of May, so it's exciting canoeing waters in June. We offer a popular excursion: a thirty-mile motorized canoe trip to McNally's, our other camp. It's a great way to see remote Maine and still sleep in a dry, warm bed. What with running canoe trips and hosting fishermen, May and June are two of our busiest months."

Regina Webster: "This recipe features the whitefish from Chamberlain Lake at Nugent's Camps. It can also be made with lake trout."

> **1 large whitefish (or lake trout), 1/2 cup flour, 1/4 tsp. pepper,
> 1 tsp. garlic salt, 3/4 cup Bisquick, 1 egg, 1 cup stale beer (or
> water), cooking oil**

Fillet a freshly caught whitefish. Cut the fillets into 1-inch cubes. On a plate, combine the flour with the pepper and garlic salt. In a bowl, mix the Bisquick with egg and beer (or water). The batter should be the consistency of pancake batter. Add more liquid if necessary. Dip the fish chunks into the flour first, then into the beer batter.

In a heavy saucepan or deep fryer, fry the fish in at least 2 inches of oil, 4 or 5 pieces at a time. Cook 2 minutes or until golden brown.

– Penobscot Lake Trout Pierre –

Paul Fichtner: "We are lucky to have a healthy population of blueback trout here at Penobscot Lake Lodge. This makes into a wonderful plate of fish that will keep your guests asking for more. It is rich, with a delicate flavor and is routinely served here as a welcome hot appetizer on still-cool spring evenings (or anytime!).

> **3 to 5 (8- to 10-inch) trout (preferably blueback trout, but brook trout will do), 1 cup chopped onion, 2 sticks salted butter (no substitutes!), salt and fresh-ground pepper to taste, 1 cup Chablis or chardonnay wine**

In a large skillet, on low heat, sauté the onions in the butter. Add the fish, sprinkle with salt and pepper, turn the heat to medium, and cook the fish. After 2 to 3 minutes, add the wine and continue to cook on medium heat until the fish is done (when it flakes with a fork at the thickest part) and the wine has cooked off.

– Spring Greens –

After months of writing this cookbook, I find myself absolutely compelled to jump in with one recipe per season. I look forward to all or part of these spring greens every May. Dandelions conveniently pop up in my asparagus patch the same time fiddleheads are ready for picking. Fiddleheads are tightly curled-up ferns that grow in sandy riverbeds or marshy areas. There is only a short window for optimum picking: One weekend they may barely be up out of the ground, and the next they could be starting to uncurl into ferns. The kind to pick has a papery tan husk and a ridge along the inside of the stem. If you harvest them carefully, they won't have much grit or sand.

> **fiddleheads, Moss-Ness dressing, dandelion greens, asparagus**

Pick 2 to 3 quarts (or desired amount) of fiddleheads. Back home, brush off the papery husks with your hands. Wash thoroughly and steam (in batches, if necessary) 3 to 4 minutes, or until color brightens and fiddleheads are al dente.

Rinse in cold water and drain. I then place them in an earthenware crock and coat them well with a Maine-made French dressing called Mos-Ness. (Ordering information for all featured Maine products, including Mos-Ness, is found in the Resources section, p. 255.)

Cover the crock and let marinate in the refrigerator for a day or two. (Refrigerated marinated fiddleheads will last for up to a month. They can also be frozen.)

After the fiddleheads have marinated for two days, gather some dandelion greens and asparagus. Dig greens that have a fully closed flower head. Remove the head and cut off the root. If you are gathering asparagus from a garden, you can simply take your fingers and slide down the stalk, bending it until it snaps of its own volition.

Cut the asparagus into bite-size pieces and steam the dandelion greens and asparagus together for 2 to 3 minutes. Refresh with cold water and drain. Place greens on small individual plates, asparagus on top of greens, and spoon fiddleheads, with some of the dressing, on top of that. *Ahhh, spring!*

– Tim Pond Salmon Royale –

Betty Calden: "Every owner will tell you it's an adventure coming in to open up camp in the springtime. Maybe the sewer backs up, or the water pump dies, or you get every vehicle stuck in the snow and there's no way out. Fortunately, this all happens before opening day! One year, I cut my finger in the new food processor and needed stitches. But there's so much to do this time of year, and so little time to do it, I just wrapped it up and went back to work.

"We have a tradition of four-thirty cocktails at Tim Pond. When the camp is full, I sometimes bring little plates of this salmon with crackers around to each of the cabins so when people come back from fishing they have something waiting for them. That way, they can relax before the dinner bell."

> **1 can red salmon, 1 (8-ounce) package cream cheese, 1 T lemon juice, 2 T chopped onion, 1/4 tsp. horseradish, 1/4 tsp. Liquid Smoke (optional), 1/2 cup finely chopped pecans, 2 to 3 sprigs fresh parsley finely chopped (or 1 T dried)**

Mix the first three ingredients together. Add the remaining ingredients. Combine well and chill for 2 hours. Roll in chopped pecans and parsley. Serve on your favorite crackers.

Soups

– The Birches Meatless Chili –

This is good for those cold early-spring fishing days.

1 package favorite chili mix, 1/4 tsp. cinnamon, 1 (14- to 16-ounce) can red kidney beans undrained, 1 (14- to 16-ounce) can pinto beans undrained, 1 (14- to 16-ounce) can chopped tomatoes with juice, 1 (6- to 8-ounce) can salt-free tomato sauce (not tomato paste), 1 large stalk celery chopped, 1 large white onion chopped, 1 green bell pepper chopped

Put all the ingredients in a pot and simmer for 3 hours, stirring occasionally. Serve with grated cheddar cheese and sour cream, if desired, on top.

– Chet's Fish Chowder –

Sue LaPlante: "We often make this with perch from Big Lake here, but any white fish, like bass or haddock, will do. Al's mom, who loved to fish, gave us this recipe. She passed away just before we bought Chet's. The cream of celery gives the chowder a rich taste and is also one of those supplies that can be kept on hand out here."

1 pound white fish fillets, 3 to 4 potatoes, 1 chopped onion, 1/2 cup finely chopped celery, 1 quart half-and-half, 2 cans cream of celery soup, butter, fresh parsley

Place the fillets in a heavy saucepan or soup pot. Pour in water just to cover and "shiver" the fish. This is a French term (Al's mother originally came from Canada) and means put the heat on high and boil the fish quickly (about 2 minutes). Turn off heat.

In a separate pot, place the scrubbed, peeled, and chunked potatoes, onion, and celery, and add water to cover. Cook until the potatoes are just barely fork-tender (still slightly firm). Drain the vegetable mixture (saving broth for another soup if desired), and add to the fish and broth in the other pot. Pour in half-and-half and celery soup. Simmer slowly until heated thoroughly, but do not boil.

Spoon into individual soup bowls and place 1 T of butter on top of each serving. Sprinkle on a little finely chopped fresh (or dried) parsley. Serves 4 to 6.

– Lakewood Cream of Fiddlehead Soup –

Robin Carter: "This is the perfect springtime soup."

2 cups fiddleheads, 1 tsp. salt, 1 can cream of chicken soup, 1 1/2 cups milk, 1 1/2 cups half-and-half, 2 T butter, 1 tsp. dried basil, salt and pepper to taste

Remove the papery husks and wash the fiddleheads. Steam or boil the fiddleheads for 1/2 hour. Drain, cool, and chop them up fine. In a soup pot, combine all the ingredients and simmer until very hot, but do not boil. Serves 4 to 6.

– Loon Lodge Bean Soup –

Linda Yencha: "The first thing you need to know about making this soup is that you need leftover ham, a leftover bone from the ham, and juice from the ham. It really improves the flavor and is also a solution for using leftovers from Easter or any other holiday."

12 cans navy beans (or use any small bean soaked overnight in water—save the water), cooked cubed ham, ham bone, ham juice, 1 bay leaf, 1 (48-ounce) can tomatoes (whole, crushed, or cubed, it doesn't matter), 3 to 4 T flour, 2 T sugar

In a big soup pot, empty the cans of beans. After you empty each can, fill it with water and pour that into the pot. (It's tastier than adding plain water and cleans out the cans.) Add the ham, bone, juice, and bay leaf and simmer the mixture for a good hour. Stir it now and then so the beans don't stick to the bottom.

Now, strain the juice from the tomatoes into a bowl and empty the tomatoes into the pot. Add the flour to the tomato juice and stir to make a paste. Add this to the soup to thicken it. Add sugar to get rid of the acid tomato taste (the tomatoes are just for color). Heat well and serve.

– Nicatous Lodge Fish Chowder –

Linda Sheldon: "This is sort of a generic recipe for whatever fish you may have caught or bought whole."

Cut the heads off the fish and skin and gut them, leaving the bones in. Place fish in a soup pot along with enough water to make desired amount of soup. Bring to a boil and boil gently for 15 to 20 minutes. Remove from heat, take out the fish, and let cool enough so you can remove the bones.

Cook $1/2$ to 1 cup of diced salt pork (or 8 to 10 pieces of cut-up bacon if you don't have salt pork). Remove salt pork/bacon to drain, and in the same skillet, sauté enough chopped-up celery, carrots, and onions to feed your guests (1 piece of celery, 1 carrot, and 1 small onion per person). Add to the fish stock along with diced potatoes (1 per person). Cook gently until the potatoes are tender.

Add 1 to 2 cans of evaporated milk and the flaked fish. Add salt and pepper to taste and serve.

– Tim Pond Trout Chowder –

Betty Calden: "Our guests fly-fish for native square-tailed trout. This chowder is from Mr. Hussey's day; he owned the camps after World War II. It's one of those recipes where they just kept a big pot at the back of the stove and added to it each day. As is typical of old recipes, there are no measurements."

Trout (enough to give $1/2$ to 1 cup cooked fish per person), cornmeal, bacon fat for cooking, onions (about 1 for every 2 people), salt pork (about the same quantity as the onions), potatoes (1 per person), milk (whole or evaporated) *or* cream (about $1/2$ cup per person), salt and pepper to taste,
Clean the trout, but leave the heads on. Roll the trout in cornmeal. Put bacon fat in a skillet and get it really hot; put in the fish and lower the heat to medium as you fry the fish. Cook until fish flakes.

Remove the heads, skin, and bones from the fish and put these in a soup pot. Add water, about one cup (or more) per person. Boil gently for 30 minutes. Remove from the heat and strain; this liquid is your stock.

Slice the onions and salt pork and fry in the skillet until golden. To the stock, add everything but the trout. Cook slowly (don't boil) until the potatoes are almost done. Add the trout and serve with biscuits.

Fish

· ·

TERMINOLOGY

Salmon and *landlocked salmon* mean the same thing in all these recipes; *togue* is another name for lake trout; *splake* is a hybrid of lake trout and brook trout.

· ·

– Alden's Shrimp Scampi with Maple Syrup –

Carter Minkel: "Alden's has seen four generations of management, guests, and staff. We
open the middle of May. Early each spring we work on new bathrooms, buy a few new
mattresses and linens, and there's always scraping and painting. If we have time, we'll also
make some maple syrup. It's a great way to survive mud season."

Chef Ellen Kiser: "This recipe has been top secret for so long that all we can bring ourselves to reveal are the ingredients and method. You'll just have to adjust the amounts to
your own taste. It's best served over linguini or rice, or let the shrimp marinate in the ingredients for several hours before placing on skewers and grilling. Have fun; it's delicious!"

**Peeled and de-veined tiger prawns/shrimp, chopped garlic,
melted butter, chopped fresh flat-leaf parsley, Dijon mustard,
maple syrup, Marsala wine**
Sauté the prawns/shrimp and garlic in butter over medium-high heat.
When shrimp is almost done (white and firming up), add parsley, a bit of
mustard, and maple syrup. Allow flavors to meld, then add a splash of
wine to finish the dish.

· ·

FISHING SEASON IN MAINE

Fishing season in Maine starts April 1 or at ice-out (which in many areas of the state
can mean closer to May 1), and goes until the end of September. Maine is blessed with
bountiful inland waters: 32,000 miles of rivers and streams and more than 6,000 lakes
and ponds, according to the Maine Department of Inland Fisheries and Wildlife, the
organization that provides fishing and hunting licenses and information (see Resources
section). In some areas of Maine, thanks to the increasing practice of catch and release,
the fishing is even better today than it was a decade or two ago. (Now, if we could only
do something about the mercury and other chemicals softly drifting and silently falling
into so many of our country's waters . . .)

· ·

– Alden's Tuna Steak with Asparagus –

Martha Minkel: "We plant a garden each spring. We've found that a lot of kids don't know what vegetables really look like, so we see the garden as a fun, educational part of camp. This recipe uses our own asparagus."

For each serving:
> **6 ounces sushi-grade yellowfin tuna steak (butterflied), 1 stalk asparagus, 1-inch strip roasted red pepper, 1 sheet Nori (dried seaweed), 1/3 cup tempura batter (below)**

Tempura Batter:
Mix equal parts pastry flour and water and stir well until completely combined.

Blanch the asparagus in boiling water until just soft. Place the asparagus and a strip of roasted red pepper inside the butterflied tuna steak. Wrap the entire steak in a Nori sheet, cutting off the excess from the ends.

Dip the wrapped steak in tempura batter and fry in 375° deep fat for 1 minute (rare).

Serve with wasabi, pickled ginger, and Soy-Mirin dipping sauce (below).

Alden's Soy-Mirin Sauce:
> **1/2 cup soy sauce, 1/2 cup Mirin, 1/2 cup sherry, 1/4 cup fish sauce, 3 T sesame oil, 1 T ground ginger, 2 cloves garlic crushed, 4 scallions minced fine**

Combine all ingredients and mix well.

– Bear Spring Baked Brown Trout –

Peg Churchill: "By the middle of May, our college students have usually arrived, and we have a full staff and are into our spring fishing season."

Ron Churchill: "Great Pond is the largest of the Belgrade Lakes, with a wide variety of fish. Beyond our twenty-eight hundred feet of shorefront is Meadow Stream, a winding waterway leading to a boggy area. It cannot be developed, so it's a great place to see birds and wildlife. One fish people catch here is brown trout. They have to be twelve inches to keep, but I've never seen one under sixteen around here. This is how I often prepare it."

1 brown trout, 1/4 to 1/2 cup oil-and-vinegar salad dressing, 2 cups plain croutons, 3 slices bacon, lemon slice(s)

Gut the fish and wash out the body cavity. Leave the skin and head on. With a sharp knife, cut from the gill to the dorsal fin.

In a bowl, combine the salad dressing and croutons. Let that set a bit and then mush it together with a fork. If it's not wet enough, add a few drops of water.

Preheat the oven to 400°. Stuff the fish with the crouton mixture and place it in a greased baking pan. Lay 3 slices of bacon over the top of the trout and bake it for 45 minutes to an hour, or until it flakes. Serve with a lemon slice or two. One large trout serves 2.

– Bosebuck's Salmon Sorrento –

Diane Schyberg: "I love this recipe. The sauce is so good!"

2 T olive oil, 5 plum tomatoes, 1/4 cup green olives chopped, 1/4 cup black olives chopped, 3 T lemon juice, 2 T chopped parsley, 1/4 cup capers, 2 tsp. minced garlic, 1/4 tsp. black pepper, 1/4 tsp. salt, 1 to 1 1/2 pounds salmon fillet

Heat oil in a large skillet. Add all the ingredients except the salmon. Simmer, stirring occasionally, for 5 to 10 minutes. Rinse the salmon and pat it dry. Push the sauce to one side of the pan and add the salmon. Spoon the sauce over the fish. Cover and cook over low heat for about 15 minutes, or until the salmon flakes easily at the thickest part. Serves 2.

– Bradford's Salmon and Peas with Tarragon Dill Sauce –

A dinner based on salmon and peas is the traditional Fourth of July meal for some folks. It combines an offering from the end of Maine's spring fishing season with one from the beginning of the summer garden vegetable season.

Karen Sikorsky: "Landlocked salmon is the dominant species here at Munsungan Lake. We encourage our guests to catch and release these beautiful native fish, and we supplement our dining table with salmon that is farm-raised and bought locally. This recipe can be made into an elegant pasta dish by using three cups of cooked salmon and mixing it with the sauce and tossing it with the pasta of your choice. Garnish either with fresh dill.

2 to 3 cups fresh or frozen salmon, 2 cups fresh or frozen peas

Poach salmon in enough water (or white wine, or combination) to come up the sides of the fish. Cover and cook until the fish flakes and is firm. Set aside.

In a saucepan, cook the peas in enough water to cover them, for 3 to 4 minutes, or until tender and bright green. (You can also steam the peas over boiling water.) Set aside.

Sauce:

2 T olive oil, 2 T butter, 1 small bunch green onions, 1/3 cup white wine, 1/2 cup sliced red bell pepper, 1 cup clam juice or fish stock from the poaching, 1 cup heavy cream, 2 T fresh dill chopped (or 1 T dried), 2 T fresh tarragon chopped (or 1 T dried), 1 tsp. Worcestershire sauce, salt and pepper to taste, fresh dill sprigs (optional)

Heat the butter and oil together in a large skillet. Add the onions and cook until softened. Add the wine and heat an additional couple of minutes until the liquid is reduced. Add peppers, clam juice/fish stock, cream, herbs, and Worcestershire sauce. Sprinkle in salt and pepper and simmer over low heat until sauce thickens.

Add the peas and pour sauce over the fish. Garnish with dill sprigs if desired.

– Cobb's Broiled Fish –

Gary Cobb: "You can do this with a trout, salmon, or togue. You want a fish at least twelve inches long, and you'll need a flat, sharp knife."

Preheat the broiler. First, you cut the head off and then lay the fish on its side. Slide the knife up one side of the backbone. Lay the fish open and put it on a piece of tinfoil, skin side down, and place that under the broiler.

When it's not quite cooked (just starting to flake and has lost its wet, fleshy look—about six to eight minutes), take it out of the broiler. Then you can just pull the backbone right out. It will all be on one side. It's an easy and thorough way to de-bone a fish.

Put it back under the broiler and finish cooking it (another couple of minutes). We don't salt and pepper them, as people like to do that themselves.

– Cobb's Salmon Loaf –

**1 one-pound salmon, 1 cup dry breadcrumbs, 2 eggs slightly
beaten, 1 can cream of celery soup, dash of salt and pepper**

Bake or broil the salmon (see Cobb's Broiled Fish recipe above). Remove
bones and flake. Place in a bowl along with the remaining ingredients and
combine well. Spoon the mixture into a buttered loaf pan and bake at
325° for at least 1 hour, or until bubbly. Let the loaf set for 5 minutes
before slicing.

– Deer Run Campfire Smelts and Potatoes –

Darlene Berry: "Here is a meal cooked over the fire with no dishes or pots and pans to wash!
You will need a hot fire to begin with; seasoned hardwood will give you the best bed of
coals for cooking."

Start the potatoes baking first. You can prep the smelts while they are cooking.

Potatoes:

**4 medium baking potatoes, 2 to 3 T oil, salt and pepper, dried
diced onion and dried minced garlic to taste**

Wash and dry potatoes and prick with a fork. Cut four 6-inch squares of
heavy-duty foil. Rub potatoes lightly with oil and place on foil. Sprinkle
potatoes with the seasonings, wrap in the foil, and place in the bed of
coals. Cover with a light bed of hot coals. Potatoes will take approximately
1 hour to cook. Serves 4.

Smelts:

**2 pounds smelts, 2 to 3 T oil, 1/4 cup chopped onion, 1/4 cup
chopped parsley, salt and pepper to taste, 2 strips bacon cut
in half**

Clean the fish and drain on paper towels. Cut four 12-inch squares of
heavy-duty foil and oil lightly. Divide the fish into 4 portions and place on
foil. Sprinkle each with onion, parsley, salt, and pepper. Place bacon on
top. Fold foil over the fish and seal the edges by making double folds.

Place fish packages on the bed of hot coals. Cook for 15 minutes,
turning twice. Serve by cutting a big crisscross in the top of each package.
Serves 4.

SMELT FISHING

Smelt fishing is a rite of spring around Maine. If you go out during the night to streams and inlets—in the middle of nowhere, perhaps—you're apt to find little orbs of lantern or firelight and people with long-handled fish nets. If you're lucky, the water will be roiling with four- to six-inch sparkling-silver smelts. It's sort of an East Coast miniature version of a West Coast salmon run. Smelts are cooked whole, generally dipped in corn-meal and fried, and are packed with nutrition. They freeze well, but are best cooked fresh. They make a great breakfast dish.

– Katahdin Lake's Fried Brook Trout –

Al Cooper: "Ninety percent of the state of Maine has brook trout. They are about the easiest type of fish to clean, and you can do it right at the water's edge. Leave the fish on the stringer (with the hook through the gills and out). Don't lay it on the dock. Cut from the vent to the gills, then pinch the gills and pull them off. Grab the viscera and throw them in the water because the fish love them. Then take your thumbnail up the backbone (where the blood supply is) and wash that out. By the time you've walked up to the lodge, the fish has dripped off."

Suzan Cooper: "Lay it on plastic wrap and fold it over until ready to cook (hopefully soon). Never put fish on tin or metal."

1 cup cornmeal, 1/2 cup flour, 1/2 tsp. lemon pepper, 3 to 4 T oil
In a shallow bowl or plate, combine cornmeal, flour, and lemon pepper. Dust the entire cleaned trout with the mixture and fry in the oil (adding more oil if necessary to fry properly). Fry each side 5 minutes, turning only once, being careful not to scrape off the coating.

– Leen's Landlocked Salmon in a Bag –

Charles Driza: "Fish like stable weather, free of big barometric changes, and they respond by becoming active. Fishermen love our early June salmon and bass fishing here in Grand Lake Stream, and often bring their catch to the lodge to be cooked for dinner. One of our guides, Tim Buskirk, enjoys cooking for his clients after a successful day on the water. This is one of his favorite recipes, as unique as it is delicious. We serve it with roasted potatoes and fresh vegetables for a memorable meal.

"You will need a clean brown paper bag—with no printing or ink on it—long enough to completely enclose the salmon."

**1 salmon, salt and pepper to taste, 1 small onion diced,
2 to 3 T olive oil**

Preheat oven to 400°. Take a whole salmon, dressed, with the gills removed. Remember to remove the long red line on either side of the spine inside the body cavity. (Do this by running your thumb along the spine.) Sprinkle salt and pepper into the body cavity and stuff with the diced onion. Rub the outside of the fish with olive oil.

Place the fish in the brown paper bag. Close up the bag well, place it on its side, and cut several small knife slits in the top of the bag to release steam. Bake in preheated oven for 40 minutes.

Remove the bag from the oven and let it cool for several minutes. Cut a big slit, opening up the top, so that the fish can be eaten right out of the bag.

– Libby's Baked Stuffed Splake (or Salmon) –

**2 to 4 whole cleaned fish, 6 to 8 slices dry bread (homemade
preferred), 1 to 2 onions chopped, 1 to 2 stalks celery chopped,
1 green and 1 red pepper chopped, 2 to 4 ounces cheddar
cheese cubed, 1/4 cup butter melted, 1/2 to 1 T Worcestershire
sauce, garlic pepper, Tabasco sauce, and salt to taste**

Place the fish in a greased baking pan. In a bowl, crumble the bread. Add the remaining ingredients and mix well to combine. Stuff the fish with the mixture. Cover the pan with tinfoil and bake fish at 350° for about 1 hour. Serve with lemon wedges.

– Moose Point Poached Salmon –

John Martin: "My uncle and aunt owned a sporting camp for some twenty years, and I worked there from seventh grade through high school. I mowed lawns, brought in wood. I always wanted to own a set of camps after I retired as state legislator from Eagle Lake. *[Representative Martin served 19 years as Speaker of the House.]* Moose Point Camps were built in 1906. I ended up with them in the fall of 1991, and now I'm back to doing what I did as a kid—mowing lawns, bringing in wood!"

Kathy McGough, camp cook: "I like filleted salmon for this recipe—either a whole side, or two pounds' worth of smaller fillets."

> **2 pounds filleted salmon, spicy brown prepared mustard, 1 tsp.**
> **to 1 T dried dill (1 T freshly minced), 1/2 cup dry white wine,**
> **4 to 6 lemon slices**

Cover a 9 x 13-inch baking pan with enough foil so that you will be able to bring it around and over the fish like a package. Lay the salmon, skin side down, on the foil and spread a thin coating of mustard over the top of the fleshy side. Sprinkle with the dill and pour in the wine around the fish. Fold up the foil so fish is completely enclosed. Bake at 350° for 20 minutes and then check with fork at the fleshiest part to make sure the fish is cooked through. Serve with lemon slices.

– Weatherby's Salmon Florentine –

Steve Clark, chef: "Salmon and fresh spinach—sure signs of spring."

Salmon:

> **1 whole side of salmon fillet (approx. 3 to 5 pounds), salt and**
> **pepper to taste, 6 to 8 T butter, 2 to 3 tsp. oil, flour, 8 cups (or**
> **2 bags) fresh spinach, 1 to 2 cups grated Gruyère cheese**

Cut the salmon into smaller fillets about 8 to 10 inches and season each with salt and pepper. Place butter and oil in a baking pan large enough to hold the fillets, and slide pan into a 350° oven to melt the butter/oil and heat the pan.

Dredge the fillets in flour and place them in the heated pan. Bake fish for 15 to 20 minutes.

While the fish bakes, wash spinach and remove the stems. Drop the prepared spinach into a pot of boiling water for 1 minute to blanch. Remove, cool quickly under running water, drain, and chop roughly.

When you remove the salmon from the oven, top it with the chopped spinach and the following sauce.

Sauce:

¹/₂ cup butter, ¹/₂ cup all-purpose flour, 2 cups scalded milk

Melt the butter in a saucepan. Add the flour, and combine with a whisk until well blended. Heat through. Add the scalded milk and stir until the sauce is smooth and thickened. Pour over the fish.

Top with desired amount of Gruyère cheese and bake for approximately 10 to 12 minutes more, or until the cheese is golden and the fish is flaky.

••

FISHING GUIDE'S SHORE MEAL

Jeff McEvoy, of Weatherby's Camps: "The village of Grand Lake Stream is noted for its guides. The guides will stop at an island or at secluded spots (which may be set up with a picnic table and a fire pit) and start a fire going. They bring cooking supplies and staples with them, and they'll cook the 'fish du jour' in a skillet with hot oil and salt and pepper.

"If their client has caught a salmon, they'll grill that in a fold-up grill on the open fire. They may have some chicken on hand as well. They boil up onions and potatoes, and generally have homemade bread, sweet pickles, and a homemade dessert.

"Fresh guide's coffee is made by mixing up coffee grounds with a raw egg—shell and all—and adding that to the coffeepot on the fire. You boil it up and then take it off the fire, let the grounds and eggshell settle to the bottom, and then serve it up."

••

Poultry/Small Game

– Bald Mountain Maple-Glazed Chicken with Rosemary* –

Bald Mountain serves an extensive menu to their guests and the public. Wait till you try this recipe with Bradford's Potatoes Mashed with Garlic and Rosemary (p. 176)!

Chef Meg Godaire: "I've kept this on the menu for years because people love it, and because it's wicked easy."

> **2 whole fryers, salt and pepper to taste, 2 lemons, 1/4 cup olive oil, 3/4 cup maple syrup, 4 sprigs rosemary leaves**

Cut chickens in half, place in a baking pan, and season with salt and pepper. Cut four slices from one of the lemons and squeeze the juice from the remainder of that lemon and the second lemon. Pour lemon juice over the chicken, then drizzle with olive oil.

Bake for 20 minutes at 350°. Remove from the oven and drizzle with 1/2 cup of the maple syrup and sprinkle with a few fresh rosemary leaves taken from each sprig. Bake for an additional 15 to 20 minutes until crispy and brown.

Drizzle again with remaining syrup, and garnish each portion with a lemon slice and a sprig of rosemary. Serves 4.

– Bear Spring's Spring Chicken –

Peg Churchill: "This is our standard meal in spring because it's easy and we don't have any time." Ron Churchill: "We live on it." Peg: "Good thing the whole family likes it!"

> **1 stick butter or margarine, 1 can cream of mushroom soup, 1 can water, 1 T minced onion flakes, 1 T fresh chives and/or parsley, 1 1/2 cups rice (regular white or brown), 1 to 2 green peppers sliced or diced (we like a lot), 6 chicken breast servings (bone-in or boneless), 1/2 tsp. salt, Emeril's Southwest Essence or your favorite spicy seasoning (if desired)**

Put the butter in a 9 x 13-inch baking pan and place the pan in a 350° oven to melt it. Remove and pour in the soup and 1 soup can full of water.

Add the remaining ingredients in the order given (the chicken will be on top, sprinkled with the seasonings). Cook uncovered for 1 1/4 hours or until both the rice and the chicken are cooked through. Serves 4 to 6.

– Bradford's Swiss Cheese Chicken Casserole –

Heritage Recipe from the time of Dave and Nancy Youland, who were the owners of Bradford Camp from 1972 to 1996.

6 skinless and boneless chicken breasts, 6 slices Swiss cheese, 1 can cream of chicken soup, 1/4 cup milk, 2 cups herb-seasoned stuffing mix, 1/4 cup butter

Arrange chicken breasts in a lightly greased pan. Lay a slice of cheese on top of each piece. In a bowl, mix soup and milk together and pour over the cheese/chicken. Sprinkle the stuffing mix over everything and dribble melted butter over the top. Bake in a 350° oven for 40 to 50 minutes. Serves 6.

– Moose Point Chicken and Peas Casserole –

Kathy McGough, camp cook: "This recipe can easily expand or contract depending on the number of people you're feeding."

Chicken pieces (amount desired to feed 4), 1 onion, 4 to 6 medium potatoes, 1 (29-ounce) can tomato sauce, 1 1/2 cups parboiled fresh peas (or 1 can, drained)

Grease a 9 x 13-inch baking pan and place the chicken pieces in it. Roughly chop the onion and sprinkle it over the chicken. Peel and coarsely chop the potatoes and arrange them on top. Pour the tomato sauce over everything and bake in a 350° oven for 1 1/2 hours, then add the peas on top. Bake for another 15 to 30 minutes or until the chicken is done and the potatoes are fork-tender. Serves 4.

– Mount Chase Oven-Fried Chicken –

Sara Hill: "You can use whatever parts of the chicken you prefer for this recipe."

**6 pieces of chicken, 2 cups baking mix (I use Bisquick),
1 T paprika, 1 T seasoned salt, 1 tsp. pepper, 1 T dried parsley,
1 stick margarine/butter**

Preheat the oven to 450°. Dredge the chicken in the flour/seasoning mixture to coat. Melt the butter/margarine in a 9 x 13-inch pan in the oven. Place the chicken, skin side down, in the pan and bake for 30 minutes. Turn the chicken and bake another 15 minutes.

Meat/Big Game

– Bald Mountain Roast Leg of Lamb –

Meg Godaire: "People love this, and it's easy to make. (I'm big on easy.) I serve it with mint jelly."

**4- to 5-pound boneless leg of lamb, 3 cloves garlic crushed,
4 to 5 sprigs fresh thyme, salt and pepper to taste, 3 T olive oil**

Rub the meat with the garlic, thyme, and salt and pepper (I go heavy on the pepper). Roll and tie the meat and drizzle with the olive oil. Bake in a preheated 425° oven for 15 minutes. Reduce heat to 350° and cook an additional 35 minutes for medium rare, up to an hour-plus for meat that is more well done. Serves 4.

– Bowlin's Baked Ham with Maple Cola Glaze –

Ken Conaster: "Bake a smoked ham in a 350-degree oven for about forty-five minutes, and then cover with my special glaze recipe."

**1 can cola or root beer, 1/4 cup brown sugar, 1/2 tsp. allspice,
1/2 tsp. cinnamon, 1/4 cup molasses, 2 tsp. maple syrup**

In a saucepan, bring ingredients to a boil. Turn the heat to low, simmer, and reduce the mixture by one-third. Pour over the hot ham and bake an additional 10 to 15 minutes (1 hour total). Reserve the ham juice/glaze to pour as gravy. Serves 8 to 10.

– Dad's Roast Pork with Fiddleheads –

Therese Thibodeau: "We're the only set of sporting camps on the Penobscot River from Bangor all the way to Medway. My late husband, Raymond, built the first cabins, in 1990. Now my daughter Karen and son Raymond Jr. help me run it."

Raymond Thibodeau Jr.: "During a typical sporting-camp year, I'm the plumber, electrician, carpenter, and groundskeeper, as well as a fishing and hunting guide. In April and May, I'll work on the grounds, water system, remove the insulating plastic from the cabin porches, look for leaks, get the place up and running. Around Mother's Day, fiddleheading starts. The Penobscot Indians own the islands on the river and we have to get a permit from them to hunt or gather on any of the islands."

Therese: "One of the ways we like to eat fiddleheads is sautéed in roast pork drippings. This pork is so good it just melts in your mouth."

Place a 10-pound pork roast (with the bone inside) on a large piece of foil in a roasting pan. Cut deep slits, about every 2 inches, all the way across the roast, and add 1 slice of onion for each cut. Salt and pepper the meat, sprinkle a few drops of soy sauce over it, and sprinkle with seasoned salt and garlic salt. Pour 2 cans of cream of mushroom soup all over the meat (I use my hands and pat it on). Wrap the meat completely in the foil. Pour 3 cups of water in the pan and bake at 350° for 2 1/2 to 3 hours.

Use the drippings/sauce from the foil for sautéing fiddleheads or other greens.

– Loon Lodge Ham Spread –

Linda Yencha: "This makes a nice sandwich spread—something different when you're sick of the same old luncheon meats. It's a family favorite. We spread it on white bread and cut it into four pieces."

2 to 3 cups minced ham, 1 onion diced, 1 small jar sweet pickles, salt and pepper, mayonnaise

Grind the meat (using a food processor or food mill) until fine. Add the onion, diced fine, and pickles (sliced or diced). Season to taste and add mayonnaise until desired spreading consistency.

– Rideout's Baked Ham with Orange Glaze and Gravy –

Bob Lorigan Jr.: "Our buildings were constructed in the 1940s, and when you come into our dining room you see a real classic lodge with the wood interior and the moose heads on the walls. Our big picture windows look out over East Grand Lake."

Bob Lorigan Sr.: "We serve Down East cooking: rib-eye steaks cooked on the open fire, roast pork on Wednesday, and every Sunday we have a traditional Thanksgiving dinner."

Jami Lorigan: "This ham is melt-in-your-mouth good. I'll just explain how we do it."

Baked Ham:

Preheat oven to 325°. Take about a 10-pound butt or shank, bone-in, pre-cooked ham and place it, cut end down, in a large roasting pan on a rack that sits up about 1 1/2 inches. Pour enough water in the bottom to come up almost to the bottom of the rack. (You want a rack high enough so the ham isn't resting in the water, and you want enough water in there to make gravy with later.)

You don't have to season the ham at all. Put heavy foil over the whole kit 'n' caboodle and seal it around the roasting pan so it will have some steaming action inside. Bake 15 minutes for every pound of ham. If you want it falling off the bone, cook it a little longer (but remember that it will want to come off in chunks instead of slices).

While the ham is cooking, make the glaze (recipe below).

Orange Glaze:

2 cups orange juice, 1 cup crushed pineapple, 1 cup brown sugar, 1 tsp. dry mustard, dash or two of ground cloves

In a heavy saucepan, mix all the ingredients together and simmer on low until it is heated through and sugar is completely dissolved. Instead of putting this on the ham while it's cooking, we serve it in a gravy bowl on the side like a sauce.

Ham Gravy:

When the ham is done, remove it from the pan. Strain the water/drippings mixture from the baking pan into a saucepan. In a small bowl, mix 1 cup flour with enough water to make the mixture the consistency of honey (just pourable). Over medium heat, gradually add the flour mixture to the strained pot liquid, stirring constantly. Add 1 tablespoon chicken-base paste. Serve on the side or pour over individual slices of ham.

We let people season everything themselves since the ham is already salty and people have different tastes and needs regarding seasoning, and they can use either the glaze or the gravy (or both, if they want).

Serves around 12 to 14.

– Weatherby's Rack of Spring Lamb –

Heritage Recipe from Charlene and Ken Sassi, who owned Weatherby's from 1974 to 2002.

Charlene Sassi: "I used to cook leg of lamb, but ended up cooking a rack and thought it was twice as good. This was a special treat for my guests, and they knew it!"

Marinade to cover two racks:

1 T minced fresh garlic, 1 T rosemary, 1 tsp. marjoram, 1 tsp. tarragon, 2 T fresh mint leaves (chopped), 2 T minced parsley, 2 cups oil, $1/2$ cup lemon juice, mint jelly if desired (to add some sweetness)

Marinate for at least 5 hours.

Before grilling, make sure to wrap the rib bones with tinfoil or they will char. Cook on an outside grill until nice and dark. (I cook them medium rare.) Serve immediately, or, when ready to serve, place in a very hot oven and reheat them fast.

– Wilderness Island Ham Kebabs –

Carol LaRosa: "Two pounds of ham serves five people, so figure accordingly. The secret to this recipe is the glaze."

For each person:

Kebabs:

4 (1-inch) cubes of baked ham, 3 pieces tomato, 3 pieces green or red pepper, 3 pieces onion, 3 mushrooms

Glaze:

1 cup packed brown sugar, $1/3$ cup peach (or other fruit) juice

Combine glaze ingredients until sugar has dissolved. Skewer kebabs, starting and ending with a piece of ham. Put in foil on a barbecue grill (or cookie sheet in the oven). Brush kebabs with the glaze. Cook 5 minutes, turn, and brush on more glaze. Cook until the vegetables are the way you like them (we like them still crunchy).

Salads/Side Dishes/Vegetarian

– Bald Mountain Spinach Cannelloni –

Meg Godaire: "We do a vegetarian meal every day, and pasta is very popular."

Stuffing:

1 box cannelloni shells, 1 package frozen spinach (or 3 cups fresh), 2 eggs, 1 (15-ounce) container ricotta cheese, 1 tsp. nutmeg, 1/2 cup Parmesan cheese, salt and pepper to taste

Cook the shells according to the directions on the package. Place in a buttered baking pan. Chop the spinach and mix together with remaining stuffing ingredients in a bowl. Stuff the shells with the mixture.

Sauce:

3 T butter, 3 T flour, 2 cups milk, 1 tsp. nutmeg, 1/2 cup Parmesan cheese

In a saucepan, melt the butter, add the flour, and stir until well combined and bubbly. Add remaining ingredients and stir well, cooking until sauce thickens. Pour over the stuffed shells.

Cover with foil and bake in a 350° oven for 25 minutes, or until hot and bubbly. Serves 4.

– Bear Spring Vegetable Salad –

Peg Churchill: "This is canned salad for when the garden isn't up yet or when you don't have time to prepare and chop vegetables. It keeps for up to six weeks in the fridge."

Salad:

1 can each drained French-cut green beans, corn, and baby peas; 1 cup each chopped green pepper, red pepper, celery, and onion; 1 T celery seed, 1 grated carrot

Mix all ingredients together in a large bowl.

Dressing:

1 cup sugar, 1/2 cup oil, 3/4 cup white vinegar

Combine in a saucepan and heat. Pour dressing over the vegetables and chill. Serve on a bed of lettuce.

– The Birches Pasta with Gorgonzola and Sun-Dried Tomatoes –

> 6 sun-dried tomato halves, 3 T walnut oil, 1/2 tsp. minced garlic,
> 2 T pine nuts, 1/3 pound thin spaghetti or pasta of choice, salt
> and pepper to taste, 1/3 cup crumbled gorgonzola or blue
> cheese

Slice the sun-dried tomato halves in half. Place them in a small bowl and pour boiling water over them to cover. Let them soak until tender but not too soft or soggy. Drain and set aside.

Heat the walnut oil in a skillet until hot but not smoking. Add garlic and pine nuts and sauté until pine nuts are golden brown. Do not burn. Set aside.

Cook pasta and toss with the pine nut mixture, and salt and pepper to taste. Lay pasta on a plate and top with cheese and sun-dried tomatoes.

– Bosebuck's Vegetable Rice Pilaf –

Heritage Recipe: Tom Rideout owned Bosebuck Camps from 1981 until 1997 (and was the manager for years before that). He was present during the discovery of Indian artifacts at the camps.

Tom: "The camps sit on a very active Indian site. When they were here, the glaciers were receding and this valley was a migration route for the caribou. The Indians used the natural barriers here (pond/river/steep banks) to slow the herd and ambush them. The tribes camped on the eastern shore, where the westerly wind helped to ward off the bugs. They stayed on the high banks where they could observe the herd. Because of the dam that created the lake in 1914, those banks are at water level right now."

> 1/2 cup oil, 1/4 cup diced celery, 1/2 cup diced onions, 2 cups
> sliced mushrooms, 5 cups chicken stock, 2 cups rice, 1 tsp.
> thyme, 2 bay leaves

Preheat oven to 350°. Pour oil in an ovenproof saucepan. Add celery, onions, and mushrooms. Sauté until soft. In a separate pot, heat up the chicken stock.

Add the rice to the vegetables, sauté, and add 4 cups of the hot chicken stock. Stir. Add thyme and bay leaves. Cover and and place in the oven. Bake for 30 minutes. Add remaining cup chicken stock, and bake an additional 15 minutes, until liquid is absorbed.

– Cobb's Fiddlehead Fettuccini –

**4 cups clean fiddleheads, 2 cloves garlic crushed, 2 T olive oil,
2 T butter, salt and pepper to taste, 1-pound box fettuccini,
1/4 cup Parmesan cheese, 1/4 cup pine nuts or walnuts (optional)**
Sauté fiddleheads and garlic in oil/butter until garlic is golden. Remove
from heat. Cook and drain pasta. Combine with fiddlehead mixture, and
salt and pepper to taste. Sprinkle with cheese and nuts, if desired.

– Cobb's "Italian Sandwich" Rice Salad –

Betty Cobb: "This is a recipe we use from my sister, Margaret Messinger."

Margaret: "I originally used a cheese garlic dressing for this. It works best, if you can
find it, but Italian or Zesty Italian will do the trick, if enough cheese is added. It tastes fine
without the ham, but the ham does give it more of an Italian sandwich taste. Making this
salad is a good way to use up any leftover veggies, because the cheese makes anything
taste good. Also, white rice, or any kind of pasta, works well with this recipe."

**1 (14-ounce) package instant brown rice, 1 (0.6-ounce) package
dry Italian dressing mix (or 8 fluid ounces), 1 (8-ounce) package
shredded sharp cheddar cheese, 1/2 cup grated Parmesan cheese
(up to 1 cup, if you like a cheesy taste), 1 large onion, 1 large
green pepper, 2 tomatoes, 1/2 to 1 cup small pitted black olives,
1 cup chopped dill pickles, 2 cups chopped ham (optional)**
Cook the rice as directed on the box. While it is still warm, mix in the
cheeses. Then add half the dressing. Cut up the remaining ingredients and
add to the mixture. Add some more of the dressing and a little pickle
juice, making sure the salad is moist but not soaked with liquids.

– Cobb's Peas Amandine –

Betty Cobb: "Fresh peas are good with nothing but a little butter. If you want, though,
here's something to fancy them up."

**3 cups peas, 2/3 cup chopped bacon, 2 T minced or grated
onion, 1/2 cup slivered almonds, 1/3 cup cream**

In a saucepan, cook peas in boiling water until just done (3 to 4 minutes). Drain and set aside. In a skillet, fry bacon and onion until bacon is crisp. Add peas, almonds, and cream. Serves 4.

– Dad's Poutine –

Therese Thibodeau: "I was one of seventeen children and grew up in New Brunswick, Canada, where we had a big garden. The men of our extended family would prepare the soil. The boys would make the rows, and the girls would plant the seeds. Then my mother covered the seeds with just the right amount of dirt. We typically put up two hundred quarts of string beans, and usually used thirty cords of wood a year, so I am used to having many people around and cooking in large quantities.

"This is a popular Canadian dish."

First, you make a chicken or beef gravy from whatever drippings are in the pan of the poultry/meat you're cooking. You mix the drippings with flour and enough water, stirring with a whisk to make a smooth gravy. Salt and pepper to taste. Next, you cook up some french fries. Divide the fries onto plates or shallow bowls. Sprinkle on lots of mozzarella (to cover fries) and pour the gravy over that.

– Harrison's Maple Syrup Squash –

1 butternut squash, peeled and cut in cubes (or 1 package frozen), 1 stick butter, $1/4$ cup real maple syrup

Place all ingredients in a heavy saucepan. Cover and cook on very low heat until the squash is soft and can be mashed with a fork or whisk. Serve sprinkled with a dash or two of cinnamon sugar.

– Long Lake Fiddlehead Pizza –

Sandra Smith: "Our very first guest at Long Lake Camps was John, from New Jersey. He still comes back in June and September. He is an avid fisherman, but hates to eat fish! We don't have a set menu, and quite often we specialize the meals for the guests. Once we learned that John loves pizza, we made sure to have it sometime during his stay.

"I am fortunate that Doug is not a guide and off for the day. He and I share all the hosting and other responsibilities. We take turns making the pizza dough, but the toppings are his specialty. Craig, our housekeeper Kim's husband, once brought us a large bag of fiddleheads—and laughed when he saw that Doug put some on our pizza!"

Doug Clements: "Use the measurements for the sauce as a guideline. I have no set way for seasoning my sauce. Sometimes it depends on the guest, and other times it depends on what ingredients are around and how I'm feeling at the moment."

The sauce does not have to simmer for very long, so you can prepare it while the dough is rising.

Pizza Dough (6 pizzas):

1 tsp. sugar, 2 1/2 cups lukewarm water, 4 T dry yeast, 1/2 cup olive oil, 2 tsp. salt, 7 cups bread flour, cornmeal

In a large mixing bowl, add sugar to the water. Sprinkle the yeast on top and let set a few minutes until the mixture bubbles. Mix in oil and salt. Add 2 cups of flour, mix, and then gradually add remaining flour and mix well. Turn the dough out on a well-floured surface and knead for 8 to 10 minutes until dough is smooth and shiny. Place in a lightly greased bowl and turn dough over to expose greased top. Cover with plastic wrap and let rise until doubled.

Preheat the oven to 500°. Punch down the dough and divide it into 6 pieces. Knead each piece for a minute, and then roll into either a circle for a round pan or a rectangle for cookie sheet. Sprinkle cornmeal onto pan(s) of choice and place shaped dough on pan(s). With thumbs, crimp or flute the edges to form a rim. Ladle on the sauce.

Sauce:

olive oil, 1 medium onion, 2 cloves garlic or 1 T garlic powder, 1 (1-pound) can crushed tomatoes, 3 (12-ounce) cans tomato paste, 1 T parsley, 3 tsp. oregano, 2 T sugar, 2 tsp. salt, 1 tsp. pepper

In a large, deep saucepan, heat enough olive oil to just cover the bottom of the pan. Dice the onion and 2 cloves of garlic (if using fresh) and sauté in the oil, then add the tomatoes and tomato paste. Stir in a can of water for each can of tomato paste. Add parsley, oregano, garlic powder (if not using fresh), sugar, salt, and pepper. Combine well and heat through.

Toppings:

olive oil, fiddleheads (1 heaping cup per pizza), 1 to 2 cloves garlic, grated mozzarella cheese, grated Parmesan cheese, oregano, olive oil

In a skillet, sauté cleaned fiddleheads and crushed garlic in enough olive oil to just cover bottom of pan—2 to 3 minutes.

Cover the pizza dough with tomato sauce and then with your favorite toppings (in this case, fiddleheads). Top with mozzarella and sprinkle with Parmesan. Add a dash or two of oregano and dribble a couple of tablespoons of olive oil over each pizza.

Start baking the pizza on the lowest shelf in the oven for 5 minutes, and then swap it to the middle rack and bake another 5 minutes, or until the crust is lightly browned and the topping is bubbling.

– Mount Chase Sunshine Rice –

1/2 cup chopped celery, 1/4 cup chopped onion, 2 T margarine or butter, 2 tsp. grated orange peel, 1/2 tsp. poultry seasoning, 1 cup orange juice, 1 cup chicken broth or water, 1 cup uncooked rice, 1/2 cup raisins

In a saucepan, fry celery and onions in margarine/butter until tender. Add remaining ingredients. Bring to a boil; then reduce heat, cover, and simmer about 20 minutes or until rice is cooked. Serves 4 to 6.

– Pleasant Point Stewed Tomatoes –

Mardi George: "This is a quick and easy recipe for a cool day."

1 large can diced tomatoes, 1/2 cup brown sugar, 1/2 cup diced onion, 1 T dried basil

In a saucepan, mix all the ingredients together and simmer for 1/2 hour or until heated through.

– Wapiti Maple Carrots –

Here in Maine, where there is dependable snow cover, carrots may be able to winter over in the garden. In fall, just cut the tops to about an inch from the roots, cover with mulch, and as soon as the soil has unfrozen enough to pull them out (mid-April to mid-May), you'll have delicious sweet carrots. Just in time for fresh maple syrup and this recipe! ·

Frank Ramelli: "I retired when I was fifty, and my wife, Anita, and I moved up here to the Shin Pond area. She was from Germany and loved to cook; I loved sporting camps. Anita loved this spot: You can see Mt. Katahdin from the porch of every cabin, and she liked that the place was started by two women, a librarian and a schoolteacher from Bangor, who leased the land in 1912. We're in transition now because Anita passed away in 2002 and I'm running the camps with our daughter, Karen, and son, Tony."

Karen: "My mother made this recipe a lot. It smells wonderful and tastes out of this world."

> Carrots ($1/2$ cup per person, plus extra $1/2$ cup), $1/2$ stick butter, salt to taste, $1/2$ cup peas (frozen or fresh), $1/4$ to $1/2$ cup real maple syrup, dash of cinnamon

Cut carrots on the diagonal. In a frying pan or saucepan with lid, melt the butter. Add the carrots and salt and simmer, covered, for 15 minutes. When the carrots are fork-tender, add the peas, maple syrup, and cinnamon, and cook only 2 to 3 minutes more.

– West Branch Pond Dandelion Greens –

Carol Kealiher: "Here's your spring tonic for another year. Serve as a starter, a vegetable, or a side salad."

> Dig up a dozen or so heads of dandelion (the leaves, flower bud, and taproot) while the flower is still tightly budded and green. Cut off the root, remove the flower, and wash the leaves in ice-cold water (4 rinses), swishing them around vigorously each time.

Place in a saucepan with 1 pint of water and 2 T salt. (This sounds like a lot of salt, but it helps tenderize the dandelion.) Cook for $1/2$ hour at the most. Serve with a shake or two of cider vinegar and a dribbling of melted butter.

Sauces

– Bear Spring Cooked Oil and Vinegar Dressing –

1 cup sugar, $1/2$ cup oil, $3/4$ cup white vinegar

Heat all the ingredients in a saucepan until sugar is completely dissolved. Pour into a jar or salad dressing carafe. Shake well before serving. Refrigerate any leftover dressing.

– Bear Spring Hollandaise for a Crowd –

Edward Pearl Sr.: "This is the amount I normally make for our Eggs Benedict, but it's easily reduced. I've made it this way for years using a round-bottom saucepan we have."

18 egg yolks, $1^{1}/2$ cups melted butter, 4 T lemon juice, salt and
pepper to taste, $1/2$ tsp. Tabasco sauce (or to taste)

Put the yolks in a (round-bottom) saucepan over low direct heat and whisk constantly for 10 minutes. Gradually add the butter and whisk again for another 10 minutes. Remove from the heat and add remaining ingredients, whisking well to combine. Serves 20 to 24.

– The Birches Newburg Sauce –

John Willard: "This is our sauce for Lobster or Crab Newburg, and will serve approximately twelve, depending on amount of crab/lobster used. If you delete the food coloring and lobster base, it can also serve as a rich white sauce for pasta."

2 quarts heavy cream, $1/2$ cup white wine, $1/2$ cup lemon juice,
$1/2$ cup dry vermouth, 1 tsp. granulated garlic, 1 tsp. fresh-
ground pepper to taste, 2 drops red food coloring, 1 T lobster
base, 3 cups butter, $2^{1}/2$ to 3 cups flour

Mix all but the flour and butter in a large sauce pot. Heat over medium heat, being careful not to burn the heavy cream. Stir occasionally.

While the sauce is warming, melt the butter in a large frying pan. Slowly add the flour and stir 3 to 5 minutes until the roux is thickened but not brown.

When the roux is ready, turn the heat under the sauce mixture to high, and immediately add the roux and stir constantly until the entire mixture has thickened. Sprinkle in additional flour if necessary to thicken to desired consistency.

– The Birches Red Wine Vinaigrette –

1 cup red wine vinegar, 1 cup good-quality olive oil, 2 tsp. sugar, 1 tsp. salt, fresh ground pepper to taste, 1 clove pressed garlic, 1 tsp. Italian spices

Combine all ingredients in a glass jar or dressing container and mix well, but do not emulsify (i.e., completely combine oil and vinegar).

– The Birches Vinaigrette Dressing –

John Willard: "There's a pattern to our year: April, we do our spring cleaning. The first part of May, fishing season starts up for lake and brook trout and salmon, and our white-water rafting season begins. We shuttle people fifty minutes from Moosehead Lake to our bases at The Forks on the Kennebec River and on the Penobscot River near Baxter State Park."

1 cup good-quality olive oil, 1 cup cider vinegar, 2 tsp. sea salt, 1 tsp. sugar, 1 clove pressed garlic, fresh-ground pepper to taste

Combine all the ingredients and emulsify in a blender.

– Cobb's "Favorite" Salad Dressing –

1 1/2 cups sugar, 1 1/2 cups salad oil, 3 tsp. salt, 3 tsp. paprika, 3/4 cup cider vinegar, 3/4 cup ketchup, 1/2 cup water, 1 to 2 T onion bits (optional)

Blend everything but the onion bits in the blender until well blended. Pour into a jar, add onion bits, and keep in refrigerator, covered with jar lid. until needed. Shake jar before use to blend ingredients again.

Desserts

– Bald Mountain Maple Bread Pudding –

Stephen Philbrick: "My grandfather came up here to the Rangeley Lakes with his dad in the early 1920s, to work as a logger. My grandparents were Mainers, French Canadian folks, and I bought the place from them."

I've found that this is also fabulous for breakfast, served warm or at room temperature, with fresh or preserved fruit sauce or warm maple syrup.

> **1 T butter, 3/4 cup real maple syrup, 6 slices day-old French bread, 2 to 3 T butter, 5 eggs, 1/2 cup sugar, 1 quart heavy cream (*or* half-and-half), 1/2 cup raisins (optional), 3 to 4 shakes of nutmeg**

Butter a 9 x 13-inch baking pan. Pour maple syrup in the pan. Butter and cube the bread slices and sprinkle on top of the maple syrup. In a bowl, whisk eggs with sugar and cream (or half-and-half). Pour over bread and sprinkle with raisins if desired.

Let sit for half an hour or more to let the bread soak up the liquids. Sprinkle nutmeg on top. Place in a larger pan and pour boiling water into the larger pan until it comes halfway up the side of the baking pan.

Bake in 325° oven for about an hour, until set (not "jiggly"). Cool slightly, cut into squares, and serve with additional maple syrup if desired.

• •

BAKING WITH MAPLE SYRUP

For cooking, use dark maple syrup. The darker the grade, the stronger the flavor.

If you want to substitute maple syrup for sugar in baking, use 3/4 cup of syrup in place of 1 cup of sugar and reduce the liquid in the recipe by 3 T for every cup of maple syrup substituted. (Another opportunity to dust off our basic math skills . . .)

• •

– Cobb's Coconut-Walnut Squares –

Betty Cobb: "This recipe was our own invention, and people seem to enjoy it."

3 cups flour, 6 T sugar, 3/4 cup margarine, 4 eggs, 3 cups brown sugar, 2 cups walnuts, 1 cup coconut, 1/4 cup flour, 2 tsp. baking powder, 1/2 tsp. vanilla

Combine flour, sugar, and margarine and press into an 11 x 17-inch pan (or into 2 smaller pans). Bake in a 350° oven for 10 minutes. Remove from the oven.

In a large bowl, combine the remaining ingredients. Pour over the crust and return to the oven for an additional 25 minutes. Cool slightly and cut into squares. Makes 24 to 30 squares.

··

RHUBARB

Rhubarb is wonderful because it comes up year after year and needs just a little mulch to keep it happy. It even thrives in town, and can serve as part of an edible backyard landscape. In Maine, the new tender stalks are ready in May. Although they look bold and beautiful in the garden, the leaves are poisonous. The stalk itself is tart (a good body cleanser), and just right to combine, in a sauce or pie, with the remaining jars of last year's homemade strawberry jam. (Or not homemade, as the case may be . . .)

··

– Cobb's Rhubarb Pie Filling –

Betty Cobb: "Gary's mother, Maud, used to make rhubarb pie like this. The recipe makes filling for a nine-inch pie."

4 cups rhubarb, 1 1/2 to 2 cups sugar (the younger the rhubarb, the less sugar it needs), 2 eggs, 4 T flour, 4 T medium cream, 1 T lemon, 1 to 2 T butter, pastry for 9-inch double-crust pie

In a big bowl, combine the rhubarb and sugar. In a small bowl, beat the eggs and add to rhubarb mixture. Sprinkle with the flour, cream, and lemon and combine well. Pour into prepared pie shell and dot the top of rhubarb with butter. Cover with top crust and bake at 350° until crust is golden and fruit is bubbling and/or soft.

Note: Instead of a top crust, the pie can be topped with a crumble mixture (your own favorite, or use the topping from the **Lakewood Rhubarb Crisp** recipe, p. 65).

– Cobb's Rhubarb Squares –

4 cups rhubarb (cut up), 1 cup sugar, 1 (3-ounce) package strawberry Jell-O, 2 cups yellow or white cake mix (used dry), 1 cup cold water, $1/3$ cup melted butter

Grease a 9 x 13-inch pan. Put the raw, cut-up rhubarb in the pan. Sprinkle with the sugar, then the Jell-O, then the dry cake mix. Gently pour the water over everything. Dribble the melted butter over the top. Bake at 350° for 1 hour. Serve warm or cold with favorite topping.

– Deer Run Strawberry Angel Dessert –

Darlene Berry: "Here is a light and refreshing dessert. It's my mom's recipe."

I doubled this (there was a bit of cake left), used a 9 x 13-inch pan, and it turned out great. (Good thing I did, too, 'cause it went in a flash!)

1 (3-ounce) package strawberry Jell-O, $1 1/4$ cups boiling water, 1 T sugar, pinch of salt, $1 1/2$ cups fresh sliced strawberries (or 1 package thawed frozen), $1/2$ pint whipping cream, half of a 10-inch angel food cake

Dissolve the Jell-O in the boiling water. Add the sugar and salt and stir well. Cool slightly. Stir in the fresh (or thawed frozen) strawberries and refrigerate until the mixture begins to thicken. Whip the cream and fold it into the strawberry mixture. Cover the bottom of a glass 8 x 12-inch or 9 x 11-inch dish with half of the cake (i.e., one-quarter of the total cake), torn into bite-sized pieces. Pour on half of the Jell-O mixture. Repeat. Refrigerate for 4 to 5 hours.

– Grant's Key Lime Pie with Pecan Crust –

Here's a dessert from Joy Russell, Grant's pastry/breakfast cook, that graces the red-checked tablecloths in Grant's dining room.

Crust:

3 packages graham crackers, 2 cups pecan pieces, 1 cup melted butter

In a food processor, make graham-cracker crumbs. Measure 2 1/2 cups of the crumbs into a bowl. Process the pecans and add to bowl along with melted butter. Mix well and press into two 10-inch pie pans.

Filling:

4 cans sweetened condensed milk, 8 egg yolks, 1 (8-ounce) bottle key lime juice

Whisk together milk and egg yolks. Add juice and combine well. Pour into pie shells and bake at 350° for 15 minutes. Chill and serve with whipped cream and a little chocolate syrup drizzled on top.

– Harrison's Sour Cream Pie –

1 cup sugar, 3 1/2 T cornstarch, 1 T grated lemon rind, juice of 1 lemon, 3 slightly beaten egg yolks, 1 cup milk (*or* half-and-half), 1/4 cup butter (1 stick), 1 cup sour cream, one 9-inch graham-cracker or chocolate-graham-cracker pie crust, whipped cream

In a heavy saucepan, combine first 6 ingredients and slowly bring to a boil while stirring over medium heat. When mixture thickens, stir in butter and cool to room temperature. Stir in the sour cream and pour into the pie crust. Refrigerate for at least 4 hours. Serve with whipped cream.

– Katahdin Lake Maple Syrup Pie –

one 8-inch baked pie shell, 1 $^1/_2$ T butter, 2 T flour, 2 egg yolks,
1 cup maple syrup, $^1/_2$ cup water, $^1/_2$ to 1 cup chopped walnuts,
$^1/_2$ to 1 cup whipped cream

In the top of a double boiler, combine butter and flour. In a bowl, beat together egg yolks, water, and maple syrup. Add to the butter/flour mixture and cook over boiling water until thick. Stir in chopped nuts and pour into the pie shell. Cool and top with whipped cream.

– Lakewood's Rhubarb Crisp –

Robin Carter: "The original camp housed the workmen who constructed Middle Dam, built to raise the water level and connect the lakes here in the Rangeley area. Loggers would arrive in the winter, cut trees, and haul them out onto the ice. Then, when the ice broke up in the spring, they would sluice [transport] the booms [encircled bundles of floating logs] down the waterways. At the dams, the loggers would jump from log to log, separating them to prevent log jams. Horribly dangerous work.

"Middle Dam regulates the level of the lake and flow of the water for the electric company. Richardson Lake is incredibly clear and pure because of the dam. The cold water at the bottom of the lake feeds through the dam and keeps the Rapid River cold year-round. When we open up camp in the spring, we try to bring whatever supplies possible across the lake before ice-out. It's always touch and go, trying to outrace Mother Nature.

"Here's a spring favorite."

Filling:
4 cups diced rhubarb, 1 cup sugar, $^1/_4$ cup flour, 2 beaten eggs,
$^1/_2$ tsp. cinnamon, $^1/_4$ tsp. orange peel

Topping:
$^3/_4$ cup brown sugar, $^3/_4$ cup flour, $^1/_2$ cup butter or margarine

In a bowl, cover the rhubarb with boiling water and let stand for 5 minutes. Drain and return to the bowl. Add the remaining ingredients and mix well. Pour into a 9-inch lightly greased glass dish. Mix the topping ingredients (sugar, flour, and butter) with a pastry blender and sprinkle that on top of the rhubarb mixture. Bake at 350° for 45 minutes. Serves 4 to 6.

– Lakewood's Sour Cream Cookies –

**1/2 cup butter, 4 cups sugar, 2 large eggs, 7 cups flour, 2 tsp.
baking soda, 2 tsp. salt, 2 cups sour cream, 2 cups raisins, sugar
for sprinkling**

In a bowl, cream together the first three ingredients. Sift together the next
three ingredients and add to the creamed mixture alternately with the
sour cream, stirring well after each addition. Add the raisins and stir well.
Drop by spoonfuls onto greased cookie sheets and sprinkle with sugar.
Bake at 350° for 8 to 10 minutes or until the cookies are a light gold color.

– Libby's Maple-Carrot Cake or Cupcakes –

Matt Libby: "Two of my great-grandfathers owned farms and a hotel, and supplied food to
loggers in the area during the 1880s. In the 1890s my grandfather, Ike, and his brother Will
got into the sporting-camp business and bought up a number of camps. The dining room
on their island camp—here on Millinocket Lake before it was dammed—was seventy feet
long. The chore boy, my uncle Charlie, used to walk a cow up the trail from Oxbow, the
nearest village [twenty-five miles away], soon after ice-out. He'd cross the Aroostook River
(swollen from the spring runoff), and then swim across the lake, leading the cow, so the
guests could have fresh milk."

*Carrot cake can be rich and dense. This one is moist and light as air. If you prefer the
former kind, no problem—see Bosebuck's Carrot Cake (page 185) for a delicious example. I
had some dried cranberries when I was testing this recipe, and sprinkled them on half the
cake. Either with or without, it was wonderful. I used it unfrosted, and also served it with
vanilla ice cream and a drizzle of warm maple syrup. (I know, I know—beyond the pale. But
who wants pale anyway?)*

Maple-Carrot Cake:

**2 cups flour, 1 cup sugar, 1 tsp. baking powder, 1 tsp. baking
soda, 1 tsp. cinnamon, 1/2 tsp. salt, 4 eggs, 1 cup vegetable oil,
1/2 cup maple syrup, 3 cups grated carrots**

In a large bowl, combine the dry ingredients. In another bowl, beat together the eggs, oil, and syrup. Stir the wet ingredients into the dry ingredients. Fold in the carrots and pour into a greased and floured 9 x 13-inch
baking pan, or fill paper-lined muffin cups two-thirds full. Bake at 350° for
30 to 35 minutes, or 20 to 25 minutes for the cupcakes. When cool, you
can frost with the following if desired.

Frosting:

> 1 (8-ounce) package cream cheese softened, 1/4 cup butter or margarine softened, 1/4 cup maple syrup, 2 cups confectioners' sugar

Combine all ingredients in a bowl and beat well.

– Maynard's Rhubarb-Oatmeal Squares –

> 3 cups rhubarb, 1 1/2 cups sugar, 2 T cornstarch, 1/2 cup water, 1 tsp. vanilla, 1 1/2 cups oatmeal, 1 1/2 cups flour, 1 cup brown sugar, 1/2 tsp. soda, 1 cup butter/margarine, 1/2 cup chopped walnuts

In a saucepan, combine the first five ingredients and cook until the rhubarb is tender and the sauce thickens. Preheat oven to 375°. In a bowl, combine the remaining ingredients and put three-quarters of this crumb mixture in the bottom of a 9 x 13-inch pan. Pour and spread the filling over the crumbs and sprinkle the remaining crumb mixture on top. Bake for approximately 40 minutes, or until the crumb mixture is cooked through. Cool and cut into squares. Serve with ice cream or whipped cream. Serves 12.

– Mount Chase Lemon Lush –

Sara Hill: "I've found that men especially love this. It's an old recipe from Patten, in this area, and can be made with chocolate or butterscotch pudding, too."

> 1/2 cup margarine or butter, 1 cup flour, 1/2 cup powdered sugar, 8 ounces cream cheese, 1 cup whipping cream (or 2 cups dairy whip), 2 small boxes instant lemon pudding, 2 1/2 cups milk, 1/2 cup chopped walnuts

In a saucepan, melt the margarine/butter and mix with the flour. Put in a 9 x 13-inch baking pan and press to form a crust. Bake at 350° for 20 minutes. Cool.

Beat the whipping cream (if using it). In a bowl, mix powdered sugar, cream cheese, and half of the whipped cream (or 1 cup dairy whip) and spread over the cooled crust. Combine milk and pudding and spread over the cream cheese mixture. Cover with remaining whipped cream or dairy whip. Sprinkle chopped nuts on top. Refrigerate before serving.

– Rideout's Banana Cream Pie –

You can find an easy reference for making graham-cracker crusts on page 250.

Jami Lorigan: "If you want a fabulous taste, you have to use real butter in your graham-cracker crust. One of the hardest things used to be keeping the bananas from turning brown. We don't want to use sulfides, so we've developed the trick of first soaking the banana slices in orange juice. Take them out with a slotted spoon to drain before using them in the pie."

1 graham-cracker crust, 1 large banana, 1/4 cup orange juice, 1 cup whipping cream, 1 large package instant vanilla pudding mix, 1 cup milk plus 1/4 cup whipping cream

Prepare graham-cracker crust. Cut banana and pour orange juice over slices to soak for 10 to 15 minutes.

In a bowl, whip 1 cup cream until peaks form. Place drained banana slices in the bottom of the crust. In another bowl, combine the pudding mix with the milk and unwhipped cream. Immediately add the whipped cream and mix well for about 1 minute to combine ingredients. Pour into the pie crust, cover with plastic wrap, and refrigerate immediately. Chill thoroughly and serve.

– Rideout's Pie Crust –

Bob Lorigan Jr.: "Our guests zoom in for lunch in spring, when it can be chilly out there. Not many camps will take the time or expense to provide a hot lunch. We also have American Plan and Housekeeping cottages mixed together, so people can do their own cooking or eat at the lodge. After June 26, we invite the general public to the dining room, Wednesday through Sunday, for dinner (by reservation only)."

1 egg, 2 T cider vinegar, 4 T ice water, 3 cups flour, 1 tsp. salt, 1 1/2 cups shortening

In a small bowl, beat the egg with the vinegar and 4 T ice water. Refrigerate. Mix flour and salt with whisk until blended through. Using pastry cutter, cut in shortening until pea-sized granules form. (Don't mix too much, as overworking will decrease the flakiness.)

Form a small well into the blended flour mixture and add the chilled liquid a little at a time. Using a dinner fork, cut the liquid into the dough. Continue to add liquid until the dough just holds together, with a few crumbs remaining in the bottom of the bowl. (Add a drop or two more cold water if necessary.)

Press the dough into a round ball. Dough can be rolled into a crust immediately, or chilled first for better rolling. Makes 3 crusts.

– Ross Lake Crumble-Top Brownies –

Andrea and Don Foley: "Communication to the 'outside' isn't always easy this far up in the woods. We don't have regular or cell phone connection, and our radio contact has been discontinued. However, we've had satellite Internet installed, so people can reach us by e-mail. Reprovisioning and transportation to and from the outside isn't always easy either. We stock up on cans and boxes of food. For this recipe, pecans are our favorite nut to use."

> **1 package (18 3/4 ounces) chocolate cake mix, 1 cup chopped nuts, 1/3 cup vegetable oil, 1 egg, 1 can (14 ounces) sweetened condensed milk, 1 cup semisweet chocolate chips, 1/8 tsp. salt, 1 tsp. vanilla**

In a mixing bowl, combine the dry cake mix, nuts, oil, and egg, and mix until crumbly. Set aside 1/2 cup for the topping and press the remaining mixture into a greased 9 x 13-inch baking pan.

In a saucepan, combine milk, chocolate chips, and salt, and cook, stirring, over low heat until chips are melted. Remove from heat and stir in the vanilla. Spread chocolate mixture evenly over the cake mixture, and sprinkle the remaining crumb topping over it.

Bake at 350° for 25 to 30 minutes. Serves 8 to 12.

– South Branch Lake Strawberry-Pineapple Pie –

Cindy Aldridge: "My mother, Teri, has done most of the baking for us for years. People actually come up and ask her to make this pie, it's so good."

Pie Crust:

2 cups flour, 1 tsp. salt, $^2/_3$ cup shortening, 6 to 7 T cold water

Into a medium-sized mixing bowl, sift together flour and salt. Cut in shortening until the mixture forms particles the size of small peas. Sprinkle cold water over the mixture while mixing lightly with a fork. Add water to the driest particles, pushing lumps to one side, until the dough is just moist enough to hold together. Form dough into 2 balls. Flatten one to about $^1/_2$-inch thickness and roll it out, on a floured surface, to a circle 1 $^1/_2$ inches larger than an inverted 9-inch pie pan. Fit the crust loosely into the pan.

Filling:

1 cup sugar, $^1/_4$ cup cornstarch, $^1/_2$ tsp. salt, 4 cups sliced fresh strawberries, $^1/_2$ cup drained pineapple tidbits or crushed pineapple, 2 T butter, $^1/_4$ cup milk

In a bowl, combine the first three ingredients, and stir in the next two ingredients. Spoon the mixture onto the pastry and dot with slices of butter. Roll out the remaining dough. Cut into strips $^1/_2$ inch wide. Crisscross over the filling to form a lattice top. Trim and seal the ends by folding the bottom crust over to cover the lattice strip and pinching dough together at the edges. Brush the strips with some of the milk. Place pie on a cookie sheet and bake in a 425° oven for 10 minutes. Lower the oven to 350° and bake an additional 30 to 40 minutes, or until the crust is golden brown and filling is bubbling.

– West Branch Pond Rhubarb Surprise –

Carol Kealiher: "Each spring, I plant a twelve-by-fourteen-foot garden because I like to provide my guests with the freshest food I can. We had a horse for years that provided the dressing for the garden. And our camp dog, 'TARI-two,' named for where we are on the map—Township A, Range Twelve [surveyed around the time of the Civil War]—helps keep the wildlife from eating up all the vegetables before I can get to them. I use our fresh rhubarb for this recipe. The surprise is that you place the rhubarb on top, but it ends up on the bottom. It's fun—and boy, the people love it!"

Cake:

$1/2$ **stick butter, 1 cup sugar, 2 eggs, $1/2$ cup milk, 1 tsp. vanilla,**
$1/2$ **cup flour, 2 tsp. baking powder**

In a bowl, cream together the butter and sugar. Add the eggs, milk, and vanilla and beat well. Sift the flour and baking powder into the wet ingredients and stir together. Pour into a greased 9 x 13-inch baking pan. Continue the recipe by making the topping (below).

Topping:

3 cups diced rhubarb, 1 cup brown sugar, 1 cup sugar, $1/2$ tsp. cinnamon, 2 T butter

Combine the rhubarb with the sugars and spoon over the cake batter in the pan. Sprinkle the top with cinnamon and dot with butter.

Bake in a 350° oven for 45 to 50 minutes. Serve plain or warm with whipped cream or ice cream. Serves 8 to 12.

Miscellaneous

– Bear Spring Critter Patrol –

Ron Churchill: "It's not just people who like our cabins. . . . Part of the changeover from winter to spring each year involves letting the wild critters know that the cabins are off-limits. I take a stick, press a cotton ball on top of that, and put a couple of drops of bob-cat or coyote urine (sold in bottles) on the cotton ball. Then I place a stick or two under each cabin. You can come around and . . . I guess I shouldn't really say . . . *refresh* the cot-ton balls from time to time. We also have high-pitched squeakers for the bats, which seem to do the trick."

– Bradford's Window-Washing Solution* –

Igor Sikorsky: "In February 1996 we called the Youlands, the former owners, and less than six weeks later we closed on Bradford's, and were in here opening up camp, having left our jobs only the week before. In less than two weeks we had ice-out, cabins cleaned, water running, twenty guests, and food on the tables!"

Karen Sikorsky: "Cleaning camp—on an ongoing basis, of course, but particularly in the spring when we're opening up—is a major task because we have eight cabins plus a lodge. So, we have dozens and dozens of windows to wash after the long winter. Igor and I have gone back and forth on how best to wash our windows. Igor believed in newspaper, but that was hard to handle and used up too much newspaper. I liked paper towels, but that wasn't good ecologically, and they left lint."

Igor: "Now we think we've got it figured out."

In a bucket combine:
1 gallon hot water, a squirt of liquid soap, 1 cup white vinegar,
1 cup rubbing alcohol
Use a sponge to apply the cleaning solution, a squeegee to dry-wipe after each sponge stroke, and then wipe the four edges of the window with a clean cotton cloth.

– Deer Run Hollow-Log Bonfire –

Robert and Darlene Berry: "Here at the camps we have a large bonfire every night from May to September. Building that many, we've tried to get 'creative' with the fires. The first and foremost rule of bonfires is safety. Our pit is dug out, free of rocks and grasses. Your cleared area for the actual fire should be quite large (ours is a ten-foot circle). We have a circle of rocks eight feet out from the edge of the fire pit, and we keep the grass around it mowed to avoid flare-ups from falling sparks. Make sure you have a clearance above from hanging tree branches so that flying sparks will not catch in a tree or limb (our pit isn't anywhere near trees). Pitchforks come in handy for moving the wood around in the fire, and two adults are necessary to attend a hollow-tree fire. A bonfire can be enchanting and mesmerizing. If done safely, it can create an evening of memories that last a lifetime!"

Find yourself a nice hollow log ("HL"), preferably at least 2$\frac{1}{2}$ feet in diameter and approximately 4 feet high. It may sound difficult, but there are many downed hollow trees in the woods. (If cutting down a hollow tree, make sure you do not have a nesting animal or bees' nest inside!) Lay two small logs down with a space between them of at least 6 inches. Set your HL upright on top of those two small logs. This will allow air to come up from underneath your HL. Stuff the HL with very dry wood and very dry fir boughs. If fir boughs are not available, crumpled newspaper will do.

Place a small amount of boughs/newspapers under the HL and light. The HL will act as a giant candle and burn for hours. As dry wood inside burns, add additional wood. Beware: As the HL and the supporting logs underneath burn down, the HL can tip. It is best to use pitchforks and tip the HL over before it falls down on its own—you need two people to do this safely. Once it is on its side, you will find the coals perfect for roasting marshmallows and hot dogs (and see **Smelts and Potatoes**, p. 40, and **Roast Corn**, p. 110).

– Indian Rock Bread Storage –

JoAnne Cannell: "April is my cooking time for the rush of May fishing. I'll cook at least twenty loaves of bread ahead of time. In order to prevent freezer burn, I put my make-ahead bread in plastic bread bags, making sure there is no air remaining in the bags. Then I place them in plastic containers I've gotten at the meat and/or fish counter at the grocery store. They'll last up to three months in the freezer that way, without freezer burn (although my twenty-plus loaves are usually gone within two weeks!).

– Katahdin Lake Maple Syrup—Five Ways –

Al Cooper: "Maple syrup runs when the sun brings the sap up into the tree system. You need warm days and freezing nights. I hand-auger our taps around March fifteenth, and we'll have sap generally until April fifteenth. We have at least thirty taps and use both red and sugar maples. It takes forty gallons of sap from a red maple to make one gallon of syrup, whereas with sugar maples the ratio is only twenty-seven to one. We get about two and a half gallons of sap per tree each day, and we'll pour that into our two-and-a-half-by-five-foot flat boiling pan. At this time of year we're cutting the wood supply for the camps [cabins], and we use the dead trees and leftover slabs for the sap boiling."

Suzan Cooper: "The bears will come out when they smell the sap, so we stay right at the sap burn—otherwise they'd tear everything to pieces."

Al: "Whichever of our three sons is at home will have target practice with their 22s (which improves their skills and keeps the bears at bay)."

Way #1:

Suzan: "We bring teacups and tea bags with us and we drink the new sap. It's delicious, and it's like a family holiday for us out there." Al: "A celebration of spring. The snowpack is still three and a half to four feet deep in March, but you know you've gotten through the winter together."

Way #2:

Al: "We collect the sap in the morning when the snow is still hard, and try to boil it down before dark. As it starts to come together, we always have snow cones. You pour syrup on the snow or scoop some into a teacup and pour some syrup over that and voilà, snow cones. Then, as the day ends, we pour the almost-ready syrup into five-gallon buckets and haul them into the kitchen to finish it off—otherwise it might boil away."

Way #3:

Suzan: "For the actual syrup, we filter it into stainless steel pots and cook it down the rest of the way on the woodstove. It works because we're in a log cabin and the logs will absorb the water/steam. But you can't do this in a kitchen with wallpaper."

Al: "The syrup is done if, one, you put a drop of it in water and it stays together, or two, the syrup is sheeting on your spoon. The official density is eleven pounds per gallon. We have canning jars heating in a big pan and pour the syrup right into them. We'll usually get sixteen to twenty quarts."

Way #4:

Al: "Next, we make maple sugar candy. You take a nine-by-nine-inch pan and coat it with butter. Boil a quart of syrup on a gas stove, approximately an hour, stirring constantly toward the end until it reaches the soft-ball stage and is foaming, and stays boiling even on low heat. Then I pour it into the pan and take the pan outside and put it on the snow to hasten the crystallizing process. After two to three minutes of cooling, it starts to change color into a light, opaque amber. Take a fork and stir it up to move those crystals around to all parts of the pan. All of a sudden, it flashes and gets hard immediately. You have to take your jackknife then and score it into little pieces before it gets rock hard."

Way #5:

For the fifth way to use maple syrup, see the **Katahdin Lake Maple Syrup Pie** recipe on page 65.

– Long Lake Dandelion Wine –

Sandra Smith: "My first taste of dandelion wine came from a Maine cousin. Her husband was making some repairs to the cellar where her wine was stored. As each trip back up the stairs became a bit harder for him to negotiate, she said to me, 'You'd better try the wine now, otherwise it might not survive the repairs!'

"I made my first batch of dandelion wine at my first sporting camp, Tea-Pond, in 1987. It came out fine, but it froze over the holidays when I left camp. Next time I made the wine I was at Penobscot Lake Lodge. I left the wine in the gas oven, where the pilot light made just enough warmth to keep it from freezing, and I had the wine for New Year's. The taste is really delicious and better than any champagne.

"Here at Long Lake Camps, my partner, Doug Clements, and I don't have many dandelions (or the time, for that matter, with fourteen cabins), but we recently opened some wine from eight years ago, and much to our amazement, it was smooth, potent, and very, very good."

> **1 gallon dandelion flower heads, 1 gallon water, 4 pounds
> sugar, 1 T dry yeast, 1 slice bread, fruit of choice: 2 oranges
> and 1 lemon *or* 2 cups raspberries, strawberries, or blueberries**

You also need a deep kettle, cheesecloth, and a large glass container with a large opening and a cover.

Pick enough dandelions (heads only) to fill a gallon container (you can use a plastic milk container to measure). Spread them out on a sheet of paper and let set for half an hour to get rid of the insects. Put the heads in a deep kettle. Add water and fruit of choice and bring to a boil. Strain the mixture into a bowl using cheesecloth. Add sugar and stir well.

Pour the wine into a large glass container. Put the slice of bread on top and sprinkle the yeast on the bread. Put the cover on loosely and let set away from the light for 1 week. Strain the mixture again with cheesecloth and pour into bottles. Put covers on the bottles loosely for the first week, then tighten. Let age 6 months in a cool, dry place.

– Mount Chase Dilly Fiddleheads –

Sara Hill: "This is basically the same recipe I use for Dilly Beans, except I use dry dill this time of year. The recipe comes from Betty Smallwood, who along with her husband, Jon, used to own Bowlin Camps."

I wait several months before serving my spring/summer pickles, to give them time to "do their pickling magic" in the jars. Especially with dilly beans and fiddleheads, the more patient you are, the better they'll be. (It's a Zen thing . . .)

4 to 6 cups fiddleheads, 2 cups cider vinegar, 2 cups water, 1/4 cup salt, 3/8 to 1/2 tsp. red pepper (cayenne) powder, 3 to 4 cloves garlic, 1 1/2 to 2 tsp. dried dill

Wash fiddleheads and remove the light brown husks. Steam them until just tender (about 4 to 5 minutes). Meanwhile, in a saucepan, bring vinegar, water, and salt to a boil and stir a minute or so. Place fiddleheads in hot pint jars, add one clove of garlic, 1/8 tsp. red pepper, and 1/2 tsp. dill to each jar. Cover with the boiling mixture. Seal. Makes 3 to 4 pints.

– South Branch Lake Oven-Cleaning Method –

Set the oven on warm for 20 minutes. Turn the heat off.

Set a small glass dish of full-strength ammonia on the top shelf. Set a pan of boiling water on the bottom shelf. Close the door and leave overnight.

In the morning, open the door and let the oven air out. Then wash down the oven with soap and water.

– South Branch Lake Wood Cleaner –

Cindy Aldridge: "Every spring we wash down every wood surface—all the log walls, the dining room tables and chairs, windowsills, all around the kitchen. This cuts into any greasy film from cooking, even smoke film from fires."

1 cup ammonia, 1/2 cup white vinegar, 1/4 cup baking soda, 1 gallon water

Combine in a bucket. Dip a heavy cotton cloth rag into the solution, wring it out, and wipe wood surface. No need to rinse!

Summer Season
July and August

Summer at Maine sporting camps is the time for family vacations and intergenerational reunions. The waters have warmed up, and there's fishing for bass and other warm-water species. There's plenty of time for swimming and boating, white-water rafting, and hiking along nearby forest trails. The earth is producing a cornucopia of vegetables from gardens—beans and peas, corn and carrots, lush lettuces and herbs, early potatoes and tomatoes—to name but a few.

White and pale yellow flowers underfoot give way to tiny, sweet strawberries in late spring and early summer. Soon raspberries bracket dirt roads and flourish in timber clearings. In fields and on hilltops, the famous Maine blueberry is ready for picking. Smaller and sweeter than the cultivated variety, Maine's official state berry is one of only three berries native to North America. Juicy blackberries round out the wild berry season. Sporting-camp cooks are known to take many a bucket of wild berries, brought in by proud, juice-stained, sunburned guests (as well as staff and family members), and transform the sweet treasures into pies and muffins, cobblers and cakes, jams and sauces.

Some guests have been at "their" particular camp longer than the owner, and it can be an endearing interpersonal dance for new owners between their own ideas and longtime guests' expectations. This is especially so in the case of favorite foods. Eventually, of course, it all sorts itself out, thanks to flexibility and a bit of gentle education on both sides.

Summer at a Maine sporting camp is like having your own cottage or cabin on a lake without the hassle of upkeep, the expense of purchase, or, at the American Plan camps, even the effort of food preparation. It's an environmentally conscious vacation as well, because people are enjoying a pristine setting without chopping it up into house lots (and thus destroying the wilderness that brought them there in the first place). It's a time to bask in the sun, go out in a canoe or kayak or putt around the lake, fish in the gentle morning light, walk along a dapple-lit path bracketed by wildflowers, listen to birdsongs, look at shooting stars. Kids can be kids, outdoors in the fresh air, using their imaginations, learning new skills, making new friends. On rainy days, families and friends gather to swap stories and play board games; or you can indulge in the luxury of reading a good book or simply daydreaming.

For many people, their week or two at a particular sporting camp is a summer tradition handed down in their family for generations. Some even share that time with friends who have set aside the same vacation time, decade after decade. People may have changed jobs, houses, or locales, but the reference point—the constant in their lives—is a certain sporting-camp cabin in Maine . . . where they know the families beside or near them, where they were all brought as kids, and where they grew up—and old—together.

Breakfast Fare

– Bald Mountain Greek Omelet –

Stephen Philbrick: "Bald Mountain Camps were started in 1897. Back then, guests came up by train and dispersed out through the Rangeley Lakes on old steamships. You used to be able to get on a train in Baltimore at seven a.m. on Friday, have three meals served to you, sleep in a Pullman car, and be here for your summer vacation by seven a.m. Saturday. The trains went out in 1889 and it's a shame, because it's a sensible and great way to travel.

"I'm the breakfast cook, and we offer a lot of selections. Every summer we have a guy in here, over ninety at this point, who always asks for a lobster omelet on his last day. I'll often kid around and put a lobster claw on the top of it.

"This Greek Omelet is requested a lot, here and at the BMC Diner I opened up in Rangeley for year-round business. The diner's turned out to be a popular place, and helps financially when the camps are closed for the winter."

> **3 eggs beaten, 1 T butter, 1 handful baby spinach, 2 T onion diced fine, 2 T tomato diced fine, 3 Calamata olives chopped, 1/2 cup feta cheese**

Whisk the eggs in a bowl with a drop or two of water. Melt the butter in a small skillet and sauté the spinach, onion, and tomato until the onion is soft and spinach is wilted (a couple of minutes). Add the olives; stir and set aside. In an omelet pan or skillet, make the omelet. Place the filling on one side, add the cheese, fold the omelet over the filling, and cook through. When it's done, slide onto a plate.

– Bear Spring Blueberry-Cranberry Muffins –

Peg Churchill: "July and August are our peak months. The camp is full of families enjoying a Maine summer, and we're serving around four hundred meals a day. At that point I'm ordering huge volumes of food. Each day, we're going through seven or eight dozen eggs and forty to fifty quarts of milk."

Ron Churchill: "Same thing's true at the waterfront. We're using about three hundred and fifty gallons of gas a week for the boats in the summer."

Peg: "Here's something that we serve on the Fourth of July."

3 cups flour, 1 cup sugar, 4 tsp. baking powder, 2 eggs,
1/2 cup oil, 1 cup milk, 3/4 cup blueberries, 3/4 cup cranberries
(dried or fresh)

Sift together the first three ingredients. In a separate bowl, combine the remaining ingredients. Mix the wet ingredients into the dry ingredients, stirring just enough to dampen the flour mixture. Spoon the batter into greased muffin tins and bake at 400° for 20 minutes. Makes 1 dozen large or 18 regular-sized muffins.

– Cobb's Two-Flour Pancakes –

Betty Cobb: "We've been making these pancakes for years. They're our special tried-and-true recipe, which everyone seems to enjoy."

2 1/2 cups white flour, 1/2 cup whole wheat flour, 1/2 cup sugar,
2 tsp. baking soda, 4 tsp. Bakewell Cream, 1 can evaporated
milk, 2 eggs, 3/4 cup melted margarine or butter

Place the dry ingredients in a big bowl. Mix the milk with enough water to make 3 cups and add to the dry ingredients, along with the rest of the wet ingredients. Mix until smooth and cook on a hot buttered griddle.

– Cobb's Zucchini-Blueberry Muffins –

Betty Cobb: "This recipe comes from Jane Wilkinson, who writes a weekly cooking column for a local paper called *The Original Irregular*. I enjoy trying some of her recipes and find they are very good."

2 cups flour, 1/2 cup sugar, 1 1/2 tsp. baking soda, 1/2 tsp. salt,
1 tsp. cinnamon, 1/2 tsp. nutmeg, 1/4 cup vegetable oil, 1/4 cup
maple syrup, 2 eggs beaten, 1 tsp. vanilla, 2 cups grated raw
zucchini (well-packed), 1/2 cup blueberries, 1 T flour

Preheat oven to 375°. Sift dry ingredients into a bowl. In another bowl, beat the oil, syrup, eggs, and vanilla. Stir the zucchini into the liquids; then add to the dry ingredients and stir until just moistened. Toss the blueberries with the flour before gently folding them into the batter. Grease two 12-cup muffin tins and fill two-thirds full of batter. Bake for 20 to 25 minutes or until golden. Makes 24 regular-sized muffins.

– Lakewood Blueberry Muffins –

Robin Carter: "The buttermilk in this recipe makes these muffins terrific."

2 1/2 cups flour, 1 cup sugar, 2 1/2 tsp. baking powder,
1/4 tsp. salt, 1 cup buttermilk, 2 eggs, 1/2 cup butter melted,
1 1/2 cups blueberries

In a large bowl, mix together the dry ingredients. In a small bowl, mix together buttermilk, eggs, and melted butter, and add to the flour mixture, stirring only until just moist. Add blueberries and mix in gently. Spoon batter into greased muffin cups and bake at 400° for 20 minutes. Makes 1 dozen.

BLUEBERRIES IN MAINE

You would think that Maine's acid, low-fertility soil and harsh winters might be an agricultural negative. Instead, those conditions support around 60,000 acres of wild blueberries and a $75 million industry. According to the Wild Blueberry Commission of Maine, blueberries were first harvested and canned commercially to feed the Union army during the Civil War.

Long before that, the various Maine Indian tribes valued this health-giving fruit. Elders say that in an ancient starvation time, the Great Spirit sent a special food down from the heavens to feed the people. You can see the token of this gift, they say, in the five-pointed star atop each berry. Native Americans ate blueberries fresh, dried them for winter use, and made juice as a cough remedy. Today, studies show that blueberries are "nature's antioxidant." In mid-May when blueberry flowers are in blossom, about a billion bees are trucked in and let loose in the blueberry barrens. Harvesting (late July to mid-August) is generally still by hand using a special rake, which looks a little like a metal dustpan with wide teeth.

Finally, in fall, the berry bushes turn a rich magenta color. If you want to see some beautiful alternative fall coloring, go to eastern Maine and drive past deep red blueberry barrens surrounded by green pines and tamaracks (conifers whose needles turn golden and fall off) under brilliant blue skies. Gorgeous. This all from a tiny little berry (and in the berry kingdom, smaller is often better and sweeter).

– Libby's Raspberry Muffins –

Matt Libby: "Ellen's homemade baked goods have saved the day many times when the fish decided not to bite or the deer decided not to appear. Without the long line of talented Libby women, our huge repeat-customer list would undoubtedly be shorter."

1/2 cup margarine/butter softened, 1 cup sugar, 2 eggs,
2 cups flour, 2 tsp. baking powder, 1/2 tsp. salt, 1/2 cup milk,
1 tsp. vanilla, 2 cups raspberries (or berry of choice),
cinnamon/sugar mixture

In a bowl, cream the margarine/butter and sugar. Add the eggs, one at a time, and mix well after each addition. Add the dry ingredients alternately with the milk and vanilla beginning with the dry ingredients. Gently fold in the berries. Spoon into 12 large greased muffin tins. Sprinkle mixed cinnamon/sugar over the muffins. Bake at 350° for 25 to 30 minutes, or until a toothpick inserted in the center of a muffin comes out clean.

– Nicatous Lodge Lobster Hash –

Linda Sheldon: "Something with a Maine flavor for an elegant brunch."

1 1/2 cups finely chopped cooked lobster, 3 cups finely chopped
cooked potatoes, 1/3 cup finely chopped onion, 1 tsp. salt,
pepper to taste, 3 to 4 T bacon fat or butter

In a big bowl, lightly toss together lobster, potatoes, and onions. Season to taste. Melt bacon fat/butter in a big skillet and spread the hash evenly over the bottom. Cook over medium heat until the underside is brown and crusty. Serves 4.

– The Pines Plain Donuts –

Steve Norris: "My dad, Charlie, when he was fifty-two, decided to leave the paper mill and run a sporting camp (with eight children and hardly a penny in his pocket). I was eight, the youngest, and so had the good fortune of growing up at Kidney Pond Camps [at Baxter State Park], in the sporting-camp industry."

Nancy Norris: "Steve's mother, Ruth, hired me as a waitress, and I basically never left! We had our wedding reception at camp."

Steve: "But in 1987 the state decided not to renew our lease because it was going to make the land part of the park. So now we had no equity and no future prospects. But we wanted to stay in the industry, so we started looking at camps. It took five years and twenty-seven places until we found this spot."

Nancy: "Steve and I spent a lot of good years with Ruth and Charlie at Kidney Pond. It's a hard business to be in if you're sick or of retirement age; you end up having to sell, thus leaving what you love. It's not really quite the right thing. Fortunately, Ruth ended up spending several summers with us here and just loved it. Fit right in, of course. She was a good cook, and people love these donuts."

> **2 eggs, 1 cup sugar, 2 T shortening, 1 tsp. vanilla, 1 tsp. nutmeg,**
> **1 cup buttermilk, 1 tsp. cream of tartar, 2 tsp. baking soda,**
> **3 1/2 cups flour**

Beat the eggs, then add sugar and shortening; beat mixture well. Add nutmeg, vanilla, and buttermilk; stir well. Sift together and add soda, cream of tartar, and flour, adding 1/2 cup additional flour, if necessary, to make dough the proper consistency to roll out. Roll on lightly floured board, cut with donut cutter, and fry in hot bacon fat or oil on one side until brown. Turn and cook on the other side until done.

– Weatherby's Pie Filling Muffins –

Heritage Recipe from Charlene and Ken Sassi.

Charlene Sassi: "I used to do all the cooking, and got it down so that if we were in full swing, cooking for forty, I could make everyone breakfast to order in twenty minutes so people could head right out fishing. After breakfast we'd have a staff meeting and plan our day. You have to be very organized so you have time in the middle of the day, because there are no days off.

"You can add almost anything to this basic muffin recipe: any fresh-picked or frozen berries, whole cranberry sauce, even crushed pineapple with walnuts. If there are pieces of pie or a cobbler left in the fridge, I remove the crust and put the fruit fillings in my muffins. Often the staff would ask, 'Where's the pie from last night?' Guess where!"

> **1 egg, 1/2 cup milk, 1/4 cup vegetable oil, 1 1/2 cups flour,**
> **1/2 cup sugar, 2 tsp. baking powder, 1/4 tsp. salt or to taste,**
> **1/2 cup berries or pie filling**

Mix first three ingredients. Add remaining ingredients and mix briefly until barely combined. Grease muffin tin and fill each two-thirds full with batter. Bake in a 350° oven for 15 to 20 minutes, or until golden brown.

Breads

– Attean's Basic Bread Recipe –

Andrea Holden: "I use this basic bread recipe for dinner rolls and sweet rolls. It's been part of the camp so long it doesn't even have a name. The yield is large, but the recipe can easily be cut in half and the extra rolls frozen."

12 T yeast, 10 cups warm water, 2 cups sugar, 2 cups dry milk,
2 2/3 cups shortening (margarine or vegetable shortening),
3 T salt, 16 eggs beaten slightly, 32 cups flour

In a large mixer or large bowl, dissolve the yeast and warm water. Add the sugar and dry milk and mix together. Add the shortening, salt, and eggs and mix together well. Add the flour gradually and mix until thoroughly combined and the dough is stiff. Turn out onto a lightly floured surface and knead until the dough is soft and elastic (5 to 10 minutes). Place dough in a large, well-greased bowl (or divide into 2 smaller bowls). Turn over so the grease is on the top. Let rise until double in bulk. Punch down, turn out onto lightly floured surface, and shape into any dinner or sweet rolls desired. Let rise, and bake at 350° for 15 minutes or until golden.

– Mount Chase Heavenly Cloud Biscuits –

2 cups flour, 4 tsp. baking powder, 2 T sugar, 1/8 tsp. salt,
1 stick margarine, 1 egg, 2/3 cup milk

In a bowl, mix dry ingredients together. Add margarine and mix with fork or pastry cutter until crumbly. In a small bowl, beat egg and milk together and add to the biscuit mixture. Turn onto lightly floured surface and knead 10 times only. Roll out to 3/4-inch thickness and cut into biscuits with glass or biscuit cutter. Bake at 450° for 15 minutes.

– Tim Pond Biscuits –

Betty Calden: "One of my fishermen once said, 'Wow! These biscuits are so big, you ought to hang one up on the wall with the other trophies.'"

**4 cups flour, 5 tsp. Bakewell Cream, 3 tsp. baking soda,
1 1/2 tsp. salt (or to taste), 1/2 cup vegetable shortening,
3 cups milk**

Sift the dry ingredients into a large bowl. Cut in the shortening (I use my fingers). Add the milk all at once and mix just lightly (the longer you mix biscuits, the harder they'll get). This makes a very moist mixture, but I put enough flour on the board—1 1/2 to 2 cups—to make the right consistency. Scoop out the mixture with a spatula onto the very well-floured board. Knead gently, incorporating the additional flour, about 6 to 7 times, until you get a soft dough. You don't have to get all the flour from the board into the dough. It should feel like soft Play-Doh (if you make biscuits enough, you'll know the feel). Roll or pat the dough out gently to a 3/4- to 1-inch thickness. Cut with a round cutter or a glass. Bake at 400° for 8 to 10 minutes. Makes 12 or more, depending on how thick you like them.

– Wheaton's Lemon Bread –

**1 cup sugar, 6 T melted butter, 2 beaten eggs, 1/2 cup milk,
1 2/3 cups sifted flour, 2 tsp. baking powder, 1/4 tsp. salt, grated
rind of 1 lemon**

In a bowl, combine all ingredients and stir until well blended. Pour into a greased 5 x 9-inch loaf pan and let stand 20 minutes. Bake in a 325° oven for 45 minutes. While loaf is still warm and in the pan, spread the following over the top:

6 T sugar mixed with the juice of 1 lemon

Cool in the pan. Remove and slice.

– Whisperwood's Zucchini Bread –

Candee McCafferty: "If you want, you can also use this recipe to make zucchini muffins for breakfast. Just fill muffin tins three-quarters full and bake for twenty to twenty-five minutes."

2 cups grated unpeeled zucchini, 3 eggs (or 1 whole egg and 4 whites), 1 cup oil, 2 cups sugar, 3 cups flour, 1 tsp. salt, 2 tsp. baking powder, 1 tsp. baking soda, 1 tsp. cinnamon, 1/2 cup walnuts (optional)

Wash, dry, and grate zucchini. In a big bowl, beat eggs, oil, and sugar. Sift dry ingredients into the wet mixture and mix well. Stir in zucchini and walnuts, if desired. Bake at 350° for 1 hour.

Appetizers

– Alden's Veggie-Cheese Strudel Bites –

If you're lucky enough to know your wild mushrooms and have a garden with basil and (at this point in the season) a second planting of spinach, you'll be well on your way to making this recipe from my archives, collected when Joe Plumstead was chef at Alden's.

It was given to me as an entrée, but my notes say: "This would be fabulous served as an appetizer, since it is very rich. For people not passionate about garlic, probably 4 cloves would do the trick." Joe offered a variation (which could serve as an entrée): "Omit spinach and basil. Substitute 1 cup diced chicken plus 2 tsp. thyme. Proceed as directed."

> **2 T butter, 6 cloves garlic chopped, $1/4$ cup fresh basil leaves finely chopped, $1/8$ cup dry sherry, 4 cups sliced wild (or store-bought) mushrooms (shiitake, crimini, and oyster are a good combination, but any other combination will do; more mushrooms is okay, but not less!), $1/2$ pound fresh spinach chopped, $1/2$ tsp. salt, $1/2$ tsp. white pepper, $1/2$ pound Muenster cheese shredded, $1/4$ pound softened cream cheese, $1/8$ cup sour cream, phyllo pastry**

Melt the butter in a deep-sided pan with the garlic. Add the spinach and cook until wilted. Add the sherry, basil leaves, and mushrooms. Cook, stirring frequently, about 2 to 3 minutes, or until the mushrooms have absorbed some of the sherry (taste one!). Remove from the heat and drain any excess liquid. Add the salt, pepper, cheese, and sour cream. Mix thoroughly and chill. When chilled, drain any remaining liquid from the mixture.

Arrange phyllo pastry 3 layers thick, brushing each layer with melted butter or spraying with pan coating. Place about a quarter of the mushroom mixture onto the pastry. Spread mixture down phyllo about two-thirds of the way and out to about 1 inch from the sides. Carefully fold the unfilledt third of the phyllo over the filling. Fold over the sides to lock in the filling and roll up the pastry. Repeat with remaining mushroom mixture and phyllo pastry.

Spray a cookie sheet with pan coating. Beat 1 egg and brush some onto the strudels. Cook at 375° for 15 to 20 minutes or until the pastry is golden brown.

– Cobb's Gazpacho –

Gary Cobb: "Each August we have a special nature-study weekend. Along with the geology of the Pierce Pond area, we do wildflower and tree identification, and we might have a tour of timber-cutting practices. There are actually wild orchids here, and we'll see sundew, creeping snowberry, pipewort, and bladderwort. This area is full of wildlife treasures."

Betty Cobb: "I serve this soup as a summer appetizer in small bowls with a little extra ground-up onion/pepper mixture and croutons on top. You can grind the vegetables in a food processor if you don't have a food grinder."

10 cups tomato juice, 2 T beef bouillon, 7 tomatoes chopped, 2 cups peeled and chopped cucumbers, 1 cup coarsely ground green or red bell pepper, 1 cup coarsely ground onion, 1 cup red wine vinegar, 1/2 cup good-quality olive oil, 3 1/2 tsp. Worcestershire sauce, 20 drops of Tabasco sauce

In a big pot, bring the tomato juice and bouillon to a boil. Stir in the remaining ingredients. Return to the boil and then turn off heat. Let sit for 1/2 hour and then refrigerate until cold before serving. Serves 12 to 14.

– Indian Rock Watermelon Starter –

JoAnne Cannell: "This is a refreshing starter on a hot day, or it can serve as an easy dessert. Everyone seems to like it."

Rainbow sherbet, watermelon

Put 2 to 3 spoonfuls of sherbet in the bottom of individual bowls. Halve a watermelon and use a small ice-cream scoop or spoon to scoop out desired amount of watermelon into each bowl. The sherbet will have melted a bit at this point, which is the way it should be.

– Jalbert's Salsa Dip –

Jalbert's (pronounced Jal-bear) is on Round Pond along the Allagash, and most people come upon the cabins while canoeing the wilderness waterway in the summertime.

Phyllis Jalbert: "This was true wilderness in 1946 when my grandfather, Willard Jalbert, and his sons built the camps. Sometimes we could boat the thirty-five miles from Allagash Village to camp in a day, if nothing went wrong. . . .

"'Moosetowner' is the name given to people who live in the Allagash area. They're mostly of Scotch and Irish ancestry, with some French mixed in too.

"Here is a dip you can use with tortilla chips, or sometimes I'll make up mini quesadillas using grilled flour tortillas, grated Monterey Jack cheese, and this salsa."

> **2 yellow (or red) tomatoes coarsely chopped, 1 small white onion minced, juice of 1 lime, 2 T chopped fresh cilantro, 1/2 tsp. salt, dash of cayenne pepper**

Combine all ingredients in a bowl and stir well. Set aside for 15 minutes before serving so the flavors can combine.

– Long Lake Before-or-After Salad –

Sandra Smith: "Doug and I liked Long Lake Camps because we thought they had a wonderful location, good for family vacations. People can go across to Canada, where there's a great chocolate factory, Campobello Island, and the Quoddy Head Light. We have golf courses nearby, hikes, canoe trips, a wildlife refuge, and the village has a couple of tennis courts. We offer guided kayak and canoe trips, wildlife and birdwatchers' tours, a women's fly-fishing school, and a photography workshop. We have all the freshwater attractions, and the ocean is only an hour away. Also, there's a small airstrip right up the road.

"This makes a refreshing summer appetizer. It can also serve as a light dessert, topped with whipped, sour, or ice cream. My ingredients depend on the season, but in a pinch, I use frozen fruits, which also work well. The following fruits are simply a guideline."

> **Wild fruits in season (strawberries, blueberries, raspberries, blackberries), watermelon, apples, grapes, cantaloupe, bananas, 1/4 to 1/2 cup light brown sugar, 1 tsp. lemon juice**

Slice the bananas and cut the apples and melons into bite-sized chunks. Combine in a bowl with sugar and lemon juice and stir gently until sugar is dissolved and the fruits start to form some juice. Refrigerate and cover the bowl until you serve.

– Maynard's Deviled Eggs –

Gail Maynard: "When the family started running the camp in the early 1900s, they charged two-fifty a day, including meals—but to give you an idea, whole loins of beef were then only fifteen to eighteen cents. There was also a daily train running up here [to Rockwood on Moosehead Lake] from Portland, so it was actually easier to get supplies back then. There was a garden, and two cows and sixty-seven chickens, so all the milk and eggs were taken care of. My late father-in-law, Roger, told of making homemade ice cream so rich that it stuck to the roof of his mouth. We still have the garden, and we still raise chickens. We'll get around twenty-five to thirty pullets in the spring and raise them for eating chickens for the family, and we'll have around forty laying chickens for the camp's fresh eggs."

> **1 dozen eggs, 3 T sweet relish, 1/2 to 1 tsp. prepared horse-radish (or to taste), salt and pepper to taste, a dash of Worcestershire sauce, mayonnaise**

In a saucepan, boil the eggs gently for 10 minutes. (I never have any problem with the whites seeping out, because the whites in fresh eggs hold together—both in frying and boiling. It's one way to tell how fresh your eggs are.)

Drain the water from the pan and cover with several rinses of cold water. Cool the eggs, peel them, and cut in half the long way. Gently scoop out the yolks into a bowl and mash them with a fork. Add remaining ingredients. (I go heavy on the horseradish because I like them hot.) and stir in enough mayonnaise to get the consistency you want for spooning or piping into the egg whites. I use a cake-decorating bag and squeeze the yolks into the egg whites with the big floret piping tube.

– The Pines Broiled Tomatoes –

After making and enjoying this, I had some extra topping mixture left over. The next day, I picked some cherry tomatoes, combined them with the topping in a salad bowl, poured some of Alden's White Balsamic Vinaigrette (p. 109, in the Too Many Tomotoes Salad recipe) over it all, and had a delicious Italian-type bread salad. (I love my job!)

Nancy Norris: "There's nothing like real tomatoes, ripe from the garden."

> **4 large ripe tomatoes, 2 T unsalted butter, 1/4 cup finely chopped onion, 1 clove garlic, 3/4 cup soft breadcrumbs,**

> 3/4 cup canned pitted black olives chopped, 3 T chopped
> parsley, 1 T grated Parmesan cheese, 3 anchovy fillets finely
> chopped (optional)

Remove the stem end and the bottom of each tomato. Cut crosswise into 3 thick slices and place on a baking pan. Preheat the broiler.

Melt butter in a large skillet over medium heat. Add the onion and garlic and sauté until soft (2 to 3 minutes). Remove from the heat and stir in the remaining ingredients. Spoon mixture onto the tomato slices. Broil 6 inches from the heat for 5 to 7 minutes, or until nicely browned.

Serve hot or at room temperature. Serves 4 to 6.

– West Branch Pond Firecrackers –

Carol Kealiher: "These are perfect for the Fourth of July. They are a little labor-intensive, but worth it. You can regulate the 'fire' part of the crackers with the amount of Tabasco sauce you use."

> 1/2 cup butter, 1/4 pound sharp cheddar cheese, 3/4 tsp. salt,
> 1/2 tsp. cayenne pepper, couple of drops Tabasco sauce,
> 1 tsp. dried dill (2 tsp. if fresh), 1 cup flour, 1 1/4 cup Rice
> Krispies

Grate the cheese and cream together with the butter. Add the seasonings, then the flour and Rice Krispies, and mix well. Shape into marble-sized balls and place on a lightly greased cookie sheet. Flatten firecrackers with a fork and bake at 350° for 12 minutes or until golden.

Soups

– Alden's Chilled Cucumber Soup –

This can be a refreshing summer appetizer or the soup portion of a soup-and-salad meal.

6 cucumbers, 1/2 cup chopped fresh parsley, 6 scallions chopped,
2 T chopped fresh dill, 1/4 cup lemon juice, 1 quart (4 cups)
buttermilk, 1 cup plain yogurt, 1 cup sour cream, salt and pepper to taste

Peel the cucumbers and cut in half lengthwise. Scrape out the seeds, sprinkle with salt, and let them stand in a colander to drain for 30 minutes.
Chop the cucumbers coarsely and put the pieces in the food processor or
blender along with the remaining ingredients (do this in batches, if necessary). Blend thoroughly and season to taste. Chill well before serving.
Garnish with a dill flower if available. Serves 8 to 12.

– Bear Spring Carrot Basil Soup –

*If you gently simmer the carrots (2 pounds) and onion (1 large) along with some chicken bones
(or use bouillon), you'll have some nice chicken broth in addition to your vegetable purees.*

6 cups cooked carrot puree, 1/2 cup cooked onion puree,
2 3/4 cups chicken broth, 6 cups half-and-half, 1/2 to 1 T fresh
basil chopped, 1 1/4 tsp. seasoned salt, 1/2 tsp. white pepper,
whole sweet basil for garnish

Cook the vegetables and puree until smooth. In a large bowl or pot,
combine the remaining ingredients, except the whole basil, and stir in the
vegetable purees. Serve chilled for a hot day, or you can warm the soup
on low heat for a cold day. Garnish with the whole basil.

– Bowlin's Bass Chowder –

Heritage Recipe from Betty and Jon Smallwood, who ran Bowlin Camps from 1968 to 1999.

Betty Smallwood: "We have four boys, who were raised at Bowlin Camps with no
running water. They were, I believe, the first and only kids in Maine who took a floatplane
to school each day."

Jon Smallwood: "They would walk two miles to Bowlin Pond in the morning to get the plane. There were no roads in here then; we had a team of horses and a buckboard to get in and out."

Betty: "Our sons were always thrilled to catch the bass for this recipe. Incidentally, here's a hint I learned over the years: Never let a guest look into your stockpot. They invariably say, 'Ugh! You're going to serve that?!' Of course, once they try this, they won't be able to get enough of it. For best flavor, make the chowder ahead and let it cool, then reheat before serving."

2 pounds bass, 5 medium potatoes, 1 small onion,
chives and parsley (we prefer fresh from our garden),
canned evaporated milk

Prepare the stock by placing the cleaned and scaled fish (with heads) in a large stockpot. Cover with water, salt lightly, and bring to a boil. Turn down the heat and boil gently until the fish is done (10 to 20 minutes). Remove the fish and set aside to cool. Discard the head, skin, and bones. Strain and save the stock.

Place peeled, diced potatoes in the stockpot. Cover with the stock. Add the diced onion and boil until the potatoes are fork-tender. Add salt and pepper to taste. Add 1 T each chopped chives and parsley (or to taste).

Let the chowder cool at least $1/2$ hour before adding the evaporated milk (as much milk as stock, or more if you want it richer). Add the fish, stirring gently so as not to break up the pieces too much, and cool completely before gently reheating to serve. Serves 6.

– Cobb's Garden Soup –

1 zucchini, 1 summer squash, 1 cup each diced onion, carrot,
and celery, 1 T minced parsley, 2 cloves minced garlic,
3 T butter, 1 pound ground turkey or beef, 2 cups tomato
sauce, 2 cups diced tomatoes, 1 can red kidney beans (un-
drained), 2 cups water, 4 chicken or beef bouillon cubes,
1 tsp. salt, $1/2$ tsp. black pepper, 1 T each finely chopped fresh
oregano and basil (1 tsp. each if using dried)

Dice zucchini and summer squash and place in a big pot with the onion, carrot, celery, parsley, garlic, and butter. Sauté until onion is soft. Add turkey or beef and sauté until meat is browning. Add remaining ingredients (use chicken bouillon with turkey, beef with beef), and boil gently for $1/2$ hour, stirring occasionally. Check doneness of vegetables and adjust seasoning to taste.

– Grant's Lemon Turkey Soup –

I always cook a turkey in the summer. You just stick it in the oven and go out and play. You then have meat for sandwiches, pasta dishes, salads, and this refreshing soup. This recipe comes from Leslie Hilyard, former chef at Grant's Kennebago Camps, who says: "Turkey is a natural sedative, and the lemon, with vitamin C, acts as a restorative."

> 3 T olive oil, 2 stalks celery, 4 carrots, 2 onions, 1 to 2 cups diced cooked turkey meat, zest and juice of 2 lemons, kosher salt and white pepper, fresh (or dried) minced parsley and rosemary to taste, 8 cups hot turkey stock, 3 T melted butter, 3 T flour

Heat oil in soup pot and sauté the vegetables and turkey. Add the lemon zest, juice, seasonings, and herbs. Stir, allowing flavors to blend, then pour in heated turkey stock. Add butter mixed with flour and stir to thicken. Taste and adjust seasonings if desired.

– Harrison's Strawberry Soup –

Fran Harrison: "For hot days, here is a cold soup that can also be used as a dessert."

> 4 pints fresh strawberries, $1/2$ cup sugar (or four 16-ounce packages frozen strawberries in syrup), 2 T confectioners' sugar, 1 cup whipping cream, 1 cup sour cream, $1/4$ cup red wine (Merlot or whatever is available), $1/4$ cup Triple Sec *or* Grand Marnier *or* $1/3$ to $1/2$ cup orange juice

Slice strawberries into a bowl. Pour sugar over berries and set aside until juices flow. (If using frozen berries, thaw them in a bowl.)

Puree berries (I use a hand blender for everything). Add confectioners' sugar and both creams and continue to blend well. Add wine and liqueur (or orange juice) a little at a time, until desired taste is achieved. Once the mixture is all blended, put it in the freezer for an hour or so until it is thickened. Serve in individual bowls with a dollop of whipped cream if desired.

Fish

– Bald Mountain Lobster, Shrimp, and Scallop Stew –

Stephen Philbrick: "For dinner, we do one seating of sixteen tables, and any tables not locked up by our guests are available to the public. We also do a lot of catering. Our dining room looks out to the west onto ten miles of protected shoreline and some spectacular sunsets. In the summer we'll have lobster feeds outdoors, and on Fridays we have a real old-fashioned guide's barbecue.

"I've been involved with this business ever since I was a little kid and saw what it was like, at the end of the fifties, when jet travel developed and the sporting camp industry and the American Plan were on the decline. Now I'm seeing it coming back. Folks are spending their dollars at places like this, where they can be served and treated like they want to be treated. It's not just rush in, rush out."

Recipe from former chef Stephanie Altstaetter.

> $2^{1}/_{2}$ T vegetable oil, 2 large onions (diced), 8 shallots (diced), 3 cloves garlic (minced fine), 3 bay leaves, $^{1}/_{4}$ cup fresh basil (or 3 T dried), $^{1}/_{4}$ cup fresh thyme (or 3 T dried), 1 tsp. cumin, $^{3}/_{4}$ cup white wine, $1\,^{3}/_{4}$ pounds new potatoes (peeled and diced), 2 quarts chicken stock, meat from two $1\,^{1}/_{4}$-pound lobsters, 2 pounds scallops, 2 pounds shelled shrimp, 3 cups half-and-half

Sauté onions, shallots, and garlic in the oil in a large soup pot. Add the herbs, wine, potatoes, and stock, and boil gently until potatoes are just cooked. Add lobster meat, scallops, and shrimp and simmer for $^{1}/_{2}$ hour. Add half-and-half and heat through. Serves 8.

– Bear Spring Pike Steak –

Ron Churchill: "We have bass and pike (as well as many other varieties of fish). Pike are bony but very sweet, like pickerel. If people don't use live bait to catch them, the biggest, ugliest lure in the bait box works great. They're big, so they're fun to fish for. A pike has to be twenty-four inches to be a keeper, and should be over thirty inches for steaks, which is no problem at all here at Great Pond."

Slice a pike into 1-inch steaks and fry in enough peanut oil to cover the bottom of the skillet. Cook about 8 minutes to a side over medium heat. Serve with a couple of lemon slices.

– The Birches Crabmeat Stuffing –

John Willard: "This is our camp-sized recipe. It can easily be halved. You can use this mixture to stuff almost any fish. Fill the fish cavity and bake until the fish is flaky. Alternatively, you can use it to stuff mushroom caps (in which case, bake the caps at 450 degrees until crusted and golden, about eight minutes)."

> 1 medium onion finely chopped, 2 T garlic, 4 cups bread-
> crumbs, 4 cups cracker crumbs, 1 to 1 1/2 cups mayonnaise, 3 T
> lemon juice, 2 pounds crabmeat

Sauté the onion and garlic in oil until soft. Put all the ingredients in a large bowl and mix together well.

– Dad's Haddock with Shrimp/Cheese Sauce –

Therese Thibodeau: "When Raymond and I first opened the camp, there was not going to be any cooking whatsoever; but our first guest, a man, didn't want to come in here if he had to cook. So I said, 'Okay—it's only one man. He can eat with us.' Well, word got around, and we started getting more and more people, and now we do a lot of cooking. When people arrive, we ask them if they have any allergies or if there's anything on our menu that they don't like (if so, I don't cook it). I never make the same meal twice during the seven days people are here, and it's all you can eat. For lunch, we give them a menu with several choices; they circle what they want, and we store it in a cooler so they can take it with them out on the river."

> 2 to 3 pounds haddock fillets, 1 can cream of shrimp soup,
> 1/2 to 1 cup mozzarella cheese grated, 1 sleeve Ritz crackers

Place the haddock in the bottom of a greased baking pan. Spoon and smooth the soup over the haddock, sprinkling cheese on top. Crumble the crackers over everything with your hand. Bake at 350° for 30 minutes, or until the fish flakes and is done.

– Deer Run Pan-Fried Pickerel Fillets –

Robert and Darlene Berry: "Many people avoid eating pickerel because they're so full of bones, but they *are* good eating. If done properly, a pickerel twenty-five inches or larger can be filleted, and then the bones are no longer a problem. A good, sharp fillet knife is also important. Believe it or not, an electric knife makes an excellent fillet knife.

"An added tip: Fish fresh from the water are always easier to fillet. The longer the fish sits, the softer the meat becomes."

enough pickerel fillets to feed your guests, vegetable oil, enough flour for dredging fillets, salt, pepper, and paprika to taste

Lay the pickerel on its side and, starting at the gills, slice down to the level of the backbone. Turn the knife sideways and cut down along the backbone to about half an inch from the tail. Flop the fillet meat over, but keep it attached at the base of the tail. With the fillet knife, cut through the meat to the edge of the skin, but do not cut *through* the skin. Follow down the meat of the fish, with the fillet knife turned sideways, cutting the meat away from the skin.

If the rib bones are still in it, take the fillet knife to where the rib bones are, and cut and roll the rib bones out. With your fingers, find the long strip of Y bones located in the center of the fillet. On the left side of the Y bones, at an angle to the left, cut the whole length of the Y bones to the end of the fillet. This will give you two long strips of boneless pickerel. Practice makes perfect, and boneless pickerel *is* possible!

Place 1/8 inch to 1/4 inch of vegetable oil in a frying pan. In a shallow bowl or plate, combine flour with seasonings and dredge the fillets, coating completely. Place fillets in hot oil. Cook 2 to 3 minutes on one side; turn and cook 2 to 3 minutes on the other side, until fish is browned and flaky. The fillets will cook quickly.

– Deer Run Baked Stuffed Pickerel –

Darlene and Robert Berry: "This recipe is good for those smaller pickerel you catch and don't want to fillet [as described in preceding recipe]. Scale the pickerel first, while it is still whole. Slit the belly and clean the inside, making sure to remove the blood vein that runs along the spine—it can be gritty and add an unpleasant taste.

Preheat your oven to 350°. Remove the head and rub the pickerel with salt and pepper. Place it on its back, belly side up, in a greased baking pan. Fill the belly with your favorite bread stuffing mix and bake 35 to 45 minutes or until the fish flakes. Remember to watch out for the bones!

– Indian Rock Campfire Lake Trout –

JoAnne Cannell: "Each summer we have what we call Celebration of Life Week, when we open the camps up, free of charge, to families who have children with cancer. The town of Grand Lake Stream is invited to our final cookout, and everyone gets involved. We started this in 1996 because of our daughter. It will always start on August 10, which is when her tumor was found (and also our wedding anniversary), and go until August 17."

Ken Cannell: "When we do our outdoor shore dinners, we never cook right on the fire, but put the food in a big, square screen and prop that up by the flames."

Lake trout, especially if they're around three or four pounds, will be oily. (It's almost like lamb tallow fat.) So you want to open the fish up and have the belly side facing the fire and slanted down so the oil can run out. If you bake them indoors, put them up on a rack to get rid of the fat that way. Cook until the fish flakes at the thickest part.

– Leen's Lemon-Pepper Lake Trout Fillets –

Charles Driza: "We have an abundance of lake trout here on West Grand Lake, and encourage our guests to keep all legal fish of eighteen inches or more. These fish are tasty and very nutritious due to the high levels of omega-3 in them."

Lake trout, melted butter, lemon pepper
Fillet the lake trout and remove all bones. Brush the fish with melted butter and sprinkle generously with lemon pepper. Broil the fillets under a hot flame until just done. This should only take a few minutes per side. It is important not to overcook the fish to the point where it is dry. The center of the fillet should still be just slightly translucent when removed from the broiler. We generally serve the fish on a bed of lettuce with sliced fresh tomatoes.

– Nicatous Lodge Lobster Pie –

Heritage Recipe from Denise and Gary Betz, who ran Nicatous Lodge from 1997 to 2003. Gary Betz Jr. grew up in a housekeeping sporting camp that his parents, Nancy and Gary Sr., still run in Grand Lake Stream.

Denise Betz: "We had an annual wild game potluck at Nicatous, and we also ran a lot of specials. This was something people really enjoyed. Adjust amounts to the number of people being served."

> **2 T butter, $^1/_4$ cup white wine, 1 cup well-packed lobster meat,
> 3 T butter, 1 T flour, $^3/_4$ cup light cream, 2 egg yolks, about $^1/_2$
> cup seasoned cracker crumbs or breadcrumbs**

In a saucepan, combine butter and wine and boil 1 minute. Add the lobster and set aside. In another saucepan, melt the 3 T butter. Add the flour and stir until the mixture bubbles. Remove from the heat and slowly stir in the cream. Drain the wine-butter mixture from the lobster and add that liquid to the cream mixture.

Return pan to the heat and cook, stirring constantly, until the sauce is smooth and thick. Remove from the heat. Stir in the egg yolks and pour the sauce into the top of a double boiler over hot, not boiling, water (the sauce may curdle if the water is boiling). Stir about 3 minutes. Add the lobster.

Spoon the mixture into a small pie dish and sprinkle with crushed seasoned crackers or breadcrumbs to cover. Bake at 300° for 10 minutes.

– Pleasant Point Spicy Lake Trout –

Mardi George: "During the summer of 2003, one of our guests, fourteen-year-old Josh, taught us this delicious way to cook lake trout. Since then, every time a guest wants to keep a trout they've caught, Clif fillets it for them and we cook it this way, and then accept the raves."

> For each trout (2 fillets):
> **1 egg, 2 to 3 T milk, $^1/_4$ cup flour, $^1/_4$ cup cornmeal, salt and/or
> pepper to taste, cayenne pepper to taste, 1 to 2 T butter**

In a bowl, beat the egg with the milk and dip the trout fillets in the mixture. Place the remaining ingredients in a baggie large enough to hold the trout. Place the trout in the baggie and shake well. Melt the butter in a skillet and sauté the trout until the flesh is flaky.

– Pleasant Point Stuffed Lobster –

Mardi George: "An unusual recipe for a sporting camp, unless you're lucky enough to have a husband who drives back and forth to the coast one day a week to tend twenty-five to fifty traps, as Clif does. We make no promises to our customers. We just tell them if he's lucky, they'll be in for a special treat."

(To kill the lobster quickly, insert a knife blade just behind the top of the "head" and pull it forward.)

1¹/₄-pound lobster (live), 1 tube Ritz crackers, 1 stick butter, dash of garlic powder

Split the lobster down the middle on its underside. Remove the green tomalley (and red roe, if you find any) and set aside. Remove the intestine (black cord in the tail). Sauté the roe and tomalley in the butter. Crush the crackers and combine with the sautéed mixture. Sprinkle on a bit of garlic powder. Stuff the lobster cavity and tail generously. Put the lobster halves in an aluminum basket, then on a cookie sheet, or place in a baking pan. Bake at 400° for 20 minutes.

– South Branch Lake Broiled Bass –

Russ Aldridge: "We're in prime bass waters, so this recipe is one of our specialties. A 'keeper' is two and a quarter pounds and up. Bass lay their eggs when it's warm, but if it gets cool they'll abandon the eggs and start all over again when it warms up, spawning up to six times that way. So, when weather changes back and forth from warm to cool, bass are on the move—which makes for the best fishing."

4 to 6 bass fillets approximately ¹/₄ pound each, 1¹/₂ sticks of butter, 2 T lemon juice, 1 medium clove garlic finely chopped, ¹/₄ to ¹/₂ cup seasoned breadcrumbs, 1 lemon, fresh parsley

To fillet the fish, you'll need a 6-inch thin-blade fillet knife. Start at the back of the head, where the fin ends, and enter with the knife approximately one inch deep. Follow down to the tailbone and repeat the process, following along the rib cage. Place the fillet, skin side down, on a cutting board. Hold the tail end down with a fork, and take the knife and cut down through the tail section. Turn the blade away from you and peel the fillet off the skin in an outward direction. Repeat process on the other side.

Pat the fillets dry with a paper towel and set aside. In a saucepan, melt the butter and add the lemon juice and garlic. Simmer gently for 2 minutes. Brush some of the butter mixture on the bottom of a large glass baking dish. Place the fillets in the dish and brush or spoon the remaining butter mixture over the fish.

Sprinkle the fillets with seasoned breadcrumbs and place pan under a broiler until the tops of the fish are golden brown and the meat is flaky (approximately 6 to 8 minutes). Garnish with lemon wedge and parsley.

For a special effect, serve with **Sherry Dill Sauce** (p. 119).

Poultry/Small Game

– The Birches Grilled Chicken Saté –

Ingredients listed are for 1 whole chicken breast; adjust amounts according to number of portions. This marinade can be made up to 2 hours ahead of time.

Saté Marinade:

2 cups teriyaki sauce, 1/3 cup fresh lime juice

Marinate a whole chicken breast in the marinade for 30 minutes to an hour before grilling. Do not marinate more than an hour. Grill chicken and serve on a bed of rice with The Birches Curried Peanut Sauce (below). Garnish with lime slices. Serves 2.

Curried Peanut Sauce:

This sauce can be prepared up to 3 days ahead of time.

1/3 cup peanut oil, 1 medium onion finely chopped, 4 cloves garlic finely chopped, 1 tsp. curry powder, 1/2 tsp. crushed red pepper flakes, 1/2 cup unsweetened coconut milk, 1/2 to 3/4 cup creamy peanut butter, 1/3 cup fresh lemon juice, 2 T white vinegar, 1 cinnamon stick, 2 T basil, 1/3 cup brown sugar, 1 or 2 bay leaves, 1/4 to 1/3 cup finely chopped peanuts (optional), 1/4 cup boiling water

Heat the oil in a large nonstick skillet over low heat. Add the onion and garlic and cook, stirring, until wilted, about 5 minutes. Add the curry powder and chili pepper and cook over low heat 2 to 3 minutes to mellow the flavors. Stir in the coconut milk (well blended) and the remaining ingredients, up to the chopped peanuts, and mix together well. Bring to a boil and immediately reduce the heat to low. Simmer gently, stirring until the sauce thickens, about 5 minutes. Stir in the chopped peanuts (optional). Remove the cinnamon stick and bay leaf. Place the mixture in a food processor and process until smooth, adding the boiling water through the feed tube to bind the sauce.

– Chet's Dutch Oven Chicken Pot Pie –

Sue LaPlante: "We run some daylong and extended canoe expeditions to places like the Allagash, Penobscot, and St. Croix Rivers. On these trips we like to do Dutch oven cooking over the open fire. This is one of many originally complex recipes that we've modified for busy camp owners cooking in the field. (It can easily be baked in a regular oven too, of course.) The pie crust called for is already rolled out and folded into quarters, and is usually found in the dairy section of the grocery store. We take it out of the package and put it into a cooler along with the other perishable or frozen items."

2 prepared double pie crusts, 4 cups cooked chicken in bite-sized pieces, 1 jar Alfredo sauce, 1 can cream of mushroom soup, 1 can chicken broth, 1 small container sour cream, 2 packages frozen stew vegetables (*or* 6 to 8 cups cooked fresh vegetables), salt and pepper to taste, butter

Line a 14- to 16-inch Dutch oven with foil. Line the bottom and part of the sides with 2 of the crusts. In a bowl combine all the ingredients except the butter and stir well. Pour into the pie lining and cover with the remaining 2 crusts. Make slits in the top crust and dot with butter. Put on the lid and place the Dutch oven on a bed of 8 to 10 coals, with 18 to 20 coals covering the top of the lid. Bake for 35 minutes without taking the lid off (this is important!).

If using a conventional oven, assemble the pot pie in a 9 x 13-inch baking pan. Bake at 425° for 35 minutes. (You can cover pan with foil for the first half of cooking time, removing it for the second half, or simply cook uncovered for the duration.)

– Cobb's Oven Barbecue Chicken –

Betty Cobb: "Our main meals are pretty standard. People know what to expect, and so do our food distributors. Every Tuesday, someone (usually Gary) goes out and picks up the bulk order that has been delivered to our garage at home. On Friday, we go out again and pick up the order of lobsters that's left in the garage. It sounds simple, but these trips eat up a better part of the day.

"This chicken turns out black on top, but people seem to like it that way."

1 quart tomato sauce, 1 cup vinegar, 1 cup brown sugar, 1 cup vegetable oil, 1 T onion powder, 1 T dry mustard, 1 T garlic powder, 1 T chili powder, 1 T black pepper

Cover cookie sheet(s) with aluminum foil. Place desired amount of washed chicken parts, skin side up, on top of the foil and smooth sauce over the top. Bake at 350° for one hour, or until chicken is cooked through.

Any extra sauce can be kept, refrigerated, in glass jars. Shake well before use.

– Wapiti Chicken Marsala –

Frank Ramelli: "The most popular meal I serve is Chicken Marsala and Sour Cream Noodles. People from all over the area will call and request it."

> **2 full boneless chicken breasts, 1 egg, $^1/_4$ cup flour, 3 to 4 T garlic olive oil, 2 green peppers, 2 T garlic olive oil, $^1/_2$ cup Marsala wine, salt and pepper to taste**

Cut each breast in half, giving you 4 pieces of chicken. On wax paper pieces, flatten each portion with a mallet. Beat the egg in a small bowl. Pour the flour onto a plate. Heat the 3 to 4 T garlic olive oil in a skillet. Dip each chicken piece first in the egg, then in the flour, and sauté in the skillet.

Meanwhile, slice the green peppers into strips and, in another skillet, sauté them in the 2 T oil. When peppers are nearly cooked, add the wine, stir, and pour the pepper/wine mixture into the chicken skillet; simmer the combined mixture until the chicken is thoroughly cooked. Serve with **Wapiti Sour Cream Noodles** (p. 114). Serves 4.

– Wilderness Island Teriyaki Chicken –

Carol and Mike LaRosa: "This can be prepared in a large fry pan if you don't have a grill (or if you just don't feel like grilling). Spray the pan with a vegetable spray and cook the chicken over medium heat, using the technique described below for grilling."

> **2 whole boneless chicken breasts (4 halves), 4 T teriyaki sauce, 2 T vegetable oil, 2 T brown sugar, 2 T cornstarch, 1 tsp. ground ginger, 2 to 3 cloves minced garlic (or 1 tsp. dried minced garlic)**

Cut chicken breasts in half and cut each half in 3 equal pieces (each whole chicken breast serves 3 people). In a bowl, combine the remaining in-gredients and stir well. Place chicken pieces in a large freezer bag and pour in the marinade. Seal the bag, mix everything well, and put in the refrigerator for 1 to 3 hours.

Preheat the grill on medium. Drain the chicken. Grill for 3 to 4 minutes, then turn pieces. Shut off the grill and finish cooking, 3 to 4 more minutes on the other side. Serves 6.

Meat/Big Game

– Attean's Barbecued Baby Back Ribs –

From my files, a recipe submitted by former camp cook Daryl Goslant.

> 37 pounds baby back ribs, 1 1/2 quarts brown stock, 1/3 cup
> onion diced fine, 1 T minced garlic, 1/2 cup salad oil, 1/3 cup
> flour, 1/4 cup sugar, 1/2 T dry mustard, 1 tsp. black pepper,
> 1/2 cup cider vinegar, 1 quart tomato puree, juice of 1 1/2
> lemons, 1/2 cup Worcestershire sauce, 1/2 T barbecue spice,
> salt and Liquid Smoke to taste

In a large pot, heat the brown stock. In a small saucepan, sauté the onion and garlic in the oil. Add the flour to make a roux, and stir until bubbly. Add about 1/2 cup of the hot stock to the roux, stir until thick and smooth, and then pour the roux into the pot, stirring well. Add remaining ingredients and simmer 30 minutes. Adjust seasonings to suit taste.

Marinate ribs in the sauce for at least 3 hours. Grill, brushing on the barbecue sauce, or cook in the sauce in a 375° oven until meat is thoroughly cooked (35 to 45 minutes). Serves 40.

– Jalbert's Seven-Layer Moose Casserole –

Phyllis Jalbert: "Here's a recipe featuring vegetables from a Maine summer garden. I use spaghetti sauce with vegetables, mushrooms, and herbs to spice this up a bit. The better the sauce, the better the dish. You can also substitute uncooked sliced carrots for the green beans, or use both. I add the cheese topping only after the first hour of cooking to allow the bacon to crisp; also, that way the cheese stays light and bubbly."

> 1 cup cooked (or canned) whole-kernel corn, 1 cup uncooked
> rice, salt and pepper to taste, 2 cups fresh (or canned) tomato
> sauce, 3/4 cup water, 1/2 cup finely chopped onion, 1/2 cup
> chopped green pepper, 1 cup cooked (or canned) green beans,
> 3/4 pound ground moose (or beef), 1/2 cup grated mild cheddar
> cheese, 1/2 cup grated mozzarella cheese, 4 slices cut-up bacon

Put the corn and rice in a baking dish or pan. Sprinkle with salt and pepper. Mix the tomato sauce and water and pour half over the corn/rice. Add the vegetables, mix the two cheeses together, and sprinkle about a third of it over the vegetable layer. Add the meat and sprinkle again with salt and pepper (if desired). Top with the bacon. Cover tightly with foil and bake in a 350° oven for 1 hour. Uncover, sprinkle top with the rest of the cheese, and continue to cook for 30 minutes longer. Serves 4 to 6.

MOOSE WATCHING

Visitors coming to sporting camps in the summer are keen to catch a glimpse of Maine's largest big-game animal. A mature bull moose can weigh between 1,000 and 2,000 pounds (a cow weighs in at 700 to 900 pounds). Several camps offer moose cruises, and most camps can offer predictable moose sightings thanks to the animal's regular eating habits. A moose eats about 40 to 50 pounds of vegetation a day, and needs three square meals: breakfast around dawn, lunch between 12:00 and 2:00 p.m., and dinner at dusk. A word of caution in this regard: If you drive on logging roads in hopes of seeing a moose, be very aware that they have dark coats and their eyes don't reflect car headlights the way other animals' eyes do. They also don't scamper away like deer and other game. Moose are the Maine animal kingdom's equivalent of logging trucks— they are heavy, potentially life-threatening, and definitely have the right-of-way.

– Jalbert's Venison-Corn Pie –

Phyllis Jalbert: "This has lots of corn; you can use fresh or canned. I like to mash my potatoes so they're very smooth before I add the butter and milk."

A helpful tip when making mashed potatoes: Add melted butter first, followed by the milk; that way, the potatoes won't get too "starchy."

2 cloves minced garlic, 1 onion diced, 1 T butter or oil, 1 pound ground venison (or moose or chuck steak), salt and pepper to taste, 1 (15^1/2-ounce) can cream-style corn, 1 (10-ounce) can *or* 1 to 1^1/2 cups fresh corn, 3 to 4 potatoes cooked and mashed

Sauté the garlic and onion in the butter/oil in a large frying pan. Add the meat and cook until browned. Salt and pepper to taste and spoon into a casserole dish. For the next layer, mix the two corns together in a bowl and spoon on top of the meat mixture. Top with the mashed potatoes and dot with butter. Bake at 350° for ^{1}/2 hour until bubbly.

– Loon Lodge Meat-Stuffed Peppers –

Linda Yencha: "My menu is simple, hearty, home-style cooking. Our meals (except lunch) are served family style, and are all you can eat. I cook like my mom: a little of this and that, to taste. Of all my jobs in this business, I love cooking the best. This recipe goes well with mashed potatoes. Use the ketchup/water gravy over the meat and potatoes."

> $^{1}/_2$ cup rice, 1 onion diced, $^{1}/_2$ stick of butter or margarine, $^{1}/_2$ pound hamburger, $^{1}/_2$ pound ground pork, 2 green bell peppers, salt and pepper to taste, 1 bottle ketchup, 1 or 2 bay leaves

Cook rice according to directions on the package. Brown the hamburger and set aside. Fry the onion in the butter until the onion is soft. Mix the onion and rice together with the meat. Cut the peppers in half and stuff each half with the meat/rice mixture. Arrange stuffed peppers in the bottom of a large heavy pot. Pour the ketchup over the top of them and add enough water so liquid comes halfway up the peppers. Add the bay leaf and simmer until the peppers are fork-tender. Serves 4.

– Nicatous Lodge Pepper Steak –

Heritage Recipe from Chris and Pete Norris, who ran Red River Camps and then Nicatous Lodge from 1984 to 1997. Pete, Steve (The Pines), and Charlene Sassi (Weatherby's) are all members of the Norris family that operated Kidney Pond Camps in what is now Baxter State Park.

> 4 fillet steaks ($^{1}/_2$ pound each), 1 tsp. salt, 3 T coarsely crushed peppercorns, 3 T butter, 1 T oil, 4 T bourbon, 2 T water

Warm a platter (in a 225° oven, or under hot water). Rub the steaks with salt and sprinkle with the peppercorns. Pound the pepper into the meat with a meat pounder. Repeat on the other side. Heat the butter and oil in a heavy skillet and sauté the steaks 4 minutes to a side. Transfer to the warm platter. Add the bourbon and water to the skillet and cook over medium-high heat, scraping the bottom to incorporate the bits of meat and fat. Boil down the sauce for 1 minute, then spoon it over the steaks and serve. Serves 4.

– Weatherby's Moussaka –

Recipe from chef Steve Clark.

**4 to 5 pounds potatoes, $1/2$ cup melted butter, $1/2$ cup flour,
2 cups scalded milk, 2 eggplants, oil, 1 large Spanish onion
thinly sliced, 4 pounds ground beef, salt and pepper to taste,
1 tsp. nutmeg, 1 tsp. cinnamon**

Scrub or peel potatoes, cut in chunks, and boil until fork-tender. Mash and set aside.

In a saucepan, melt butter, add flour, and mix thoroughly with a whisk. Add scalded milk and whisk on medium heat, bringing just to a boil, until mixture is smooth and thickened. Set aside.

Slice the eggplants thinly lengthwise (either with or without skin) and lightly fry in oil to cover the bottom of a big skillet. Remove from pan with a slotted spatula. Add onion to the pan and sauté until soft. Remove to a separate dish with the spatula. Add the beef to the skillet, along with salt and pepper and spices, and fry until browned.

In a 10 x 14 x 2-inch pan, or 2 smaller baking dishes, layer as follows: Place eggplant on the bottom. Top with the beef and the cooking juices in the skillet. Place the onions on the beef. Top with the mashed potatoes. Finish by pouring on the sauce. Bake in a 350° oven for 30 to 35 minutes.

Salads/Side Dishes/Vegetarian

– Alden's Too-Many-Tomatoes Salad –

Martha Minkel: "Our dining room is also open to the general public, by reservation. There is always a vegetarian dish on the menu. Most sporting camps serve one set entrée per meal; we generally have over half a dozen choices. This recipe is perfect for that season we await all during the spring months—when our garden tomatoes are abundant and the basil could use some pruning! This salad says summertime to us at Alden Camps."

> **Sliced fresh tomatoes, thin slices of red onion, cubed fresh mozzarella cheese**

Combine in a bowl and marinate in the dressing (below) for several hours prior to serving.

White Balsamic Vinaigrette:
> **4 cloves garlic, a handful of fresh basil, 2 cups white balsamic vinegar, 1 cup honey, 6 cups olive oil, salt and pepper to taste**

Combine all ingredients (reducing amounts if necessary) in a food processor until basil and garlic are thoroughly chopped.

– Bear Spring Fettuccini with Creamy Tomato Sauce –

Peg Churchill: "We always add a salad and/or pasta-type entrée for the evening meal in the summer. It's nice to be able to get a few ingredients from our herb garden."

> **1/4 cup chopped onion, 2 crushed cloves garlic, 2 to 3 T oil or butter, 2/3 cup ricotta cheese, 1 T fresh basil, 1 T fresh chives chopped, 2 tsp. sugar, 1/8 tsp. pepper, 1 (14.5-ounce) can of tomatoes (undrained and broken up) or the equivalent amount of fresh stewed tomatoes, 1 pound fettuccini**

In a saucepan, sauté the onion and garlic in the oil/butter over medium heat until tender. Add remaining ingredients (except the pasta), reduce the heat, and simmer the sauce for at least 5 minutes. Prepare the pasta according to directions on the box. Spoon the sauce over the pasta in individual servings, or toss pasta with sauce in a bowl and serve. Garnish with additional chives, if desired.

– The Birches Bean and Corn Salsa Salad –

**1 1/2 cups mild salsa, 1 cup canned cooked black beans (drained
and rinsed), 1/2 cup fresh (or canned) cooked corn, 1/2 tsp.
cumin, 2 T fresh lime juice**

In a bowl, mix all the ingredients together well. Cover and let stand in the
refrigerator overnight to blend the flavors.

– Deer Run Roast Corn –

Darlene Berry: "Another possibility for bonfire cooking (see **Deer Run Campfire Smelts
and Potatoes**, p. 40) is summertime corn."

Husk the number of ears desired to feed the number of people on hand.
Place them individually in double-thick squares of heavy-duty aluminum
foil. Add a small pat of butter to each and salt lightly. Wrap and seal edges
with a fold. Place on top of the coals and cook for about 6 minutes, turning once or twice.

– Enchanted Outfitters' Harvard Beets –

Gloria Hewey: "This is my husband, Craig Hallock's, favorite dish. I don't have my own
garden here at camp. Even though I'd have time to tend it in the summer, come fall, I would-
n't have time to harvest it. So, I either buy fresh beets or use canned for this recipe."

**1/2 cup sugar, 1/2 cup vinegar, 1/2 T cornstarch, 2 T butter, 1 can
(1 pint) beets—*or*, if you're taking them out of the garden,
about 6 medium-sized beets cooked until fork-tender, peeled,
and sliced**

In a saucepan over medium heat, combine the sugar, vinegar, and cornstarch and cook until the sauce thickens. Add the butter and beets, stirring
gently; heat thoroughly.

– Katahdin Lake Zucchini Loaf –

Suzan Cooper: "If you need to deal with a large zucchini, you can cut it in quarters the long way and grate it, or use diced small zucchini. This is a satisfying one-dish meal for a Saturday night supper. You can serve it cold on a hot day or hot on a cold day."

> 3 cups diced/grated zucchini, 1/2 tsp. baking soda, 1/2 cup oil,
> 1/2 tsp. oregano, 1/4 tsp. salt, 1 cup flour, 1 tsp. baking powder,
> 1/2 cup grated Parmesan cheese, 4 beaten eggs, 1 cup grated
> cheddar cheese

In a bowl, mix all ingredients together (except the cheddar cheese) until well blended. Spoon into a greased bread pan and sprinkle the top with the cheddar cheese. Bake in a 350° oven for 40 to 45 minutes. Let it set for 10 minutes before slicing and serving. Serves about 6.

– Lakewood's Orzo and Feta Salad –

Robin Carter: "This is wonderful when it's hot out. It's popular, too, so you may want to double it right off!"

> 1 cup orzo, salt and pepper to taste, 1 head broccoli, 2 T white
> wine vinegar, 1/4 cup olive oil, 1 red bell pepper, 1 bunch
> scallions, 1/4 cup fresh mint, 4 ounces feta cheese crumbled

Cook the orzo in boiling water for 6 minutes and steam the broccoli over boiling water for 5 minutes. Drain orzo and broccoli. In a large bowl, combine the orzo with salt and pepper, vinegar, and olive oil. Toss lightly and allow mixture to cool. Chop pepper, scallions, mint, and cooled broccoli, and add to the orzo along with the feta. Toss salad and refrigerate 1 hour to chill before serving.

– Libby's Zucchini Casserole –

I cooked this the first time in an uncovered casserole dish for the recommended time, and the vegetables were slightly crunchy and delicious. Next time, I sautéed the vegetables in butter a few minutes first and covered the casserole dish as suggested, and the vegetables were not crunchy, but still delicious. Choices, choices . . .

4 cups zucchini, 1 cup chopped onion, 1 cup chopped green pepper, 1 cup mayonnaise, 2 eggs, 1 cup Parmesan cheese, salt and pepper to taste, $^1/2$ cup breadcrumbs

In a big bowl, mix everything together but breadcrumbs. Spoon into a greased casserole or 9 x 13-inch baking pan and sprinkle the mixture with the breadcrumbs (using more if you like a lot of crumbs). Bake at 350° for about 30 minutes.

– Long Lake Fried Corn –

Sandra Smith: "Fresh corn on the cob from the Calais Farmer's Market is such a treat that we often buy too much. Frying the corn is a different and tasty way to serve the leftovers."

Leftover corn on the cob, butter, olive oil, salt

Cut the corn off the leftover cobs. Melt butter and oil in a frying pan (2 parts butter to 1 part oil). Add the corn and salt to taste. Fry until the corn is slightly brown.

– Loon Lodge Potato Pancakes –

Linda Yencha: "This is one of my mother's Polish recipes. It's tasty and nutritious when it's so hot outside you don't feel like eating."

3 large raw potatoes (either boiling or baking type), 1 egg, 3 T flour, 1 onion diced, salt and pepper to taste

Grate the potatoes on the smallest hole of a hand grater. Place everything in a blender and mix until well blended. Let rest for 15 minutes. It should be the consistency of pancake batter. Add more flour if it's too thin; add

milk if it's too thick. Pour batter, by big spoonfuls, onto a generously
greased frying pan. Fry until lightly browned. As they are done, place on
a plate covered with paper towels and keep warm. Serve with sour cream
or ketchup.

– Maynard's Potato Salad –

Bill Maynard: "I don't follow any recipe really, so I'll just tell you what I do. It's really two
salads in one, and people seem to like it a lot."

You first make up a potato salad the way you like it. Then you prepare a
regular salad (except without lettuce): sliced onions (I like a lot of onions),
carrots, radishes, cucumbers, tomatoes, green pepper, celery, and anything
else you'd like to add. Then you combine the two salads, heap it all on a
bed of lettuce in a bowl or on a plate, and that's about it.

– Moose Point Old-Fashioned Green Beans –

Kathy McGough, camp cook: "This is camp owner John Martin's favorite recipe. He has a
garden here, and it gets full sun, so our beans are fresh from the garden, cooked in the
classic old Maine way, with salt pork. There are really no set amounts—it depends on how
many green beans you have and the number of people you're going to serve, so I'll just tell
you how it goes."

Slice salt pork (get some with a nice amount of meat on it) into $1/8$-inch
slices. Snap the vine-end of the beans. Then, in a soup pot or saucepan,
put down a layer of salt pork slices and cover that with a layer of green
beans. Do this two more times so you have three layers in all, and cover
everything with water. Bring to a boil, then lower the heat and keep at a
slow, steady boil for 45 minutes to an hour. Check it now and then to make
sure it's covered with water, and add hot/boiling water when necessary.
Drain and serve.

– Wapiti Sour Cream Noodles –

Frank Ramelli: "This is something my late wife, Anita, liked to cook. It goes well with her **Chicken Marsala** recipe (p. 103). I let people add their own salt and pepper, and I usually add another handful of cheese at the end—it's up to individual tastes."

1 package Pennsylvania Dutch wide egg noodles, 1 cup sour cream, 1 T dried parsley, 1 cup grated Parmesan cheese

In a large pot, boil the noodles until just done and drain. Add the remaining ingredients and stir well to combine.

– West Branch Pond Potato Salad –

Carol Kealiher: "This is how my father, Cliff, made potato salad, and I still do it this way. Tradition is important around here, and I like to use the old recipes."

4 medium boiling potatoes, 4 eggs, 1/4 cup cider vinegar, 1/4 cup olive oil, 1/4 cup chopped celery, 2 T diced onions, 1 T (heaping) mayonnaise, dash of paprika

In a saucepan, bring scrubbed or peeled potatoes and eggs to a boil. Turn off the heat and let stand for 15 minutes. Take the eggs out first; take the potatoes out when they are fork-tender.

In a medium bowl, stir together vinegar and oil and slice eggs and potatoes into that. Stir gently and refrigerate, to marinate for several hours. Remove from refrigerator. Add celery, onion, and mayonnaise, and stir gently. Serve on a bed of lettuce and sprinkle with paprika. Serves 2.

– Wheaton's Late Summer Casserole –

4 cups summer squash and/or zucchini, 1/2 cup chopped onion, 1 can cream of chicken soup (condensed), 1 cup sour cream, 1 cup shredded carrots, 1 (8-ounce) package stuffing mix, 1/2 cup melted butter

Cook the squash and onion in boiling salted water for 5 minutes. Drain. In a big bowl, combine sour cream and soup. Stir in carrots; fold in squash.

In another bowl, combine the stuffing mix with the melted butter and spread half in the bottom of a greased 9 x 13-inch baking pan. Cover with vegetable mix and top with remaining stuffing mix. Bake in a 350° oven for 30 minutes. Serves 10.

– Whisperwood's Zucchini-Tomato Pie –

Candee McCafferty: "For this dish, I use the recipe right on the Bisquick box. This is a quick and easy way to use summer produce."

2 cups chopped zucchini, 1 cup chopped tomato, 1/2 cup chopped onion, 1/3 cup grated Parmesan cheese, 1 1/2 cups milk, 3/4 cup Bisquick, 3 eggs, salt and pepper to taste
Preheat oven to 400°. Grease a 10-inch quiche dish or 10-inch deep-dish pie plate. Sprinkle first four ingredients in the bottom of dish/pie plate. Beat remaining ingredients until smooth and pour over vegetable/cheese mixture. Bake until a knife inserted in the center comes out clean (about 30 minutes). Cool 5 minutes before serving. Serves 6.

– Wilderness Island Zucchini-Basil Salad –

Mike LaRosa: "Ever since 1985, we have worked to improve the mostly clay soil of our garden by composting food scraps and using horse manure. Now we have a beautiful garden! We let our guests pick their own vegetables for supper if they want."

4 zucchini (8- to 10-inch), 1/2 Bermuda onion sliced, about 20 basil leaves washed and drained, Caesar salad dressing
Cut each zucchini in half and scoop out and discard the seeds. Slice zucchini into matchstick-sized strips. Place in a shallow bowl and stir in the onions. Drizzle a few tablespoons of salad dressing over the mixture. Chop half the basil leaves and add to the mixture. Marinate in the refrigerator for at least 1/2 hour. Drain and add remaining chopped basil leaves and additional dressing to taste. Serves 4.

Sauces

– Bald Mountain Fresh Fruit Sauce –

Meg Godaire: "This is delicious over sliced duck breast. You can use whatever berry is in season. It's a very versatile sauce, and easy to make."

> 1 pint fresh fruit, $1/4$ cup water, $1/2$ cup sugar, $1/4$ cup raspberry vinegar, 2 T cornstarch

In a saucepan, combine all ingredients and stir gently until sauce thickens and is bubbly.

– The Birches Berry Cabernet Sauce –

> 1 bottle Cabernet Sauvignon, 4 T butter, 2 T brown sugar, $1/2$ tsp. freshly ground pepper, $1/4$ tsp. dried parsley

Simmer mixture, cooking until it is reduced to $1/3$ cup. Serve over berries of your choice.

– The Birches Sweet Red Pepper Vinaigrette –

This is a delicious use of end-of-summer garden peppers. You can also use the fresh shallots and sage available at this time.

> 2 cups roasted sweet red pepper, 4 cups good-quality balsamic vinegar, 6 cups good-quality olive oil, 2 cups water, 5 T brown sugar, 4 tsp. dried shallot, 4 tsp. dried sage

Roast peppers under the broiler for 2 to 3 minutes; remove, turn, and roast the other side. Cool and chop coarsely. Add remaining ingredients and emulsify in blender.

You can reduce amounts or process in batches at home.

– Cobb's Fruit Salad Dressing –

Gary Cobb: "The camps were founded in 1902, and my parents, Floyd and Maud Cobb, brought the family to Pierce Pond in 1958. One of my most graphic memories as a kid was of the magnificent forest and the sense of remoteness. There were no roads and very few trails until the mid-sixties. Large areas had never seen an axe. A booklet in the main lodge, *Birds of Pierce Pond,* states, 'Birds are an ecological litmus paper. Many different species are a sign of a healthy ecosystem.' The long list of species that have been spotted here is proof of the area's still-pristine habitats."

> 1 (46-ounce) can pineapple juice, 2 T butter, 1/2 cup sugar,
> 2 T flour, 1 egg

In a saucepan, heat the juice. In a small bowl, mix the butter, sugar, and flour together and add to the hot juice. Beat an egg in the same small bowl, add to juice mixture, and cook until thickened, but do not boil. Chill and serve over fresh fruit salad.

– Cobb's Ginger-Soy Marinade –

Betty Cobb: "This is good with any meat; just marinate for several hours or overnight, and then bake, broil, or grill."

> 1/2 cup soy sauce, 1/4 cup oil, 1 1/2 tsp. garlic powder, 2 T brown
> sugar, 1 T cider vinegar, 3 chopped scallions, 1 tsp. ginger

In a blender, food processor, or by hand, mix all ingredients well. Store in a jar with lid for future use, if desired. Shake jar prior to use.

– Cobb's Tomato Salad Dressing –

Betty Cobb: "I cut up tomatoes, sprinkle finely chopped onions and fresh basil on them, and drizzle this dressing over everything."

> 1/2 cup wine vinegar, 1 1/2 cups olive oil, 2 cloves garlic minced,
> 2 tsp. Worcestershire Sauce, 1/2 tsp. black pepper, 1 tsp. salt,
> 1 tsp. sugar

Combine all ingredients in a jar and shake well. Chill and serve.

– Jalbert's Fruit Salsa –

Nancy Thibodeau, camp cook: "I use this over cooked salmon. You could also serve it as an appetizer or a fruit salad."

**1 pint blueberries, 2 pints strawberries, 1 mango, 1/2 honey-
dew melon, 1/4 cup Amaretto liqueur, 1/4 cup sugar**

Pour the blueberries into a large bowl. Hull and cut the strawberries into small pieces and add to the bowl. Peel and dice the mango and add to the fruit. Scoop out the melon and cut into small pieces. In a small bowl, mix the liqueur and sugar and stir well. Pour over the fruit mixture and refrigerate the salsa before serving.

– The Pines Buttermilk Dressing –

Nancy Norris: "This is the amount I make, but it's easy to halve."

**2 cups buttermilk, 2 cups mayonnaise, 2 cups sour cream,
1/2 cup vinegar, 1 cup sugar, 1/2 cup garlic powder, 1/4 cup dill
weed, 1/4 cup onion salt**

Blend all ingredients. Refrigerate.

– The Pines Chicken Marinade –

Nancy Norris: "This works equally well for a barbecue or when baking your chicken in the oven."

**1/2 cup lemon juice, 1/3 cup vegetable oil, 1 T sugar, 2 tsp. hot
pepper sauce, 2 tsp. chicken bouillon, 1 tsp. thyme leaves,
1/4 tsp. oregano, 1 T minced garlic**

Mix everything together and marinate chicken either overnight or most of the day. This makes enough for 3 whole chicken breasts.

– The Pines Green Goddess Dressing –

Nancy Norris: "I use this on sliced cucumbers and tomatoes on lettuce for a summer appetizer, or it's great on a regular side salad."

3/4 cup mayonnaise, 1 T finely chopped onion, 2 T finely
chopped parsley, 2 cloves mashed garlic, 1 tsp. tarragon
vinegar, 2 to 3 anchovies *or* 2 to 3 tsp. anchovy paste

Mix together well and refrigerate.

– Rideout's Sweet Mustard Dressing –

Jami Lorigan: "My mother-in-law, Annie Lorigan, helped run Rideout's for years and is still very much a part of the place. She created this recipe, and people really like it. You need to use Country Dijon mustard; nothing else works quite the same."

1 cup oil, 1 cup vinegar, 1 T Country Dijon prepared mustard,
1/2 cup sugar, 1 tsp. salt, 1/4 tsp. pepper

Combine everything in a jar or salad dressing decanter and shake well.
Serve at room temperature and shake well just before serving.

– South Branch Lake Sherry Dill Sauce –

Russ Aldridge: "One of the things we do in the summer is our youth contest. The kids write an essay about why they'd like to spend a week at a traditional Maine sporting camp. Then we carefully read each one, awarding the child (and a responsible adult) with a weeklong stay here at camp. The only thing we ask is that they spend a day with me, both on the river and on the lake, and that they meet our local game warden and visit the local fish hatchery. Then, for a week, they get to experience the beauty and peace we enjoy every day."

Cindy Aldridge: "For this, or any sauce, if you ever have lumps that won't blend in, you can always strain the mixture and return it to the saucepan and heat. We serve this over bass, but once you taste how good it is, you may want to try it on other dishes as well!"

1/4 pound butter, 2 T flour, 1 pint light cream (not whipping
cream), 2 T dill weed, 1 T sherry (cooking sherry will do)

Melt butter in a saucepan over low heat. Sprinkle in flour and stir the roux with a whisk until smooth. Do not burn! Slowly add cream and blend until smooth. Add the dill and sherry. Stir until smooth and let set for 10 minutes before pouring or spooning over food.

Desserts

– Alden's Raspberry Chocolate Cake with Chocolate Ganache –

Ellen Kiser: "This is a very popular cake."

Cake:

4 cups flour, 4 cups sugar, 4 tsp. baking soda, 2 cups unsweetened high-quality cocoa, 2 cups mayonnaise, 4 eggs, 4 cups
brewed coffee (cooled), 3/4 to 1 cup raspberry jam

Preheat oven to 325°. Line two 9-inch cake pans with parchment. Set
aside. Sift and set aside dry ingredients. In a Hobart/Kitchen Aid–type
mixer, with the paddle attachment, blend together the wet ingredients,
except the jam. Gradually add sifted dry ingredients and combine well.

Pour into the cake pans and bake 35 to 40 minutes or until a toothpick or cake tester inserted in center comes out clean. Cool on cake racks
and remove from pans. Assemble cake on a cake plate, spreading jam
between the layers.

Ganache:

1 (6-ounce) bag chocolate chips, 1 T heavy cream, 1 tsp. vanilla,
2 T sweetened condensed milk

In a double boiler, slowly melt the chocolate chips and the cream. Take off
the heat and add vanilla and milk. Pour over the assembled cake. Smooth
the top and sides and chill before serving so the frosting hardens a bit.

– Bear Spring Cherry Pie –

*It was in one of the cabins at Bear Spring Camps one summer that E. B. White wrote the fol-
lowing (used by permission from his book* Once More to the Lake):

*". . . none of us ever thought that there was any place in the world like that
lake in Maine. I guess I remembered clearest of all the early mornings, when the
lake was cool and motionless, remembered how the bedroom smelled of the lum-
ber it was made of and of the wet woods whose scent entered through the screen
. . . those summers had been infinitely precious and worth saving."*

Pie Crust:
> 1 cup flour, $1/3$ cup sugar, $1/2$ cup soft butter or margarine,
> $1/8$ tsp. salt

Mix all the ingredients in a bowl and press firmly into a 9-inch pie pan.
Bake at 350° for 15 minutes.

Filling:
> 1 can (21 ounces) cherry pie filling, $1/4$ tsp. almond extract

Combine and pour into the slightly cooled crust.

Topping:
> 8 ounces cream cheese, 1 egg, $1/2$ cup sugar

Beat the topping ingredients together in a bowl and pour over the pie filling. Bake pie an additional 30 to 35 minutes, or until firm.

– The Birches Raspberry Bavarian Pie –

John Willard: "There's been a big change in land ownership around Moosehead Lake: private individuals buying up thousands of acres, gating off their property, and putting up 'no trespassing' signs. Fortunately, there's a movement now to use federal land, water, and conservation money from offshore drilling and leasing to buy development rights on a lot of the land up here. If they can get enough, I think Moosehead will be okay."

> 2 T Knox gelatin, 3 T cold water, 2 (16-ounce) bags frozen raspberries (thawed), 1 cup confectioners' sugar, 1 T lemon juice, 1 cup whipping cream, 1 single 9-inch baked pastry shell

In a small bowl, soak gelatin with cold water. In a saucepan, add sugar and lemon juice to the berries and cook until the mixture comes to a boil. Remove from the heat. Stir in the gelatin until dissolved. Cool in the refrigerator. When almost set, whip the cream and fold it into the fruit mixture. Pour into
the pastry shell and refrigerate.

– Castle Island Peach Cobbler –

6 T butter, 1 cup sugar, 1 cup flour, 2 tsp. baking powder, 2/3
cup milk, 4 cups sliced peaches, 1/4 cup orange juice (or juice
from canned peaches)

Cream the butter and sugar. Sift the flour and baking powder and add to
the creamed mixture alternately with milk. Place peaches in an 8 x 11 1/2-
inch baking pan. Cover with the batter and pour the juice over the batter.
Bake at 350° for 45 minutes. Serve warm topped with ice cream or
whipped cream if desired. Serves 8.

– Cobb's Blackberry Gingerbread –

Betty Cobb: "Some people don't like the seeds in blackberries. If that's the case, you can
use blueberries instead. I make this in a 10 1/2-by-18 1/2-inch pan, which is bigger than most
people have at home. I guess you'll just have to experiment with two smaller pans or
reduce the ingredient amounts."

1 1/2 cups margarine, 1 1/2 tsp. salt, 3 cups sugar, 3 eggs, 3 cups
sour milk, 6 cups flour, 1 1/2 tsp. ground ginger, 3 tsp. cinnamon,
3 tsp. baking soda, 1/2 cup molasses, 3 cups blackberries

If you don't have sour milk, measure milk into a bowl and add 1 tablespoon of lemon to the milk, stir, and set aside to sour.

Mix together 3 T of the sugar and 1 tsp. of the cinnamon and set
aside. Cream margarine, salt, and sugar. Add eggs and beat well. Sift together dry ingredients (including the 2 T remaining cinnamon), add to batter alternately with molasses and milk, beating well after each addition.
Pour into greased pan. Sprinkle with reserved cinnamon-sugar mixture.
Bake at 350° for 50 to 60 minutes. (Check after 40 minutes if using smaller
pans, and use toothpick or cake tester to test for doneness.)

– Cobb's Chiffon Cake –

2 cups cake flour, 1 1/2 cups sugar, 3 tsp. baking powder, 3/4 tsp.
salt, 7 eggs, 1 1/2 tsp. lemon juice, 1 tsp. vanilla *or* orange extract, 1/2 cup oil, 3/4 cup water, 1/2 tsp. cream of tartar

Sift the first four ingredients together into a bowl. Separate the eggs.
Make a hole in the center of the flour mixture and pour in the 7 egg

yolks, the lemon juice, vanilla/orange extract, oil, and water. Beat well. Beat the egg whites until they hold soft peaks. Add cream of tartar and beat until stiff peaks form. Fold whites into batter and pour into a greased and floured tube pan. Bake at 350° for 1 hour or until golden and cake tester comes out clean.

· ·

SAVING THE WILDERNESS

Guests coming up to "get away from it all" at a Maine sporting camp enjoy pristine views and a variety of wildlife, but for sporting-camp owners, maintaining that environment is an ongoing challenge. Fortunately, a number of owners across the state have begun to get help from guests, community groups, and environmental and business organizations that recognize not only the ecological, but also the economic value in setting aside tracts of wilderness land for the future. For example, Pierce Pond's entire 10,000-acre watershed ecosystem has been protected from development, thanks in part to the efforts of loyal guests at Cobb's and Harrison's.

· ·

– Eagle Lodge Banana Cream Crepes with Raspberry Sauce –

Heritage Recipe from Tami and John Rogers.

Tami Rogers: "These crepes can be made a couple of weeks in advance, wrapped tightly in plastic, and frozen. The sauce can also be made up to a week ahead and frozen."

Nice to be able to whip out a gourmet dessert at a moment's notice! A tip from bitter experience ages ago: If you put wax paper between the crepes, you won't have one conglomerate mass to disentangle when you remove them from the freezer.

Crepes:

1 3/4 cups flour, 1/4 cup confectioners' sugar, 1/4 tsp. salt,
4 large eggs, 2 1/2 cups milk, 3 T vegetable oil, 1 tsp. vanilla

In a medium bowl, combine the flour, sugar, and salt. In another bowl, use a wire whisk to beat the remaining ingredients. Add the flour mixture, whisk well, and then let set for 5 minutes to thicken. Heat a nonstick 8-inch frying pan over medium heat. Spray lightly with a cooking spray. Ladle a scant 1/4 cup of batter into the pan. Tilt the pan, covering the bottom completely. Cook the crepe until the top has set (about 2 minutes). Carefully turn and cook the other side briefly. Set aside until ready to use.

Banana Cream Filling:

> 2 cups heavy cream, 1 (3-ounce) package softened cream
> cheese, 1/4 cup confectioners' sugar, 6 very ripe mashed
> bananas, 1/4 tsp. cinnamon

In a medium bowl, using a hand mixer, blend the cream, cream cheese, and sugar on high. Beat until stiff peaks form. In another bowl, mix together bananas and cinnamon. Fold 1 cup of the cream mixture into the bananas, then fold banana mixture into the remaining cream until well combined.

When ready to serve, warm the banana cream mixture in a microwave briefly (or leave at room temperature). Place 1/3 cup of the filling into the center of each crepe. Fold both sides of the crepe toward the center, covering the filling. Place on a plate and drizzle with the raspberry sauce (see below).

Raspberry Sauce:

> 2 cups fresh (or frozen) raspberries, 1/3 cup sugar, 2 T brandy
> (optional)

Using a food processor or handheld mixer, blend ingredients until smooth. Refrigerate until ready to use.

– Grant's Raspberry Squares –

John Blunt: "In the summertime, we have tables on some of the beaches around the lake so people can picnic and possibly see a moose. For some people, a family vacation means driving somewhere, and then a week later driving back home—and you've hardly done a thing together. But when you're in our atmosphere, you can be hiking, picnicking, canoeing, and fishing together. Kids will come out of the dining hall while their parents are finishing dinner, get a carrot from the kitchen, and go feed the rabbits or play on the swings. Mom and Dad know right where they are, and since we're at the end of the road, they don't have to worry about traffic or safety, and can just relax."

> 4 cups flour, 2 tsp. salt, 1 1/2 cups vegetable shortening, 2 cups
> raspberry jam (or other favorite jam)

Cut shortening into sifted flour and salt. Add enough ice water (about $2/3$ cup) to make the mixture hold together. Roll out half for the bottom crust and place on a lightly greased cookie sheet (with sides).

Spread jam on the bottom crust. Roll out remaining crust and place over jam. Cut slits on the top to let air escape. Bake at 400° until golden, about 25 minutes.

– Katahdin Lake Wild Blueberry Crumble –

Suzan Cooper: "When people ask me how many this serves, I have to say, 'Not many—it's too good!'"

1 quart fresh wild Maine blueberries (if possible), $1/2$ tsp. cinnamon, 1 cup flour, 1 cup sugar, 1 stick butter

Place the berries in the bottom of a 9 x 9-inch pan. Mix the remaining ingredients with your fingers, a fork, or in food processor until crumbly, and sprinkle over the berries. Bake in a 350° oven for 45 minutes. Serve warm with whipped cream or ice cream if desired.

– Katahdin Lake Wild Blueberry Pie –

Suzan Cooper: "The small Maine wild blueberries are sweet and delicious. This pie is food for royalty."

1 single pie crust, 3 cups fresh wild Maine blueberries (if possible), 1 cup sugar, $1/2$ tsp. cinnamon, 4 T flour, 1 cup cream (or half-and-half, evaporated milk, or whole milk)

Preheat the oven to 400°. Place berries into a bowl. Sprinkle the sugar, cinnamon, and flour over them and stir gently. Pour the berry mixture into the prepared pie crust and pour the cream/milk over the top. Bake for 10 minutes in the preheated oven. Reduce heat to 350° and bake for an additional 25 minutes, or until mixture is firm in the middle.

– King and Bartlett's Blueberry-Cranberry Crisp –

Wild blueberries are ready to harvest before cranberries, so one of these can be fresh/wild while the other will need to be store-bought or frozen.

Cathy Charles: "What makes or breaks it for a place like this, and affects the guests' experience, is how well the staff works together. We're very fortunate, as the camp managers, to have an exceptional cook, Donna Beloin, who has worked here for years. She takes care of all the ordering as well as the food preparation, which frees up Jeff and me to do all the other things that need doing each day."

Fruit Filling:
1 pound blueberries, 2 pounds cranberries, 1/2 cup flour,
1 1/2 cups sugar, 1 tsp. freshly grated or ground nutmeg

In a 2-quart casserole, add the berries. Mix together the flour and sugar and pour over the berries, blending together well. Sprinkle fresh or ground nutmeg over the top.

Topping:
2 cups all-purpose flour, 1 1/2 sticks butter or margarine,
1 cup brown sugar, 1 cup quick oatmeal

Cut the butter into the flour as you would for pie crust. Add the brown sugar and mix gently with a fork. Add the oatmeal and sprinkle the mixture over the top of the berries. Bake until the top is golden and the berries are bubbling, 45 minutes to an hour. Serve warm with vanilla ice cream.

– Lakewood's Blackberry Pie –

Heritage Recipe from Stan and Sue Milton and Janne Provencher (also the camp cook) who ran the camps from 1976 to 2001. They were only the fifth owners in more than 125 years.

If you're planning to use wild blackberries, make the dough for a double pie crust ahead of time and refrigerate it while you're off berrying (see index for pie crust recipes). Then, when you return with your wild treasures (hopefully!), you can roll out and prepare the crust during the 15-minute break called for below.

Janne Provencher: "If you use frozen berries, thaw them and drain off half of the juice before adding the other ingredients."

4 cups blackberries, 3/4 cup sugar, 2 1/2 T tapioca, 1/2 tsp. cinnamon, 1 T lemon juice, 1 1/2 T butter or margarine

In a bowl, combine all ingredients except lemon juice and butter. Let set
15 minutes. Place in the bottom of a double-crust pie shell. Sprinkle with
lemon juice and small pieces of butter. Cover with top crust and seal
edges. Bake on the lower rack of a 400° oven for 30 to 40 minutes.

– Long Lake Wild Raspberry Pie –

Sandra Smith: "Raspberries grow wild in Maine, and we have had good patches of them at
all three of the sporting camps where I've lived. Our golden retriever, Brookie, loves them
too, and eats them right off the bush. Raspberries have such a delicate flavor that I decided
to work on a recipe for a one-crust pie that featured the fruit rather than the crust. In June,
I substitute strawberries in this recipe. Our guests just love this dessert."

Prebaked single pie shell, 3 T cornstarch, 3/4 cup sugar, 1/2 cup
water, 4 cups raspberries, 1/2 tsp. lemon juice

In a saucepan, mix the cornstarch and 1/2 cup of the sugar. Gradually add
the water and 2 cups of berries. Over medium heat, stirring constantly,
bring the mixture to a boil. Turn heat to low and simmer until the mixture
is clear and thick, again stirring all the time. Add the remaining 1/4 cup
sugar and mix in until it dissolves. Add and stir in the lemon juice. Remove
from the heat and carefully stir in the remaining 2 cups of berries, trying
to keep the berries somewhat whole. Pour into the prebaked pie shell.
Cool and serve with whipped cream.

– Loon Lodge Cheesecake –

Linda Yencha: "For this recipe I use packages of cheesecake mix that come with two
envelopes; one is for the filling, the other is for the crust. I tweak the box recipe by adding
cream cheese to improve the taste, and then I use fresh berries or pie filling on top."

2 packages no-bake Jell-O Cheesecake, 2/3 cup butter or margarine, 1/4 cup sugar, 8 ounces cream cheese softened, 3 cups
cold milk, fresh berries or fruit pie filling

In a bowl, combine contents of crust mix packages, butter, and sugar. Press onto a lightly greased cookie sheet (with sides). In a mixing bowl, beat the cream cheese and half the milk until smooth. Gradually add the rest of the milk and the contents of the filling packages. Beat until smooth (mixture should be thick). Pour over the crust and refrigerate until ready to serve. Sprinkle berries or spoon pie filling over the top of each piece.

– Pleasant Point Peach Crumb Pie –

Mardi George: "This is a family recipe I've brought to camp."

**1 stick butter softened, 3/4 cup flour, 1 tsp. cinnamon,
1/2 tsp. salt, 1 cup brown sugar, 2 cups fresh peaches
(peeled and sliced)**

In a bowl, combine all ingredients except peaches, and cut in with a fork or pastry cutter until you have a crumb mixture. Butter a pie plate, pour in the sliced peaches, and cover with the crumb mixture. Bake at 400° for 10 minutes, then lower heat to 350° and bake an additional 15 minutes. Serve with real whipped cream and watch this treat disappear.

– Red River Cheesecake –

Crust:

**2 cups graham-cracker crumbs, 1/3 cup melted butter,
1/3 cup sugar**

In a bowl, mix all ingredients together and press into the bottom and a bit up the sides of an 8-inch springform pan.

Cheesecake:

**3 (8-ounce) packages softened cream cheese, 1 cup sugar, 2 tsp.
vanilla, 3 eggs, 1 cup sour cream**

In a big bowl, mix cream cheese well. Add sugar, vanilla, and eggs and beat until smooth. Fold in the sour cream and pour into the prepared crust. Bake at 350° for approximately 1 hour or until set (when center is firm).

Turn off heat, but leave in the oven with the door ajar so it cools slowly. Then chill in the refrigerator for 4 hours. Top with fresh raspberries, blueberries, or cherries.

– Red River Creamy Peach Pie –

Mike Brophy: "The camps are located on Public Reserve Land, which supports the arctic sandwort, a plant of national significance found in only one other place in New England and nowhere else in Maine. And over on Deboullie Pond is a cave where there's ice even in the middle of summer. There's really just so much that's unique here—we're talking about twenty-three thousand acres open to our guests! Since 1982, for a week each summer, we turn the camps over to special-needs guests and their staff support. (We still take care of the cooking and cleaning.)

"This pie is a real favorite. A tip for serving is to set the pie plate over a large bowl of hot water for fifteen seconds to release the crust from the pie plate."

> 1 1/4 cups crushed graham cracker crumbs, 1/3 cup melted
> butter, 1 (29-ounce) can of sliced peaches, 1/3 cup peach juice,
> 1 1/2 tsp. plain gelatin, 1 (8-ounce) package cream cheese,
> 1/4 cup granulated sugar, 2/3 cup evaporated milk (well chilled),
> 2 T lemon juice

In a bowl, blend the crumbs and melted butter and form a crust in a deep 9-inch pie plate. Chill the crust while you make the filling. Drain and dice the peaches. Reserve 6 slices for the garnish. In a small bowl over hot water, dissolve the gelatin in the peach juice. In a bowl, blend the juice/gelatin mixture with softened cream cheese and sugar. In a bowl set over another bowl of ice, whip the chilled milk until light and fluffy. Add the lemon juice and beat until stiff. Beat in the cheese mixture and fold in the diced peaches. Pour into the chilled crust and garnish with 6 peach slices. Chill 3 hours before serving.

– Summer Cream Pie –

This is a family favorite. It's refreshing and sumptuous, just right for celebrations. I adapted it from an old Gourmet *magazine recipe, and used to make it on Valentine's Day because strawberries look like hearts to me. This is luscious in early summer with a new batch of strawberry-rhubarb jam and fresh strawberries.*

> 1 prebaked pie shell, 1 envelope plain gelatin, 2 T cold water, 1
> cup milk, 4 egg yolks, 1/3 cup sugar, dash of salt, 1 tsp. vanilla,
> 1/3 cup strawberry or strawberry-rhubarb jam, 1 quart fresh
> strawberries, 3/4 cup whipping cream, 1 cup semisweet choco-
> late chips (or 2 to 3 squares bittersweet baking chocolate)

In a small bowl, sprinkle the gelatin over the cold water. As the gelatin softens, pour the milk into a small saucepan and put on medium heat to scald. Meanwhile, in a heavy medium-sized saucepan, beat the eggs, sugar, and salt together with a whisk until the mixture is thick and light. Add the by-now scalded milk in a stream while beating. Cook the custard over low heat, stirring, for 2 to 3 minutes, or until mixture thickens a bit. Add the softened gelatin and stir until it is completely dissolved. Remove from the heat, add vanilla, stir, and place saucepan in the refrigerator.

While the custard cools and thickens, take the pie shell and spread jam in the bottom. Hull and halve enough strawberries to cover the jam. Save aside 8 of the biggest and most beautiful berries, with their green stems, for later. While you're getting out the whipping cream, check the custard, and whisk it a bit (you don't want it to set up on you, just cool and thicken a little). Whip the cream and fold it into the custard. Pour the custard into the shell and refrigerate the pie for several hours.

When the custard is firm, carefully cut the saved strawberries in half (including the green top parts). Melt the chocolate and gently dip the tips of the strawberries in it. Place the strawberry halves, cut side down, around the edge of the pie with the chocolate tips pointing to the center. Refrigerate until ready to serve.

– West Branch Pond Raspberry Cobbler –

Carol Kealiher: "This is a quick, easy, and delicious way to serve raspberries. When our three boys, Jack, Nathan, and Eric, brought in their berries, this is what they wanted."

Filling:

   1 quart raspberries, 1/2 cup sugar, 2 tsp. cornstarch, 1 cup water

Place the berries in the bottom of a greased 9 x 13-inch baking pan. In a small bowl, combine the sugar and cornstarch and sprinkle that over the berries.

Topping:

   1 cup flour, 1/2 tsp. salt, 1 1/2 tsp. baking powder, 1/4 cup sugar, 1/2 stick butter, 1/2 cup milk, 2 T sugar

Sift the first four ingredients into a bowl. Slice the butter into that and blend well with a pastry blender. Add the milk and stir well. Drop by spoonfuls (not a soup spoon, but regular sized) onto the berry mixture. Sprinkle with the 2 T sugar. Bake in a 400° oven for 30 minutes.

– West Branch Pond Secret Chocolate Chip Cookies –

Long-term guest and right-hand man Charles Furbush offered me this recipe as astonished staff and owner Carol Kealiher listened in. Apparently, no one had been able to pry it out of him over the years. Guess we just got lucky!

Charles Furbush: "When I was in denial about my parents' divorce, I told my mother, 'You can't leave without giving me your cookie recipe!' It was a matter of survival. This recipe developed out of a lot of trial and error. No two chocolate chip cookies are the same in this world. They're like snowflakes."

> 2 cups flour, 3/4 tsp. baking soda, 1 tsp. salt, just under 1 cup
> sugar, just under 1 cup dark brown sugar packed down lightly,
> 2 sticks margarine (not butter), 1 tsp. vanilla, 1 1/2 large eggs
> (figure it out—it's crucial!), 1/4 tsp. water, 6-ounce bag
> chocolate chips

Sift flour, baking soda, and salt together in a bowl and set aside. Measure the sugars into a bowl and set aside.

In a saucepan, melt the margarine and stir a handful of the chocolate chips into the melted margarine. Stir until chocolate melts. Pour this into the sugars, but leave a couple of teaspoons in the saucepan (this is part of the ritual). Add the vanilla, eggs, and water, plus the sifted dry ingredients, and mix with a wooden spoon. Add 3/4 to 1 cup of chocolate chips (I use a 6-ounce bag).

Refrigerate the dough 15 to 20 minutes.

Preheat oven to 350°. Drop dough by tablespoonfuls onto an ungreased cookie sheet. Watch the cookies while baking. Halfway through (about 4 to 5 minutes), when the cookies have puffed up, open the oven door, pick up the cookie sheet, and drop it down on the counter or inside oven door to flatten the cookies down so they cook evenly. Return to oven and finish cooking until light brown.

– Wheaton's Blueberry Buckle –

Jana Wheaton: "We started here in 1979, and those first few years were hard. I was trying to learn the business, be a manager, do the cooking, and keep everyone happy while Dale was out guiding. I guess the blueberry buckle story says it all. One afternoon, some people arrived unexpectedly. I'd been out straight all day and had just cleaned the oven and then made a blueberry buckle and put it in to cook. I had a million things on my mind, and as many things that needed to be done, and here I am trying to be cordial.

"Well, just as Dale was coming in off the lake from guiding, and could take over answering all their questions, my blueberry buckle boiled over—all over my clean oven. I was at the end of my rope! I went out on the back porch and chucked that buckle as far as I could chuck it. I mean, blueberry all over everything. After a few choice words to Dale, I got in our car and went hell-bent for election down the road. About five miles out of town I started feeling sorry for him because dinner was coming up and I'd left him high and dry.

"When I got back, Dale was in the kitchen with a cookbook open, wondering how he was going to put a meal together. Thankfully, we can laugh at all that now. And I still make the blueberry buckle!"

> 3/4 cup sugar, 1/2 cup shortening, 1 egg, 2 1/2 cups flour, 2 1/2
> tsp. baking powder, 1/2 tsp. salt, 1/2 cup milk, 2 cups Maine
> blueberries, 1/2 cup sugar, 1/2 tsp. cinnamon, 1/4 cup butter

Beat sugar and shortening until fluffy. Add egg and beat well. Combine 2 cups flour, baking powder, and the salt. Add flour mixture and milk alternately to batter and beat until smooth after each addition. Spread in a greased 8 x 8 x 2-inch pan. Top with blueberries. Combine remaining 1/2 cup flour, 1/2 cup sugar, and cinnamon. Cut in butter until crumbly. Sprinkle over blueberries. Bake at 350° for 45 minutes.

Miscellaneous

– Katahdin Lake Zucchini Relish –

Suzan Cooper: "This is a delicious way to use up those big zucchini that appear out of nowhere in the garden!"

>   10 cups grated zucchini, 4 cups grated onion, 2 green peppers,
>   5 T salt

Combine everything in a big cooking pot and let mixture set overnight. Next morning, drain, rinse with cold water, and drain again. Return to pot and add the following:

>   2 1/2 cups cider vinegar, 4 1/2 cups white sugar, 1 T each dry
>   mustard, nutmeg, turmeric, cornstarch

Bring to a boil and cook for 2 minutes. Pack in hot, sterilized jars.

– King and Bartlett's Preserved Fresh Soup Pot Herbs –

A recipe from former chef Karen Clarke Bishop: "This is my favorite mix. Packed into pint jars and refrigerated, it keeps for months. I use it to flavor soups just before serving. Careful—just use one tablespoon at a time."

>   5 to 6 large bunches of curly parsley, 3 large bunches
>   flat-leaf parsley, 6 leeks well cleaned and with 3 inches of
>   green, 4 bunches summer savory, 2 to 3 bunches thyme,
>   2 cups kosher salt

Chop all the herbs and leeks fine and mix in the salt.

– The Pines Hot Dog/Hamburger Relish –

>   1 dozen cucumbers, 6 onions, 3 sweet peppers (red or green),
>   2 T salt, 1 1/2 quarts cider vinegar, 4 cups sugar, 1 tsp. turmeric
>   powder, 1 1/2 tsp. mustard seed

Chop fine (or grind in a food grinder) the cucumbers, onions, and peppers. Place in a large cooking pot and add salt. Let set for a minimum of 2 hours,

or overnight. Drain, return to pot, and add remaining ingredients. Boil for
45 minutes or until mixture turns a light yellowish color. Seal in hot jars.

– Tim Pond Fruit Punch for a Crowd –

Betty Calden: "You can use some of the lemonade from the **Lemonade for a Crowd** recipe
(see below). Make sure all the ingredients are cold to begin with."

> 2 1/2 **cups liquid fruit punch, 8 cups water, 2 cups lemonade,**
> 1/2 **cup lemon juice, 1 cup orange juice (not from concentrate,**
> **with or without pulp), 12 ounces ginger ale**

Combine all ingredients in a large punch bowl and float some ice on top
to keep punch cold.

– Tim Pond Lemonade for a Crowd –

Betty Calden: "Each 'preparer' has different tastes on this recipe. Add either more sugar
or more lemon juice to suit your taste buds."

> **6 cups sugar, 3 gallons water, 2** 1/2 **(15-ounce) bottles**
> **lemon juice**

In a large (punch) bowl or serving pot, pour 1 gallon of warm water, and
the sugar. Stir until the sugar dissolves and add the remaining 2 gallons of
water, this time ice cold, along with the cold lemon juice. Take a taste and
adjust to your preference. Serve with or without ice.

Fall Season
September, October, November

As fall arrives and the school year begins, guests and activities at sporting camps are as varied as the autumn colors. Singles, seniors, couples, and couples with young children fill the cabins. Some couples bring large family groups because September is a popular time for getting married at a favorite sporting camp. Fall is also the time to harvest the final largesse from the camp garden, for brisk, bug-free hiking, for the fall fishing and hunting season, and for enjoying colorful foliage. By the end of the season, owners are preparing the cabins and water systems for the winter to come.

In the garden, pumpkins and squash, beets and carrots, and tomatoes and herbs are all ripe for the picking. Up in northern and eastern Maine, community activity revolves around the potato harvest. There is usually a lovely warm spell in September—Indian Summer—which extends the growing season slightly in some areas, and offers achingly gorgeous days with crystal-clear skies both day and night.

In the mountainous woodlands, northbound Appalachian Trail hikers have reached Maine (from their start in Georgia months ago) and are wending their way along about 280 miles to Katahdin, the northern terminus of the 2,160-plus-mile trail. A few sporting camps are very near the trail, and most are close to hundreds of other excellent hiking opportunities. Maine citizens have been forward thinking in setting aside wilderness areas for future generations. Several sporting camps surround Baxter State Park, which gives them more than 200,000 acres of wilderness protection. The woods are a beautiful part of the state's landscape and an important part of the economy. Timber is Maine's number-one cash crop, and the fall foliage season, at the beginning of October, brings in people from around the world.

As the air and water cool, trout/salmon fishing picks up and hunting season starts. More than 200,000 people hunt in Maine, and a number still rely on their catch for most of their winter supply of meat. The season generally begins with bear, then moose, followed by deer. Sporting-camp owners often double as guides during one or more of these hunts, and the camp is on the move early, so everyone is busy and the days are long. Fall is also time for small game: turkey, woodcock, pheasant and ruffed grouse (or partridge), and migratory birds. Trained dogs may be used in small-game hunts, which adds another dynamic to the camp experience.

Many guests and owners say that for them fishing and hunting mainly serve as a good excuse for getting outdoors and appreciating the surroundings. There's nothing like going out into the woods on a crisp fall day—when the musky, crunchy leaves underfoot have fallen from the trees and opened up distant vistas. Or heading out on the lake early in the morning, when columns of earth-scented mist glide past you. The sun comes down cliffs and hills like a window blind, illuminating a blaze of color. The last migratory loon raises a yearning cry, and a moose steps out into a bog nearby. All around, animals and nature are quietly gathering in for the coming storms and cold. Camp owners and staff have been busy chopping wood, and cozy fires and warm food await.

Breakfast Fare

– Cobb's Pumpkin Muffins –

Betty Cobb: "Patty, our son Andy's wife, makes these, and they're really good."

**2 cups flour, 1 cup sugar, 3 tsp. baking powder, 1 tsp. baking
soda, 1 tsp. salt, 1/2 tsp. cinnamon, 1/2 tsp. ground cloves,
1 cup pureed pumpkin, 1/4 cup vegetable oil, 3/4 cup milk,
1 egg, 1/2 cup nuts and/or raisins (optional)**

In a big bowl, combine dry ingredients. In a medium bowl, combine wet
ingredients and stir until combined well. Add wet ingredients to the dry
ingredients, and stir until just moistened. Fold in nuts/raisins if desired. Do
not overmix. Spoon into greased muffin tins and bake in preheated 350°
oven for 25 minutes. Makes approximately 24.

– Enchanted Outfitters' Plain Donuts –

Gloria Hewey: "I don't share this with many people; in fact, it will be weird to see it in print
since it's been like a special family secret. I've been making these donuts since back when
I was living in a log cabin. We were raising pigs then, and I would make homemade ren-
dered lard during butchering time. It made the most delicious donuts. It has become a
family tradition to make these donuts for my grandchildren every Christmas after they
open their presents. One year I lost the recipe and went into major withdrawal. As soon
as I found it, I made a couple of copies so that would never happen again! It's amazing how
a certain recipe or two can be so important in one's life."

**3 T melted butter, 1 1/2 cups sugar, 2 eggs, 1 cup buttermilk,
4 cups flour, 3 tsp. baking powder, 1/2 tsp. baking soda,
1 tsp. salt, 1 T nutmeg (freshly ground if possible, as it has
more flavor), 1 tsp. cinnamon, 4 to 5 pounds lard or vegetable
shortening**

In a bowl, combine the first 4 ingredients and beat until light and fluffy.
Sift the dry ingredients over the wet ingredients and stir together well.
Refrigerate dough for several hours. (I usually make the dough the night
before and bring it with me for Christmas morning.)

Start heating 6 inches of lard/shortening in a deep fryer or deep pot over the stove. Turn dough onto a floured board and knead until smooth. Roll to a ¼-inch to ½-inch thickness. (Don't roll too thin because that will make the donuts crunchy.) Cut dough with a donut cutter.

Check that lard/shortening is at 380° (use a candy thermometer). Cook in batches. The donuts will fall to the bottom and then rise again, and they need enough room to move around. Be careful to maintain a steady temperature with the fat. Drain on paper towels. Makes about 36.

••

MAINE CRANBERRIES

There are three berries native to North America: wild strawberries, blueberries, and cranberries. Cranberries were harvested by Maine Indian tribes, and later by the early European settlers. Most commercial harvesting died out in the nineteenth century; however, a fledgling cranberry industry started up in Maine during the 1990s. Today, there are around 250 acres of cranberry bogs located across the state, producing two to three million pounds of fruit a year. According to grower Harry Ricker, it takes ten to twelve years to get into full production. Like most wild fruit, cranberries produce on a two-year cycle.

Ricker notes that, contrary to popular belief, cranberries are not grown in water, but in sand. They must be irrigated one to two times a week, making them the most expensive fruit to grow per acre. Cranberry plants can live to be a hundred years old. Studies are indicating that the berries are beneficial for stroke victims and can help fight urinary tract problems and tooth tartar. Their harvest time is in October—just in time for the holidays.

••

– Grant's Apple-Cranberry-Nut Coffee Cake –

The basis for this recipe is the mixture for Grant's Apple-Cranberry Pie Filling (in the Fall Desserts section). Pastry and breakfast cook Joy Russell uses strong *in the old way, meaning "heaping."*

Apple-Cranberry Mixture:
2 large apples (peeled, cored, and sliced), ⅓ cup cranberries chopped, 1 rounded T brown sugar, 2½ T sugar, ¼ tsp. cinnamon, ⅛ tsp. nutmeg

Coffee Cake:
> 4 cups flour, 4 tsp. Bakewell Cream, 2 tsp. baking soda, 1 tsp.
> salt, 1 tsp. cinnamon, "strong" 1/2 cup vegetable shortening,
> apple-cranberry mixture, 4 eggs, 1/2 cup water

In a large bowl, mix dry ingredients and shortening together with pastry cutter, hands, or fork. Add apple-cranberry mixture. In a small bowl, beat the eggs and water together and mix into other ingredients to make a consistency like muffin batter. Spread batter into a 10 x 14-inch greased pan and cover with brown sugar topping.

Brown Sugar Topping:
> 1/2 cup brown sugar, 1/2 cup white sugar, 1/2 tsp. cinnamon

Mix together and sprinkle over the top of the coffee cake. Bake at 375° for 35 to 45 minutes, or until a toothpick inserted in the center comes out clean. Let the cake cool slightly and drizzle with glaze.

Glaze:
> 2 cups powdered sugar, 3 T melted butter, enough milk to
> make it "drizzly" (I use canned evaporated)

Pour glaze over the top of coffee cake and sprinkle it all with 1 "strong" cup chopped walnuts.

– King and Bartlett's Buttermilk Pancakes –

> 2 cups buttermilk, 2 eggs, 4 T oil, 2 cups flour, 4 T sugar, 2 tsp.
> baking powder, 1 1/4 tsp. baking soda, 1 tsp. salt

In a bowl, combine the first three ingredients. Sift together the remaining ingredients and add to the wet ingredients. Stir until well blended. Pour onto a hot, buttered griddle and cook pancakes until bubbles form on top and edges are crisp. Flip pancakes and cook until brown on other side.

– McNally's/Nugent's Apple Muffins –

John Richardson: "This is my favorite muffin that Reggie makes." Reggie (Regina Webster): "You can also substitute cranberries, blueberries, or peaches for the apples."

1/4 cup oil, 1/2 cup sugar, 1 egg, 1 tsp. nutmeg, 1 cup milk,
2 cups flour, 5 tsp. baking powder, 1 cup diced apples,
cinnamon/sugar mixture for topping

In a bowl, mix together oil, sugar, egg, nutmeg, and milk. Sift flour and baking powder and add to the wet ingredients. Stir just enough to moisten and then fold in the apples. Spoon into greased 12-cup muffin tin and sprinkle with the cinnamon/sugar mixture. Bake at 400° for 15 to 20 minutes. Yields 12 medium muffins.

– McNally's/Nugent's Breakfast Casserole –

Regina Webster: "I use this a lot during hunting season because John and I are up very early. We can be getting things ready to head out while it bakes. It's also good on these cool days because it's hearty."

6 slices homemade (or store-bought) cubed bread, 1 pound
hot sausage (cooked and drained), 1 cup grated sharp
cheddar cheese, 2 cups milk, 6 eggs, salt and pepper to taste,
1 tsp. dry mustard

Cover the bottom of a large casserole dish or 9 x 13-inch pan with the bread cubes. Layer sausage on top and sprinkle with cheese. Beat the eggs, milk, and seasonings together and pour over the cheese. *Refrigerate overnight.*

Next morning, bake at 350° for 45 minutes. Serves 6 to 8.

– The Pines Cran-Apple Muffin Cake –

2 1/4 cups all-purpose flour, 1/2 cup sugar, 1/2 cup finely chopped
pecans or walnuts, 1 T baking powder, 1 cup (1 medium) peeled
and cored tart apple (coarsely chopped), 1/2 cup butter melted,
3/4 cup milk, 1 egg, 1 tsp. vanilla, 1 cup sweetened dried
cranberries (coarsely chopped)

Preheat the oven to 400°. In a large bowl, combine first 4 (dry) ingredients. In a medium bowl, stir together the next 5 (wet) ingredients. Add wet ingredients to dry ingredients and stir until just moistened. Stir in cranberries. Spread in a greased 9-inch round cake pan. Bake 35 to 45 minutes or until toothpick inserted in center comes out clean.

Let stand 10 minutes on a rack and then remove from pan. Make a glaze by combining 1/2 cup powdered sugar and 2 to 3 tsp. milk, stirring well. Drizzle glaze over the cake. Serves 10 to 12.

– Tim Pond All-Bran Muffins –

Betty Calden: "To get here back in the 1800s, people would take railroads to Kingfield, then get on a stagecoach, and finally transfer to a buckboard [open wagon] at the end. Once folks were here, they usually stayed for the summer. Back then, the cost was $2.50 a day, but this was at a time when many people only made about $1.50 a day."

**2 cups All-Bran cereal, 1 1/4 cups milk, 1 1/4 cups flour, 1/2 cup
sugar, 1 T baking powder, 1/4 tsp. salt, 1 egg, 1/4 cup oil**

In a bowl, combine the All-Bran and milk and let stand for 5 minutes. While the bran is softening, combine the remaining ingredients in another bowl. Add the bran mixture and stir well (the batter will be thick). Spray muffin tins with cooking spray and fill the cups three-quarters full. Bake at 400° for 20 minutes. Makes 12 muffins (using 2 1/2-inch muffin cups).

– Wapiti Zucchini Breakfast Soufflé –

Frank Ramelli: "In the fall I'm busy with bear-hunting season. In fact, we're the oldest bear-hunting camp in the Patten area.

"This is a good warm breakfast dish."

**8 eggs, 2 cups whole milk, 2 cups flour, 4 T sugar, 2 tsp. baking
powder, 1 1/4 tsp. baking soda, 1 tsp. salt, 2 medium zucchini
sliced, 1 (12-ounce) package shredded Monterey Jack/Colby
cheeses (or other favorite cheese), salt and pepper to taste**

In a large bowl, whisk together the eggs and milk; add the remaining ingredients and combine well. Pour into a 7 x 9-inch buttered baking pan and bake in a 425° oven for 25 minutes. It will puff up.

Let the soufflé sit for 5 minutes (it will sink back down), then slice into squares and serve. Serves 4.

– Whisperwood's Pumpkin Apple-Streusel Muffins –

Candee McCafferty: "Some of what I serve comes right from a recipe on the can or box. This is one from a can of pumpkin puree."

Muffins:

2 1/2 cups flour, 2 cups sugar, 1 T pumpkin pie spice, 1/2 tsp. salt,
1 tsp. baking soda, 2 eggs lightly beaten, 1 cup pumpkin puree,
1/2 cup vegetable oil, 2 cups peeled finely chopped apples

Preheat oven to 350°. In a large bowl, combine first five ingredients and set aside. In a medium bowl, combine eggs, pumpkin, and oil. Add wet ingredients to dry ingredients and stir just until moistened. Gently and briefly stir in apples. Spoon into greased muffin tins (or tins lined with paper cups), filling three-quarters full.

Streusel Topping:

2 T flour, 1/4 cup sugar, 1/4 tsp. cinnamon, 4 tsp. butter

In a small bowl, combine first three ingredients. Cut in butter until the mixture is crumbly. Sprinkle over muffins and bake them for 35 to 40 minutes (40 to 45 minutes for giant muffins), or until toothpick inserted in the center of a muffin comes out clean.

Breads

– Alden's Honey-Pumpkin Bread –

Martha Minkel: "We cook and puree all the pumpkin that we harvest from our garden in the fall and freeze it in increments that suit our favorite recipes—this being one of them. We also use the honey that Carter collects from his bees."

Carter Minkel: "I got our hive from Martha's father for a Christmas present one year. We get a new batch of bees each May: a queen and sixty to seventy drones (worker bees). That number will expand to around two thousand over the summer, and contract way down to almost nothing in the winter. When we're ready to harvest the honey in the fall, I'll leave two deep supers (two deep frames) inside the hive—one as a brood box and the other for the bees' honey supply over the winter. The bees seal their honey in white, waxy combs. At the end of October or beginning of November, I take the frames of honeycombs to a guy who runs a hot knife down the frames and puts the combs into an extractor machine, which then spins the honey out and drops it into containers. We usually get around sixty to seventy pounds of honey a year."

> $3\,^{1}/_{2}$ cups all-purpose flour, 2 tsp. baking soda, $1\,^{1}/_{2}$ tsp. salt, 1 T cinnamon, 1 tsp. each nutmeg (freshly grated if possible), allspice, and ginger, $^{1}/_{4}$ tsp. ground cloves, 2 cups sugar, $^{3}/_{4}$ cup honey, $^{1}/_{2}$ cup water, 1 cup vegetable oil, $^{2}/_{3}$ cup pureed pumpkin, 4 large eggs beaten; optional ingredients: 1 cup chopped pecans, $^{1}/_{2}$ cup golden raisins, $^{1}/_{2}$ cup dried sour cherries

Preheat the oven to 325°. Grease 2 loaf pans (9 x 5 x 3-inch) and set aside.
Sift the flour, baking soda, spices, and sugar together in a large bowl. With a wooden spoon, stir in the honey, water, oil, pumpkin, and eggs until you have a smooth batter. Fold in whatever optional ingredients you desire. Pour the batter into the prepared pans and bake for 50 to 60 minutes, or until a toothpick inserted in the center of the loaf comes out clean. Cool in the pans on a wire rack before inverting.

– Cobb's Fat-Free Oatmeal Bread –

> 3 packages yeast, 2 cups warm water, 2 cups oatmeal, 4 cups boiling water, 1 cup molasses, 2 tsp. salt, 12 cups flour

In a bowl, dissolve the yeast in warm water. Set aside to bubble. In a large bowl, combine the oatmeal, boiling water, molasses, and salt and let the mixture cool. Pour yeast mixture into oatmeal mixture and add approximately 12 cups flour, or enough flour to make the dough come away from the bowl. Turn onto a floured surface and knead until smooth and elastic (dividing dough if necessary to make it easier to handle).

Place dough in cleaned and greased bowl(s) and turn dough so top is greased. Let rise until double in bulk. Turn out onto floured surface, divide into quarters, and knead again. Shape loaves and place in 4 greased bread pans, turning dough so tops are greased. Let rise to top of pans. Bake in a 350° oven for 35 minutes. Cool slightly on racks and turn out to finish cooling. Makes 4 loaves.

– Lakewood's Biscuits –

Heritage Recipe from Sue and Stan Milton and Janne Provencher.

2 cups flour, 5 tsp. baking powder, $1/2$ tsp. salt, 3 T (heaping) vegetable shortening, $1/2$ cup milk, $1/2$ cup water, $1/4$ cup melted butter or margarine

In a bowl, sift together flour, baking powder, and salt. Mix in shortening with a pastry blender. Add milk and water and mix with a fork only until all ingredients are just combined. Turn out onto a floured board and knead 6 to 10 times. Roll out to a 1-inch thickness. Cut with a biscuit cutter. Place in a greased baking dish so they are touching but not crowded. Brush with a little melted butter/margarine. Bake at 425° for 15 minutes. Makes 8 to 10 biscuits.

– Nicatous Lodge Apple Bread –

3 cups flour, 2 tsp. baking powder, 1 tsp. baking soda, $1/2$ tsp. salt, 1 cup white sugar, $1/2$ cup vegetable oil, 2 eggs, $1/2$ tsp. vanilla, 1 cup shredded apple, $3/4$ cup chopped walnuts

Preheat oven to 350°. Grease one $4 1/2$ x $8 1/2$-inch loaf pan. In a bowl, sift together first five ingredients. In another bowl, combine oil, eggs, and vanilla and stir well. Add dry ingredients to liquids along with apples and walnuts, and stir only until ingredients are moistened. Bake for 35 to 40 minutes, or until a toothpick inserted in the center of the loaf comes out clean. Cool slightly before inverting on rack.

Appetizers

– Bald Mountain Wedding Mushrooms –

Stephen Philbrick: "We typically have weddings scheduled every week in September. It's a beautiful time of year up here."

Meg Godaire: "This is something I often serve at the weddings; you can adjust amounts to the size of the gathering."

> **24 stuffing mushrooms, 1 (8-ounce) package cream cheese, 1 pound crabmeat, 1/2 cup celery diced fine, 4 T onion chopped fine, 1 cup grated Parmesan cheese, salt and pepper to taste**

Place mushrooms on a cookie sheet. Mix remaining ingredients in a bowl and stuff the mushrooms. Bake in a 350° oven until brown and bubbly (about 15 minutes).

– Bradford's Homemade Tuber Chips –

Igor Sikorsky: "For fall hunting season we have thousands of acres of excellent cover for grouse, deer, and bear."

Karen Sikorsky: "Over the years that we've owned the camps, many trusts and funds have been established in Maine to protect large tracts of land. In 1999, we became members of the steering committee that helped put together the largest conservation easement, to date, in the United States: three-quarters of a million acres surrounding us. It will allow the timber and sporting-camp industries to continue to coexist in an environmentally responsible way without fear of development.

"We enjoy the produce, including potatoes of different varieties, from our garden. Plan on one to two potatoes, sweet potatoes, parsnips, or a combination, per person."

Igor: "These usually don't even make it out of the kitchen!"

> **Potatoes/sweet potatoes/parsnips, vegetable or peanut oil (fresh, not reused), salt and pepper to taste (cayenne pepper is a good addition to the sweet potatoes)**

Peel potatoes if desired, or scrub and leave the skins on. Peel sweet potatoes and parsnips. Slice the tubers to about a 1/16-inch thickness, using the slicing blade of a food processor, or a knife. Soak the regular potatoes in cold water for 15 minutes, then towel-dry. Meanwhile, using either a deep saucepan or an electric fryer, heat about 3/4 inch of oil to approximately 375°. Gently place some of the slices into the heated oil, frying only enough at one time so the temperature isn't dramatically reduced by overcrowding. When nicely browned, turn, using tongs.

The order of deep-frying should be: white potatoes, parsnips, then the sweet potatoes (if frying all three). Drain on paper towels and sprinkle liberally with salt and pepper (or cayenne pepper) as desired. Check the oil temperature before frying each batch.

If the cooked chips are not immediately eaten, you may keep them warm in an oven on low while you complete the frying.

– Cobb's Deep-Dish Tomato Pizzas –

Betty Cobb: "In September, when my college girls leave, I recruit four people to help me with the cabins and/or meals, and we get two guys to help Gary, because the place is busy with serious fall fishermen who'll come the same week year after year. It's the exact situation as in May, only in reverse (when we need to recruit people because the college students haven't arrived yet and we're deluged with spring fishermen).

"This will make up into three nine-inch pies. They can be used as an entrée or sliced up a little thinner for a nice appetizer."

Crust:
>   4 cups flour, 4 tsp. Bakewell Cream, 2 tsp. baking soda, 1 tsp.
>   salt, 1/2 cup shortening (Crisco or margarine), 1 1/2 cups milk

Combine dry ingredients in a large bowl. Add shortening and cut in with pastry cutter (or 2 knives or forks) until mixture resembles dry oatmeal. Add milk and combine lightly, forming into 3 balls. Press dough into pie plates sprayed with nonstick cooking spray.

Filling:
>   3 large tomatoes, 1 cup mayonnaise, 1 cup grated cheddar
>   cheese, 3 tsp. parsley, 3 tsp. garlic powder, 1 1/2 tsp. oregano,
>   salt and pepper to taste, desired pizza toppings

Slice tomatoes in one layer on the bottom of each pie crust. Mix mayonnaise and cheese together and spread over the tomatoes. Season each pie with 1 tsp. each of parsley and garlic powder and 1/2 tsp. of oregano. Add 1/4 to 1/2 cup of any combined toppings desired (chopped onion, peppers,

mushrooms, hamburger, pepperoni, and so on) for each pie. Bake at 375°
for 35 to 45 minutes, or until crust is golden and vegetables/meats are
cooked. Let set 10 minutes before serving.

– Leen's Grouse Nuggets –

Charles Driza: "With the onset of autumn, I'm never quite sure who is more excited about
the bird-hunting season—the hunters or the dogs! We both eagerly anticipate exploring
the covers, cloaked in the bright fall colors, and smelling the boreal forest. At the end of
a successful day, the hunters gather in our dining room and are delighted by the following recipes [woodcock to follow] that are prepared from the fruits of their labors."

**Boneless grouse breasts (allow 1 or 2 birds per person), 1 egg,
Italian flavored breadcrumbs, $1/4$ cup olive oil**

Remove the breast meat from the grouse by pulling back the feathered
skin and running a sharp boning knife along the breastbone. Cut the meat
against the grain into $1/2$-inch-wide strips about 2 to 3 inches long. Beat
the egg and dip the breast meat into the egg. Pour some breadcrumbs
into a shallow bowl and roll the grouse nuggets in breadcrumbs to cover.
In a skillet, fry the nuggets in hot olive oil until they are golden brown
(a maximum of 5 minutes), being careful to retain as much coating as possible while turning them. Serve plain or with your favorite dipping sauce.

– Leen's Woodcock Rumaki –

Charles Driza: "By the time bird-hunting season starts in the fall, my dogs have been training for months. I've introduced the new puppies to pigeons (I place a pigeon in a location
for a minute or two and the dog tries to scent out the spot where it has been). The dogs
are such a critical part of the hunt. They bring a depth to the game that can only be realized when hunting behind one of these graceful companions, whose razor-sharp senses
lead you to your elusive quarry. A pointing dog locked up on a woodcock in an old apple
orchard unleashes primal feelings in this hunter and fills me with joy."

**12 woodcock breast medallions, $1/2$ cup teriyaki sauce, 6 bacon
slices cut in half, water chestnut slices, sliced jalapeños**

Peel back the skin on the feathered breast and cut off the breast meat

using a sharp boning knife. Cut each medallion in half. Soak the breast
meat in teriyaki sauce for several hours or overnight.

Wrap each breast piece in bacon with a water chestnut or a slice of
jalapeño pepper. Secure with a wooden toothpick. Place under a hot broiler
and cook until the bacon is done. Do not overcook, as meat should still be
rare. Serve with dipping sauce of choice.

– Mount Chase Venison Liver Appetizer –

Sara Hill: "This is delicious and a real treat. I'm giving the amounts for half a liver."

**1/2 fresh deer liver (approx. 2 1/2 pounds), 1 cup flour,
1 tsp. seasoned salt, 1/2 tsp. pepper, 1/2 cup oil, 1 T butter,
1/2 cup red wine**

Soak the fresh liver overnight in cold water to cover. When ready to serve,
slice the meat as thinly as possible (like London broil). A serrated knife
works well.

In a shallow bowl or plate, combine the flour, salt, and pepper and
coat the meat slices with the mixture. Melt the butter and oil in a large
skillet and fry the liver, on medium high, for about 1 minute per side (or
until the meat turns from red to light brown; don't overcook). Remove the
meat and add the wine. Stir the wine and deglaze the pan. Place the meat
on small individual plates and pour the sauce over. Serve immediately.

– West Branch Pond Prosciutto-Apple Roll-Ups –

Carol Kealiher: "This was created right off the cuff one day when I had some apple pie mixture left over and wanted to celebrate a gift of prosciutto with friends. It's as simple as it
comes, but a real treat—a perfect fall appetizer."

**1/2 to 1 cup sliced apple, pinch of nutmeg, 1 package
prosciutto slices**

Slice your favorite fresh eating apple into a small bowl and sprinkle with
nutmeg. Let it set for a few minutes. Separate the prosciutto slices and
wrap one around each apple slice. You don't need toothpicks because the
prosciutto sort of sticks to itself.

Soups

– Castle Island Venison Stew –

Rhonda Rice: "You can use any vegetables you want in this stew, and the quantity can vary according to taste. You can substitute beef for the venison, and the herbs should be your preference too. The recipe will just give the general idea. This is really delicious for those cold late-fall days when you're out chopping wood, doing yard work, or just outdoors a lot. You come inside, and your meal's ready."

> **1 pound venison cubed, 4 to 5 medium potatoes cubed, 2 onions cubed, 4 large carrots sliced, 10 to 12 mushrooms sliced, 4 to 5 celery stalks chopped, 1 tsp. oregano, salt and pepper to taste, 1 can beef broth, 1 can tomato puree**

In a Crock-Pot, add all the ingredients and cook on low for 5 to 6 hours.

– Grant's Tomato Basil Soup –

John Blunt: "You really have a sense of history when you're up in the Rangeley Lakes area. Indians used to summer at the ocean and come back to live here on the shore of Kennebago Lake, which means 'sweet flowing waters.' It was a caribou migratory route, and the last caribou seen in Maine was on Kennebago."

This recipe is from Joy Russell, camp cook.

> **1 #10 can tomato sauce (about 1 gallon), 1 large bunch celery rough chopped, 2 large onions rough chopped, 1/2 cup fresh basil (divided), 1 #10 can diced tomatoes (about 1 gallon), 2 T pepper, 1 cup butter, 8 cups chicken stock**

Place tomato sauce, celery, onions, and 1/4 cup of the basil in a blender or food processor. Blend and then pour into a large soup pot. Add diced tomatoes with juice, 1/4 cup basil chopped fine, butter and chicken stock to pot and heat, stirring occasionally, until hot. Yields 3 1/2 to 4 gallons.

– Harrison's Tomato Bisque –

$^1/_2$ stick butter, 1 T minced garlic, 1 onion chopped fine,
sherry to taste (optional), 1 can diced Italian tomatoes, 3 fresh
tomatoes chopped, 1 can tomato puree, 2 cans tomato soup,
2 T sugar, $^1/_4$ cup grated Parmesan cheese, 1 to 2 cups half-
and-half, salt and pepper to taste

In a heavy soup pan, melt the butter and sauté the garlic, onion, seasonings, and a couple of shakes of sherry (if desired) until the onion is clear.
Add the remaining ingredients, up through the $^1/_4$ cup Parmesan, in the
order given, and mix together. Simmer the soup slowly for about 1 hour.

Add half-and-half (and more cheese and/or additional different
seasonings if desired) until it reaches desired thickness and taste.

– Leen's Wedding Soup* –

Charles Driza: "The most popular time for weddings here at camp is actually in the fall, in
September. We serve this soup often, and it is very popular. We use beef for our guests,
but any ground meat or combination of meats will do. This is a family recipe from Italy."

2 pounds ground meat, 2 eggs, 1 cup seasoned breadcrumbs,
2 tsp. garlic powder, 1 tsp. Italian seasoning, 16 cups chicken
broth (4 quarts), 1 cup sliced carrots, 2 packages baby spinach,
1 cup uncooked pastina, 4 beaten eggs

In a big bowl, mix first 5 ingredients. Combine well and make meatballs
the size of marbles by rolling in the palm of your hand. Roast on cookie
sheets in a 400° oven for 10 minutes.

In a large soup pot, combine the chicken broth, carrots, and meatballs. Heat until the carrots are tender. Add spinach and pastina and cook
until pasta is just done.

Drizzle the beaten eggs into the hot soup and serve immediately.
Serves 12 to 16.

– Libby's Moose Chili –

Ellen Libby: "This is a delicious use for ground moose meat, although you can use any ground meat of your choosing. I use homegrown canned tomatoes and sauce, but here again, you can easily use store-bought."

> 1 to 2 pounds ground moose (or other ground meat), 1 cup chopped onion, 3/4 cup chopped green pepper, 3/4 cup chopped celery, 1 pint canned tomatoes (or a 1-pound can of tomatoes), 1 (8-ounce) jar/can tomato sauce (or your favorite spaghetti sauce), 1 can red kidney beans, 1 tsp. salt, 2 tsp. chili powder (or to taste), 2 T sugar

Brown the ground meat in a skillet. Add the vegetables and cook until tender. Transfer the mixture to a Crock-Pot, add the rest of the ingredients, and cook on low for 4 to 5 hours. Serve as is or with your favorite chili toppings. Serves 4 to 6.

MAINE'S MOOSE LOTTERY

Maine's moose population is estimated at about 30,000, and the hunting season is the end of September through early October. Bull moose are most active during mating season, from mid- to late September.

Each year the quota of moose allowed to be taken from the various Wildlife Management Districts is specified, which determines the overall number of hunters allowed for the year. The hunters are then selected by means of a lottery. Around 3,000 permits are currently issued, and some of the money collected goes to the Maine Conservation School, which teaches ecology and outdoor skills.

– Long Lake Corn Chowder –

Sandra Smith: "In the cool, crisp days of fall, a hot chowder is always welcomed. Not everybody likes seafood, but corn chowder usually has all takers. You can serve this with any kind of crackers. (My favorite is pilot crackers.) For large groups, this chowder also holds well in a Crock-Pot."

**1 medium onion, 2 strips bacon, 2 potatoes, 2 cups boiling
water, 1 can cream-style corn (about 2 cups), 1 cup whole corn,
2 cups evaporated milk, salt and pepper to taste**

Cut the onion into small pieces. Fry the bacon in a large saucepan until crispy. Remove from the pan and place on paper towels to drain. Sauté onion in the bacon fat until it is almost transparent. Chop the potatoes into small pieces. Carefully pour the boiling water into the pot and add the chopped potatoes. Cook about 10 minutes and then add the two types of corn and milk. Stir the mixture and season to taste. Still stirring, let the soup just come to the boiling point, but do not boil. Serves 4.

– Maynard's Pheasant Soup –

**2 T butter, 1 pheasant (or other small bird) quartered, 1 clove
garlic minced, 2 small onions chopped, 1 stalk celery chopped,
2 carrots scrubbed and sliced thin, 8 cups chicken stock,
1 pound sliced mushrooms, 1 sprig thyme, salt and pepper
to taste**

In a large, heavy kettle, melt the butter and sauté the pheasant until browned. Remove from the pot and add the onion, garlic, celery, and carrots. Sauté the vegetables until they are fork-tender. Then add the stock and pheasant and simmer 10 minutes. Add the mushrooms, thyme, and salt and pepper and simmer until the meat is tender (another 10 to 15 minutes).

Remove the pheasant, cool slightly, take the meat off the bones, and cut into bite-sized pieces. Return to the kettle and heat thoroughly. Serves 6 to 8.

– The Pines Cream Soup Base –

Nancy Norris: "This is a great base for vegetables like broccoli and cauliflower. For cream of broccoli, I add two teaspoons lemon juice, plus one-quarter teaspoon garlic powder, to the steamed and finely chopped broccoli."

1/4 cup butter, 1/4 cup finely chopped onion, 1/4 cup finely chopped celery, 3 T flour, 1/4 tsp. salt, a pinch of pepper or to taste, 1 1/2 cups chicken broth, 1 1/2 cups milk, 1 to 2 cups cooked broccoli, cauliflower, or other vegetable of choice

Over medium heat, cook butter, onions, and celery together, stirring, until soft. Sprinkle with the flour, salt, and pepper and stir gently. Add broth and milk and stir until hot, not boiling. Add other cooked vegetable(s) and seasonings. Cool, puree if desired, and reheat to serve.

– The Pines Italian Bean and Vegetable Stew –

1 cup chopped onion, 1 tsp. olive oil, 1/4 cup water, 2 cups sliced zucchini, 2 cups chopped fresh tomato (or canned peeled tomatoes with juice), 2 cups precooked white navy or kidney beans, 1/3 cup chopped bell pepper, 2 T minced garlic, 2 T finely chopped fresh basil (or 1 T dried)

In a large, heavy skillet over medium-high heat, sauté the onion in the oil and water until soft but not brown. Add the remaining ingredients, reduce heat to medium, and cover. Simmer 15 minutes, stirring occasionally. Add water, if needed, to prevent scorching. Before serving, puree 1 cup of the stew in a food processor and add back to the pot. Serves 2 to 4.

– Wheaton's Sherried Wild Rice Soup –

1/2 cup chopped onion, 1 1/2 cups sliced fresh mushrooms, 1/4 cup butter, 5 1/3 cups chicken broth, 1 1/3 cups water, 1/2 cup chopped celery, 1/2 cup sliced carrots, 1/2 cup rinsed uncooked wild rice, 1/2 tsp. Kitchen Bouquet or similar product, 2 to 3 T dry sherry, salt and pepper to taste

In a soup pot, sauté onions and mushrooms in the butter. Add remaining ingredients and boil gently until vegetables and rice are cooked (around 30 to 40 minutes). Serves 4 to 6.

Fish

– Alden's Scallops in Garlic-Dill Cheese Sauce –

Former chef Joe Plumstead: "This recipe is very versatile. It's great on pasta or can be served in a casserole."

> 6 T unsalted butter, 3 T flour, 1 1/2 pounds sea scallops
> (de-bearded), 6 cloves garlic finely chopped, 6 T fresh dill
> finely chopped (or 3 T dried), juice of 1 lemon, 1/8 cup dry
> white wine, 1 cup cream, 3/4 cup freshly grated Asiago
> or Parmesan cheese

Melt the butter in a sauté pan over medium heat. Toss the scallops in the flour, add to pan, and stir-fry for 2 minutes. Add the garlic and dill and stir-fry 2 minutes. Add lemon juice and stir-fry 1 minute. Add wine and cook 1 minute. Add the cream and bring to a boil. Add cheese and stir until the cheese dissolves into the mixture.

Serve over pasta or put in a casserole dish, top with herbed bread-crumbs, and bake at 375° until crumbs are browned.

– Bald Mountain Crusted Baked Haddock –

> 1 1/2 pounds fillet of haddock, 4 slices day-old white bread,
> 1/2 cup sun-dried tomatoes, 1/4 cup melted butter, 1 tsp. lemon
> juice, salt and pepper to taste, 1/2 cup shredded Parmesan
> cheese

Place the fish in a buttered baking pan. Cube and then pulse the bread in a food processor to make soft breadcrumbs. Dice the dried tomatoes fine. In a bowl, mix the breadcrumbs, tomatoes, and remaining ingredients together and spoon over the fish. Bake in a 325° oven for 25 minutes or until topping is browned. Serves 4.

– The Birches Haddock Sicilian –

This serves 1; adjust measurements according to the number of people you are feeding.

**1 haddock fillet, 1/4 cup chopped fresh parsley, 1 tsp. Parmesan
cheese, 1 tsp. breadcrumbs, 1 heaping T sliced black olives,
1/3 cup Red Wine Vinaigrette dressing (see p. 60)**

In a pan, loosely roll or fold haddock fillet so that it is flat on top and
slightly indented.

In a bowl, with a fork, toss parsley, cheese, and breadcrumbs together.
Sprinkle over the fish and top with the olives. Spoon 3 to 4 T vinaigrette
dressing over the fish. Bake in a 350° oven until the fish is done and
flaky. Spoon additional dressing over the fish before serving if desired.

– Bosebuck's Stuffed Rainbow Trout –

Bob Schyberg: "Our wilderness area has been protected for over a hundred years, first by
private ownership and by its remoteness, and now by restricted access and conservation
regulations under Maine's Trophy Trout Waters Initiative."

Diane Schyberg: "We buy farm-raised trout; it's two hours away, but en route to the
grocery store. Our supplier dips them out of his pond and cleans them while we wait."

**1 or 2 cleaned rainbow trout for each person (leave the heads
and tails on)**

Stuffing for each trout:

**1/4 cup chopped celery, 1/4 cup chopped onion, 1/4 tsp. poultry
seasoning, salt to taste, 1 to 2 T butter for cooking**

Sauté the celery, onion, and seasonings in the butter until vegetables are
just tender. Fill the cavity of fish with this mixture.

Wrap each fish in a piece of foil and place on a cookie sheet or
baking pan. Bake at 375° for 30 to 40 minutes or until the fish is flaky.

– Castle Island Crappie, Broiled or Fried –

John Rice: "Crappie are similar to sunfish. They're in the bass family, and are not too
bony—and we have huge ones here. To give you an idea, 'The One That Didn't Get Away
Club' for trophy fish requires a two-pounder to get in, and we get that, and more, regularly.

Crappie are not native to the lake—they were illegally stocked at some point. They travel in schools, like white perch, so if you catch one, there will probably be more right around it. These recipes can also be used for some of the other fish we have here, like northern pike, perch, and brown and brook trout."

Broiled:

Before you fillet the fish, wrap it in a plastic bag and refrigerate it for at least 24 hours. Then, keeping the head on, take a knife (we use an electric knife) and cut down along both sides of the backbone.

Preheat the oven to broil. Cover a cookie sheet with aluminum foil. Place the fish fillets on it, brush with some melted butter, and sprinkle on some Old Bay Seasoning (or similar herb blend). Broil on the middle rack until fish is lightly white throughout (about 3 to 5 minutes). Serve with lemon and tartar sauce.

Fried:

Fillet the fish as for broiling. For each fillet, beat up 1 egg white and dip the fillet in that, and then dip it into flour that has been mixed with seafood seasoning (or your favorite seasoning mix). Then you flash-fry it in hot oil in a skillet for 3 to 5 minutes. If you cook it too long, it will get soggy and oily. We break a piece open to make sure it's white throughout.

– Eagle Lodge Island Haddock –

Heritage Recipe from Tami and John Rogers.

John Rogers: "This should be called 'The Fish Chowdah That Wasn't.' My day started out quite normal. I loaded my boat with fishing tackle and supplies for the day's float. The menu was to be fish chowder. The only thing lacking was the half-and-half, which I planned to pick up on the way to the Penobscot River. After a wonderful day of smallmouth bass fishing, we arrived at our lunch spot, a.k.a. 'the island.' My client asked what was for lunch, and when I said, 'fish chowder,' I got a silent response.

"By the time I had the potatoes on to boil and the onions and butter frying, I realized I'd forgotten the half-and-half! I hung my head in embarrassment for a second, and then quickly went into the improvise mode. I looked in my five-gallon bucket to see what I had for spices. Both Tami and I use something we call 'river spice.' It's a combination of garlic salt, pepper, basil and oregano, celery salt, and cayenne pepper (see p. 234, in the **Black Beans and Rice** recipe). Praise the river gods, we now had lunch!

"I cooked the potatoes with very little water until tender, then drained the water and turned the potatoes into home fries. I covered a plate with a generous amount of 'river spice' and coated the two haddock fillets well on both sides. (Allow six to eight ounces per person.) I then seared the fillets on both sides in the heated frying pan with the sliced onion and two to three drops of vegetable oil and butter until the fish was flaky. As we sat down to lunch my client, Alan, gave me a big smile and said, 'I hate fish chowder. This is really great!'"

– Lakewood Baked Haddock –

2 pounds haddock fillet, 1/2 tsp. salt, 1/4 tsp. paprika, black pepper to taste, 2 to 3 T lemon juice, 2 T butter, 2 T flour, salt and pepper to taste, 1 T dry mustard, 1 cup milk, 1/2 cup buttered crumbs, 1 T chopped fresh parsley

Lay fish in a shallow baking pan and season with the salt, paprika, pepper, and lemon juice. In a saucepan over low heat, melt the butter, add the flour, and whisk together. Add the salt and pepper, mustard, and milk and continue to whisk until the white sauce has thickened. Pour sauce over the fish. Sprinkle top with breadcrumbs and parsley. Bake at 350° for 35 minutes, or until the fish is cooked and flaky. Serves 2.

– Weatherby's Fish with Hush Puppies –

When you go out with a Registered Maine Guide, you not only get the benefit of their local knowledge and fishing/hunting expertise, you often get a delicious guide's cookout in the bargain using fish (such as salmon, trout, bass, white perch, or pickerel) you've just caught. A Heritage Recipe from Charlene and Ken Sassi.

1- to 2-pound fish, salt and pepper to taste, 2 slices lemon

Scale and clean the fish and remove the eyes. Place on a square of tinfoil. Salt and pepper the stomach cavity and add lemon slices. Fold the foil over the fish securely and cook slowly over hot coals, 15 minutes on each side.

Serve with hush puppies.

Hush Puppies:

1 egg, 1 cup cornmeal, water, oil, or bacon fat to generously cover bottom of frying pan

Mix egg and cornmeal with water to make a mixture thick enough to drop off a spoon. Heat oil/fat over an open fire. Drop the batter by spoonfuls into the fat and fry until golden on each side.

Poultry/Small Game

– Bald Mountain Duck Breast with Teriyaki Sauce –

Meg Godaire: "In the fall I often use teriyaki sauce for duck, while in summer, I'll serve it with **Bald Mountain Fresh Fruit Sauce**" [p. 116].

> 4 whole duck breasts (8 pieces), 2 cups of your favorite teriyaki
> sauce, $1/2$ cup orange juice, 2 T chopped garlic, 1 T cornstarch,
> 1 T sesame seeds

In a bowl, combine teriyaki sauce, orange juice, and garlic. Place duck breasts in a pan and pour marinade over. Marinate for the afternoon.

Remove the duck breasts from the marinade and set the liquid aside. Place the meat in a baking pan, and cook in preheated 400° oven for 15 to 20 minutes. (I serve them medium rare, so cook according to your preference.)

While the duck is cooking, whisk in the cornstarch into the marinade and cook over medium heat, stirring until sauce thickens. Add the sesame seeds.

To serve, slice duck breasts on an angle and spoon the sauce over them.

WATERFOWL

Early October is the beginning of Maine's waterfowl season. Various species such as mallards, wood ducks, and black ducks migrate through the state each year. They like to swim along shorelines where oaks are dropping acorns into the water for easy eating. Hunters canoe into grassy beds or sit near the water's edge with dogs eager to retrieve the quarry.

– Bald Mountain Grilled Thyme Pheasant –

> 4 pheasants (18 to 20 ounces each), 1 cup white wine, $1/2$ cup
> olive oil, $1/4$ cup lemon juice, 1 T thyme, salt and pepper to taste

Prepare the pheasants by removing the backbone with a pair of poultry shears. Then remove the wishbone and breastbone with a boning knife.

Mix all the remaining ingredients together in a large bowl. Place the pheasants in the bowl and marinate for 12 hours or overnight.

Preheat the grill. Cook the pheasants, first on the skin side, for 6 to 7 minutes. Then finish on the other side for 10 to 15 minutes, or until the juices run clear. Serves 4.

– Bowlin's Ruffed Grouse Cookout –

Heritage Recipe from Jon and Betty Smallwood's time. This is a guest recipe with comments that give a clear and personal picture of what it's like at many of the sporting camps around Maine this time of year:

Jon Smallwood: "Every year we'd have a group in hunting ruffed grouse—'partridge.' The season is from October 1 to November 30. Their visit included a great deal of banter, some practical jokes, close camaraderie, and, oh yes, some hunting."

Guest Tim Murphy: "While hunting partridge, you can talk to each other; it helps flush them up. They have to be in full flight before you shoot them. They weigh about a pound and they're good eating. With bird hunting, you get a lot of exercise by walking. One time I came back to camp around two thirty. It was beautiful. The sun was shining, the trees were in full color, and I said, 'Ah, to heck with it—I'm not going to hunt anymore.' And I just sat there. It's so peaceful, it gives you a chance to really think. You don't think about work but about things you maybe take for granted every day. I sat on that porch, fell asleep, and spent about two hours in the rocking chair. And it's just something I'll remember.

"We'd have a cookout in the woods each year. Along with the partridge and beans, we'd also have brown bread in a can, and when everything was done, we'd sit out in the woods and eat."

Take each bird and skin it while it's fresh by standing on the wings, holding on to the legs, and just pulling up. Take out the breast and fillet it into pieces.

Heat a little olive oil in a pan and season the fillets with some Mrs. Dash or a similar blend, and fry the bird with about 1/4 cup of finely chopped onion. Just get the bird lightly browned.

Meanwhile, heat the baked beans in an 8-inch-round cooking pan. Put the browned grouse in with the beans.

– Cobb's Turkey Lasagna –

Betty Cobb: "Here's a recipe for leftover turkey, or you can substitute chicken."

> 8 lasagna noodles, 1/2 cup small-curd cottage cheese, 1/2 cup
> sour cream, 1 (10-ounce) can cream of mushroom soup,
> 1 (10-ounce) can cream of chicken soup, 1 cup onion finely
> chopped, 1 clove garlic minced, 1/4 tsp. poultry seasoning,
> 1/2 tsp. each dried oregano and tarragon, 3/4 cup Parmesan
> cheese, 4 cups cooked turkey cut in bite-sized pieces, 2 cups
> grated sharp cheddar cheese, 2 cups grated mozzarella cheese

Cook the noodles according to the directions on the package. Drain and set aside.

In a large bowl, mix the turkey sauce (all ingredients from the cottage cheese through the turkey). Butter a 9 x 13-inch pan and arrange four noodles in the bottom. Cover with half of the turkey sauce. Next, sprinkle on the cheddar cheese. Add another layer of noodles, the remaining turkey sauce on top of that, and top off with the mozzarella cheese.

Cover with aluminum foil and bake at 350° for 40 minutes. Remove the foil and bake 10 minutes more to lightly brown the cheese. Let stand 10 minutes before cutting. Serves 8.

MAINE'S WILD TURKEY SEASON

In Maine, turkey hunts take place in both spring and fall. The number of spring hunters is determined by a lottery in May, and according to the Department of Inland Fisheries and Wildlife, there are about 12,000 permits issued. The fall hunt (without a lottery, but still requiring a permit) occurs during the last 10 days of October. Turkeys are skittish, wary birds, and turkey hunters need patience and skill along with their camouflage outfits.

– Dad's Duck in Sherry –

Raymond Thibodeau Jr.: "We have wood ducks, mallards, black ducks. You prepare duck for cooking the same way as the woodcock [see Dad's Woodcock in Hot Sauce recipe, next page]. Wood ducks and blacks are the best tasting. If you're cooking more than one or two ducks, add more of everything.

"When you sauté the duck cubes, pour in a little cooking sherry. Don't overcook or the meat will be tough. Place the duck in a saucepan. Pour in a can of cream of mushroom soup and a can of water. Sauté some fresh mushrooms if desired, and add to the saucepan. Slow-cook for an hour, adding more water if necessary. We serve this with rice or spaghetti."

– Dad's Woodcock in Hot Sauce –

Raymond Thibodeau Jr.: "Woodcock season is from the first week in October through November. They are brown birds, about the same size as quail, and have long beaks and no tail. They live along riverbanks where the ground is soft and they can bore for worms. You use dogs to point them, and they take off like a helicopter, straight up. Woodcock has a taste all its own; it's a strong bird. You should figure on three birds per person."

woodcocks, olive oil, salt and pepper to taste, ketchup,
Tabasco or Texas Pete or other favorite hot sauce
Cut off the wings with heavy shears. Peel back the skin on the feathered breast and cut the breast meat off the bones using a sharp knife. Dice the breast into bite-sized cubes.

In a skillet, heat enough olive oil to cover the bottom, and sauté the woodcock over medium-high heat briefly until seared. Season with salt and pepper and put into a saucepan or Crock-Pot with ketchup and hot sauce (adapt quantities to suit the number of birds and the taste buds of people present).

Slow-cook for an hour, adding water if necessary. Serve over rice or spaghetti.

– Indian Rock Deep-Fried Turkey –

Ken Cannell: "We use a commercial deep fryer, but some guys around Grand Lake Stream have made their own stainless steel canisters. That way, they only need a small amount of oil. Either way, the turkey is done quicker, it's not greasy, and it's delicious."

8- to 10-pound turkey, peanut oil, candy thermometer
Place the turkey in the fryer and add enough peanut oil to just cover it. Cook for 45 minutes to an hour after oil is up to temperature (350° to 400°). Check with a candy thermometer if there is no gauge on the fryer.

– Indian Rock Duck Baked on a Plank –

Ken Cannell: "Take a cleaned and plucked black duck, say, and put it on a nice oak plank. Heat the oven to 375°. Put the duck in the oven and baste every twenty minutes for one and a half hours. Pull it out of the oven and throw the duck as far as you can into the woods and eat the oak plank. (That's what I think about eating duck!)"

– Indian Rock Woodchuck and Venison Dinner –

Ken Cannell: "Other than duck [see above], I enjoy most wild game. Every year before Thanksgiving, we used to have a dinner of the various wild game I had caught, plus vegetables from our garden. Woodchuck meat is tasty because they eat greens—generally from your garden! You need to skin and gut it immediately, hang it up, and keep it cool. After a week of curing, it will be ready (whereas deer meat takes two to three weeks). Bake in a 350-degree oven until the meat is fork-tender and cooked through.

"With the deer, I beat up eggs with some shakes of garlic salt, and let a slice of meat sit in that for four to five hours in the refrigerator. Just before I'm ready to eat, I'll melt some oil and butter in a skillet. Take the meat out of the egg mixture and roll it in flour to coat both sides. Cook it on medium-high heat until it's done the way you like it."

– King and Bartlett Sautéed Breast of Pheasant –

Former chef Karen Bishop: "I like to serve this with a mixed-grain pilaf of white and wild rice and barley, and a vegetable puree or sautéed fresh spinach. Bar-le-Duc, a French conserve, can be found in specialty shops, or you can use red currant jelly. I just like Bar-le-Duc better because it has berries in it."

> **Breast meat of 2 pheasants (reserve legs for another use, such as broth, if desired), 2 T garlic-infused olive or canola oil, salt and pepper to taste, $1/3$ cup port wine, 1 jar Bar-le-Duc conserve**
>
> Heat a sauté pan and, when hot, add oil. Swirl oil around the pan and re-duce heat to moderate. Quickly sauté breasts until light brown. Turn and sauté other side. This will take a total of 5 minutes, maximum. Salt and pepper meat, remove to a dish, and cover with wax paper. Add port wine to pan, over low heat, and stir to deglaze. Add the conserve, stir, and remove from heat. Pour sauce over the breasts and serve immediately. Serves 2.

– Libby's Grouse and Baked Beans –

Ellen Libby: "I use yellow-eye beans for this, but it's up to individual preference."

**2 pounds dry beans, 1 large onion, 1/3 to 1/2 cup brown sugar,
1 tsp. dry mustard, 1/3 to 1/2 cup molasses, 12 ounces salt pork,
4 to 8 grouse fillets**

In a soup pot, cover the beans by at least an inch of water and let them soak overnight. (If you forget to soak them, you can instead pour boiling water over them to soak in the morning, and they'll be ready to cook in about an hour.)

Drain the beans and place them, along with the rest of the ingredients except the grouse, in a Crock-Pot. Cover with water and cook on high for 8 to 10 hours. Check after several hours to see if they need more water.

About an hour before the beans wil be done, add the grouse fillets and cook thoroughly.

– Rideout's Turkey Pot Pie –

Jami Lorigan: "We have a real Thanksgiving dinner each Sunday, with stuffing and gravy and the works. We then serve this pot pie on Tuesday, using any leftovers from that meal, including the rich turkey gravy. I think this is to die for. It also has a great biscuit recipe that makes up enough so there'll be some left over for strawberry shortcake!"

Filling:

**2 cups turkey gravy (you can use prepared chicken bouillon to
make the gravy), 3 to 4 cooked diced carrots, 3 to 4 cooked
diced potatoes, 1 to 1 1/2 cups peas (cooked or uncooked),
2 cups cooked cubed turkey**

Place the gravy into a 5-quart saucepan and heat on low until smooth, stirring occasionally and being careful not to let it burn on the bottom of pan. Add remaining ingredients and heat through. (Add water or chicken bouillon mixed with boiled water if the mixture becomes too thick; it should be the consistency of stew.)

Simmer while you prepare biscuit dough (next page).

Biscuit Dough:

**4 cups flour, 4 tsp. baking soda, 2 tsp. Bakewell Cream,
pinch of salt, $^1/_2$ cup vegetable shortening, 2 cups milk**

Sift the first four ingredients into a big bowl. Cut in the shortening with a fork. Add milk and blend lightly with the fork. Dough should have a slightly sticky consistency. Sprinkle a countertop with some flour and spoon dough onto flour.

Gently form a dough ball and pat all surfaces with flour. Flatten dough to a 1- to 1$^1/_2$-inch thickness with palm, then roll out to about $^1/_2$-inch thickness. Using round cutter (glass, can, or biscuit cutter), cut as many biscuits as possible. Gently compact remaining dough, then flatten to proper thickness with palm. Repeat until dough is used up, handling it as little as possible.

Pot Pie:

Preheat oven to 350°. Pour heated turkey mixture into a 2-quart casserole dish, filling it to just over three-quarters full. Place cut biscuits over entire top of casserole (approximately 9 biscuits; the remaining biscuits can be baked separately in a well-buttered small pan). Bake the pot pie for 30 minutes. Turn heat up to 425°, put the pan shortcake biscuits in the oven, and bake everything together for 10 more minutes.

– Ross Lake Cranberry Chicken –

Donald Lavoie: "We came here in the middle of a snowstorm on a fishing trip and, during our nine-hour ride home, made plans to buy the place. The camps were built in the early 1960s, and we're only the fourth owners. We both love fishing. Andrea was the Key West Master Angler two years in a row, and I have a captain's license and was a fishing guide there. We're in a beautiful remote area and have over 160,000 acres available for our guests."

Andrea Foley: "By the third week in September, bear season is wrapping up and we have a couple of days to relax and regroup before the moose and bird hunters start rolling in. Here is something quick but delicious."

4 to 6 servings of skinless chicken (leg quarters, thighs, and/or breasts), 1 small bottle of Russian salad dressing, 1 can whole cranberries (not jellied)

Arrange chicken pieces in a glass baking dish. In a bowl, mix together salad dressing and cranberries and pour over the chicken. Bake at 350° for approximately 1 hour. Serves 4 to 6.

– Ross Lake Partridge Sandwich –

Don Lavoie: "This is an upland bird hunter's favorite. I like my sandwich with ketchup, and Andrea likes hers with ranch dressing. For the spicier crowd, you can use ground pepper instead of seasoned salt."

6 to 8 T butter, 8 ounces mushrooms sliced, 1 large onion chopped, 1 cup flour, 1 T seasoned salt (or spice of preference), 8 partridge breast fillets (without birdshot!), 8 slices Swiss cheese, 8 kaiser rolls (toasted or not)

In a skillet, melt 2 T butter and sauté mushrooms and onion until the onion is soft and transparent. Mix flour with seasoned salt, dredge moist fillets in flour mixture. In another fry pan with lid, melt 4 T butter. Sear both sides of the fillets over medium-high heat. Cover pan and reduce heat. Turn partridge once while cooking, trying not to destroy the breading.

When the meat is done and breading is brown, turn off the heat, add the onions and mushrooms on top of the fillets, and cover each with a slice of cheese. Cover the pan to melt the cheese.

If you like the rolls toasted, melt 2 more T of butter in the onion/mushroom frying pan, and toast the rolls. With a spatula, place the partridge fillets on the rolls.

Meat/Big Game

– The Birches Grilled Pork Tenderloin –

John Willard: "We generally get our pork tenderloins two to a package, each piece usually weighing twelve to sixteen ounces. Plan on half a tenderloin per serving. The following recipe is for two tenderloins, or four servings."

> **2 (12- to 16-ounce) pork tenderloins cut in half, 3 T kosher salt,**
> **$3/4$ cup sugar, 2 cups hot water, 2 cups cold water, Spice Rub or**
> **favorite seasoning blend**

In a medium bowl, dissolve the salt and sugar in the hot water. Stir in the cold water to cool the mixture to room temperature. Add tenderloin and cover the bowl with plastic wrap. Refrigerate 1 hour to brine. Do not over-brine. *(Brining can be omitted if the tenderloins are fresh and not frozen.)* Remove the tenderloins from the brine, rinse well, and dry thoroughly with a paper towel. Rub meat with the spice mixture and set aside.

Bring grill to medium-hot temperature and place tenderloins on the grill, cooking well until browned on all sides (about 2 $1/2$ minutes per side). Move tenderloins to the cool part of the grill and cover with an over-turned aluminum roasting pan. Continue to cook until the instant-read thermometer inserted in the thickest park of the tenderloin registers 145° (or until just slightly pink in the center). Move the pork to a cutting board, cover with the roasting pan or a foil tent, and let it rest for 5 minutes.

We often serve this with **Cranberry-Onion Salsa** (p. 181).

– Bosebuck's Corn-Stuffed Pork Chops –

Heritage Recipe from Tom Rideout.

> **$1/4$ cup chopped onion, $1/4$ cup chopped green pepper, $1/2$ cup**
> **chopped mushrooms, 1 T butter, 1 beaten egg, 1 $1/2$ cups toasted**
> **breadcrumbs, $1/2$ cup cooked whole-kernel corn, 2 T chopped**
> **pimiento, $1/2$ tsp. salt, $1/4$ tsp. ground cumin, dash of pepper,**
> **4 thick center-cut pork chops**

In a skillet, cook onion, pepper, and mushrooms in butter until tender. Set aside to cool. In a bowl, combine egg, breadcrumbs, and remaining ingredients. Pour cooled skillet mixture over breadcrumb mixture. Toss lightly. Add a little water, if necessary, to moisten.

Preheat oven to 325°. Slice into each chop, creating a pocket, and fill pocket with stuffing mixture. Bake chops for at least an hour, or until the pork is cooked through.

HUNTING IN MAINE

Maine is divided into Wildlife Management Districts. Sunday hunting is illegal for big game, and hours are "half and half": from half an hour before sunrise to half an hour after sunset. Downed moose, bear, deer, and wild turkey must be tagged and brought to a registration station to be weighed and recorded. This procedure helps to regulate the hunting season and safeguard the health of wildlife populations.

Maine has an Outdoors Women program aimed at introducing women to the skills and techniques involved in fishing and hunting. There is also an organization called "Hunters for the Hungry," which distributes portions of various catches to various soup kitchens around the state.

(See Department of Inland Fisheries and Wildlife in Resources section.)

– Dad's Pig Roast –

Raymond Thibodeau Jr.: "Our fall bear-hunting season starts at the end of July for me, when I put out our bait barrels and tree stands. I'm baiting by August, and then by the beginning of September I'm ready for the bear season. This pig roast is something else we do in the fall."

We have a fifty-five-gallon drum that's been cut in half; it has a welded grate grill with chicken wire on top of that. I take twenty pounds of charcoal briquettes and burn them down until there's a bed of coals in the bottom of the drum. Then I take a hundred-pound pig, quartered, and put it on the grate, hide side down. I get out a six-pack of beer and a bottle of wine (red or white) and pour a little of each over the pig to tenderize it (beer) and give it flavor (wine). Next, I cover it (using the other half of the drum, which has a welded handle) and cook it for six to eight hours. I baste it now and then with the beer/wine. You want it to reach 180° on the meat thermometer, and ensure that it cooks through slowly. If it's cooking too fast, pour on a little water (the steam helps to keep the meat moist).

– Dad's Stuffed Loin of Pork –

Therese Thibodeau: "Have the butcher cut [butterfly] the pork, or you can cut it round and round yourself to make it come out flat. This just melts in your mouth, it's so tender."

1 boneless loin of pork, 1 box prepared stuffing mix, 1 can chicken broth, 1 package grated mozzarella cheese, 1 can cream of mushroom soup, 3 to 4 cups water

Place the flat pork loin in the bottom of a baking pan. In a bowl, mix the stuffing mix and other ingredients with enough water to make a stuffing you can spread over the pork loin like you would frosting on a cake. Save aside about 2 cups of the stuffing mixture and spread the rest over the pork. Roll up the meat and spread the remaining mixture over the top. Pour a soup can of water in the bottom of the pan, cover the meat with a tent of tinfoil, and bake in a 350° oven for 2½ hours. If the bottom of the pan gets dry, add a little more water.

– Enchanted Outfitters' Barbecued Spareribs –

Gloria Hewey: "Thursday of nearly every week, I make these pork spareribs. People really like them. The sauce keeps well, and you can use it on any kind of meat or poultry."

4 T vegetable oil, 2 onions chopped, 6 cloves minced garlic, 3 cups ketchup, 1 cup cider vinegar, ½ cup Worcestershire sauce, ⅔ cup sugar, 2 T chili powder, 1 tsp. cayenne pepper, enough spareribs to feed the number of people serving

In a heavy saucepan, heat the oil over moderate heat and sauté the onion and garlic for about 5 minutes, stirring occasionally. Add the remaining ingredients and simmer, uncovered, for at least 20 minutes to thicken. Pour over desired number of spareribs and cook in a 350° oven until tender, cooked through, and dark brown on top (about 30 to 40 minutes).

– Katahdin Lake Bear Liver and Onions –

Al Cooper: "My bear activity goes from August, when I'm baiting certain areas, through to December with the muzzle loading. But the big season is basically in September, and it's a great boon to sporting camps such as ours.

"The fresher the liver is, the better. You want to eat it that day (whereas beef liver is fine even weeks later). An average bear weighs around a hundred and fifty pounds, so one liver will feed about six people."

"Bear liver is just as tender and sweet as any liver you'll ever taste because bears feed on beechnuts, which have a mild flavor. Actually, the way it works in nature, every other year is a good beechnut year.

"Bears are amazing. If they don't get enough food, a mast crop of either beechnuts or acorns, it triggers them to go into their dens early. Females den first in a situation like this. The boars and females never den together because the females have their babies in January, and she doesn't want the male in the den because he would kill the babies. (They breed in June, but the egg doesn't implant until she goes into the den. Her overall condition when she goes in determines how many eggs will implant.) For the whole six months of hibernation, they don't defecate or urinate in the den at all. As soon as they're into the den, the urine somehow changes over into protein and is reused to help them survive the winter."

First, rinse the bear liver in cold water. Then take a sharp knife and cut the edges of the lobes to drain the remaining blood, and place the liver in a container in the refrigerator. When you're ready to eat, slice the liver into 3/8-inch pieces, starting at the bottom of the lobe and working toward the heavier veins at the top so you can discard the heaviest veins.

In a pie pan, thoroughly mix 1 1/2 cups of flour with 1/2 tsp. pepper. Dust each slice in the flour mixture.

Heat 1/4 cup of safflower oil in a large cast-iron fry pan and fry 1 to 2 chopped onions until they are lightly browned. Lay the onions on a platter and keep them warm at the back of the cookstove. Place sliced and floured liver pieces in the fry pan, adding more oil if necessary, and fry about 5 minutes to a side, or until no juice comes out when you pierce it with a fork and the outside is brown and crispy—*NEVER leave bear meat rare.* Place slices on platter with the onions and serve. Serves 6.

– King and Bartlett's Pork Loin with Root Vegetables –

Jeff Charles, manager: "Prior to 1991, the camps were in and out of private hands. We have fourteen lakes and ponds, we fish four streams, and hunt over thirty-six thousand acres of territory (nearly all of which is leased exclusively by King and Bartlett), and we own forty acres right around the camp. Hunting season is a very busy time here for all of us."

Former cook Karen Bishop: "A four- to five-pound bone-in roast will serve six people. For boneless, allow eight ounces of raw meat per serving."

Pork Loin:

> 3 cloves garlic, coarse salt and freshly ground pepper to taste, fresh rosemary sprigs, fresh root vegetables (such as potatoes, carrots, rutabagas, parsnips, baby onions), olive oil

Peel the garlic and cut it into slivers. Make small gashes about every 2 inches all over the roast, and insert the garlic slivers. Salt and pepper the meat and sprinkle with minced fresh rosemary. Roast the meat in a 325° oven until the internal temperature is 140°, or about 1 1/2 hours for a 5-pound roast.

Roast the root vegetables in a separate pan. Quarter the new potatoes and cut the remaining vegetables into comparable-sized pieces. Drizzle lightly with olive oil and sprinkle with coarse salt and freshly ground pepper. Sprinkle liberally with minced rosemary. Cover with foil and bake for 45 minutes. Remove cover, stir, and allow to brown for about 15 minutes more.

Gravy:

Pour the fat out of the roasting pan and deglaze the pan with homemade (or canned) stock of choice. Mix 1/2 cup of pan juice with 1 T cornstarch, add to the pan; cook over medium heat, stirring, until thickened. If necessary, add more cornstarch (mixed with a little liquid) until gravy has reached desired thickness.

– Lakewood's Venison Strips –

Heritage Recipe from owners Stan and Sue Milton and owner/cook Janne Provencher. Janne explains how she got her supplies: "We ordered our food once a week. It was then trucked up to a store in Oquossoc, where a man picked it up and brought it to my winter home, storing it in the freezer. Stan would go out in the morning to Rumford, pick up whatever else we needed, pick up the food stored in my freezer, and return to camp. Nothing was easy. Driving out from camp is probably forty hard, slow miles; from Oquossoc to the freezer is twenty miles; and Rumford's probably sixty miles. Stan did this every week, all summer long, leaving around eight a.m. and returning around four p.m."

2 pounds venison (or chuck/round steak), $1/2$ cup soy sauce,
2 T sugar, 1 tsp. garlic powder, 2 T olive oil, 1 T minced onion,
1 T sesame seeds

Mix everything, except the meat, in a large bowl. Thinly slice the meat across the grain. Place in the marinade and mix well until coated. Refrigerate for 1 hour (or up to 2 days). When ready to cook, drain off excess marinade. Stir-fry in very hot frying pan that has been coated with a little oil.

DEER SEASON

Although deer season starts in September and ends in December, the prime month is basically November. For some Maine hunters, a rite of fall includes heading out for deer hunting in the morning, and returning later for the Thanksgiving meal. Deer season involves a lot of work for sporting-camp owners. Uninsulated cabins require periodic woodstove tending, and hunters need to be up for a 5:00 a.m. breakfast (which of course means owners are up around 3:30 to 4:00 a.m., day after day). This schedule allows the hunters to be out and hunting half an hour before sunrise. They hide behind a tree or blind and wait, or they'll track a quarry if they're quiet enough.

Deer are large in Maine, with bucks averaging more than 200 pounds. The Maine Department of Inland Fisheries and Wildlife puts the state deer harvest at between 19,000 and 35,000 annually for the past fifteen years. In spite of these numbers, the major forces culling the Maine deer herd are harsh winters, the cutting of their black-spruce deeryards (which provide food and keep the snow cover low), starvation, and predators such as coyotes.

– Leen's Pork Tenderloin with Cabernet Sauce –

2 pounds pork tenderloin, 2 T rosemary, salt and pepper, 1 T
tarragon, 1 T butter, 1 T olive oil, 1 cup Cabernet wine, 1 tsp.
cornstarch, $1/2$ cup water

Slice the pork tenderloin into 1- to $1 1/2$-inch pieces. Place the pieces between wax paper and pound to $1/4$-inch to $1/2$-inch thickness. Mix the rosemary, salt and pepper, and tarragon, and rub this mixture on the pork. Heat the butter and olive oil in a skillet until very hot. Add the pork and cook until slightly browned on the outside and light pink on the inside (about 3 to 4 minutes). Remove to a warmed platter while you prepare the sauce.

Sauce:

Add wine to skillet and reduce for several minutes. Mix cornstarch and water in a small bowl and pour into the sauce to thicken. Stir until well combined. Pour sauce on the plate and place pork over the sauce.

– Libby's Deer Liver –

Ellen Libby: "During our first deer season, in 1977, a hunter brought in the liver from the deer he had just shot. I had never eaten any kind of liver before, much less deer liver, and had absolutely no clue what to do with it. To me it was huge (it took up most of the sink) and bloody.

"Anyway, this old fellow told me to fry it with onions. I did that, but if it didn't taste just like shoe leather, I doubt it was that good! I know I didn't eat any of it.

"This recipe comes from a great cook I know, and it's the only way I prepare deer liver now (and I don't serve any other kind of liver). Deer liver is one of those things I can serve in the dining room, since it needs to be absolutely fresh."

> 1 humongous deer liver, milk, 1 to 2 pounds bacon,
> 4 to 6 chopped onions, 2 cups ketchup, $1/4$ cup vegetable oil,
> 1 cup flour

Slice the liver across the grain and remove any bloodshot meat. Soak the liver in milk to cover for several hours (or overnight).

In a skillet, fry the bacon in batches and remove to paper towels. In the bacon fat, sauté onions until they are soft. In a saucepan, crumble the bacon, add the onions, and pour in the ketchup. Stir and keep warm.

Pour out bacon fat from the skillet (no need to wash), and heat vegetable oil in it. Drain the liver and dredge the pieces in flour. Fry liver until done to your preference. Serve with bacon/onion/ketchup sauce poured over the meat.

– Maynard's Venison Pot Roast –

Gail Maynard: "In addition to the regular fall hunting season, each year we do a turkey shoot every Sunday in October. And every Labor Day weekend we have a pig roast as a fund-raiser for cystic fibrosis. Here is a recipe from my neighbor Rowena Marin; it makes a delicious pot roast."

2 cloves minced garlic, 1 large sliced onion, 2 T brown sugar,
1 tsp. dry mustard, 1 T Worcestershire sauce, 1/4 cup cider
vinegar, 1 (14 1/2-ounce) can crushed tomatoes, 4-pound
venison roast, salt, 2 T flour, oil

In a bowl, combine the marinade ingredients (up to the can of tomatoes).
Place the venison in the marinade, refrigerate, and let it marinate overnight. In the morning, remove the venison, season it with salt to taste, and
roll it in the flour. Brown the meat in a hot skillet that has oil enough to
cover the bottom. Place meat and marinade in a Crock-Pot. Cover and
cook all day (8 to 10 hours).

– South Branch Lake Cinnamon and Garlic Roast Pork –

Russ Aldridge: "I sort of came up with this recipe, and guests love it. I've found that a glass
baking pan works better than a darker/metal roasting pan, which will sometimes promote
burning. This is a fall favorite with new apples."

Starting with a 6- to 8-pound pork roast, lance the top of the meat with
a dozen cuts, 3/4 inch deep and approximately 1 inch apart. Cut 4 cloves of
garlic into thirds lengthwise and place a segment into each cut. Sprinkle
and rub ground cinnamon over the whole roast. Sprinkle 1/4 tsp. basil over
the roast and place in a 350° oven for approximately 3 1/2 hours. Do not
pierce the roast while it is cooking. Serve garnished with freshly sliced
apples and oranges. Serves 8 to 10.

– Tim Pond Stew in a Jar –

Betty Calden: "If you bottle your deer, caribou, or moose meat in a pressure cooker or canning pot instead of freezing it, you will not have to worry about freezer burn or the meat
spoiling on your next camping trip or the next time you're without electricity. If you add cut-
up carrots and potatoes and a few onion layers, you end up with an instant stew in a jar!"

Dice up whatever meat you are using and place in quart canning jars. Add
desired vegetables, 1/2 tsp. salt, and enough water to cover ingredients by
about 1 inch for each jar. Boil in a canner for 3 hours to process and seal.

Salads/Side Dishes/Vegetarian

– Bear Spring Tomato-Basil Salad –

Ron Churchill: "By September we switch over from big family groups to couples, couples with young kids, and seniors. The foliage is beautiful, and there's fall fishing. We still wash our boats—twenty-three of them—every Saturday (using a pressure wash, not soap). I get ten cords of wood delivered each year, at the beginning of the season, from a fellow who cuts it off our back lot. Once the cool weather starts, the guys on the staff finish splitting the wood during the week."

4 medium tomatoes, 1 small Spanish onion sliced thin, 2 cloves chopped fresh garlic, 8 to 10 good-sized leaves of fresh basil, 1/4 tsp. each salt and pepper, 3 T olive oil, 3 T balsamic vinegar

In the morning, slice the tomatoes into a bowl and cover with the remaining ingredients. Cover and refrigerate all day to marinate. At suppertime, serve on leaf lettuce with a scoop of cottage cheese, if desired.

– Bear Spring Italian-Style Zucchini –

Peg Churchill: "Here's a great way to use this abundant vegetable. We serve it as a side vegetable for our main noon meal. I don't use exact measurements. We use a large eighteen- to twenty-four-inch roasting pan and a number-ten can of diced tomatoes."

Slice enough small- to medium-sized unpeeled zucchini to feed the number of people being served. Cover the zucchini with slices of mozzarella, cheddar, and American cheeses. Sprinkle with dried oregano, basil, and salt and pepper to taste. Cover everything with canned diced tomatoes (undrained). Cover the baking pan with foil and bake at 400° for about 1 hour, or until zucchini is tender.

– Beets Four Ways –

I guess I have beets on my mind because I just picked the last of them as I write this (mid-October). Here's how I make use of the entire vegetable:

Way #1: Spiced Beets (adapted from an old Bell canning booklet)
2 to 3 dozen beets, 4 sticks cinnamon, 2^1/2 cups sugar, 4 cups cider vinegar, 2 cups water, 1^1/2 tsp. salt, 1 sliced onion

Wash the beets and cut off all but ^{1}/4 inch of the stalks. (Set aside the leaves and stalks for the following recipes.) Cook beets in gently boiling water to cover until fork-tender (varies with size and age of beets). Drain and rinse with cold water. Pull off and discard the skins.

Place 1 stick of cinnamon in each of four 1-pint canning jars. Place the beets in the jars, slicing the large ones and keeping the small ones whole (stalks removed). Save some small beets aside—about 8 per person—for use in Way #4 (see below).

In a big saucepan, bring the remaining ingredients to a boil, and boil for 2 minutes. Pour over the beets (you should have some liquid left over to use in the beet relish), seal the jars, and process the jars in a hot-water bath for 5 minutes.

Way #2: Beet Relish

Dice the beet stems and dice an onion and add them to the remaining spiced liquid mixture in the saucepan. Gently boil the relish for 3 to 4 minutes. Spoon into small canning jars, seal, and process.

Way #3: Beet Green Pesto

Cull any insect-nibbled or bruised greens and use the remainder in place of, or in addition to, basil and make up into pesto using your favorite recipe. Set aside about ^{1}/4 cup of pesto per person. Put the rest into half-cup canning jars and refrigerate or freeze.

Now, it must be time to eat! So cook up some of your favorite pasta while you sauté the small beets in a little olive oil or butter. Drain the pasta, toss with the fresh beet green pesto, top with the sautéed beets, and, *voilà:*

Way #4: Spaghetti and Beetballs! *(Ouch! But it's good!)*

– Bradford's Potatoes Mashed with Garlic and Rosemary –

Igor and Karen Sikorsky: "We are fifty miles by logging roads to the town of Ashland. From there, we drive an additional twenty miles to Presque Isle once a week for groceries. The last part of the drive has scenic views of potato fields all around, with a backdrop of mountains and forests. In the fall, it's fascinating to see the huge truckloads of potatoes being transported from field to storage. Our proximity to what's called 'The County' gives us access to freshly grown potatoes, and we can also serve our guests potatoes and herbs from our own spacious gardens."

> 6 baking potatoes, 3 garlic cloves, 1 tsp. salt, 3/4 cup milk
> (*or* half-and-half *or* buttermilk), 3 T butter, 1/4 cup Parmesan
> cheese (freshly grated if available), 1 T rosemary (if using
> dried, use a bit less), salt and pepper to taste

Peel and quarter the potatoes and place in a saucepan of cold water. Add salt and garlic cloves. Bring to a boil and cook, uncovered, until fork-tender. Drain well. Add milk (or half-and-half or buttermilk—a combination of these works well) and butter. Using an old-fashioned potato masher, mash until the mixture is well combined. Add the cheese and rosemary, salt and pepper to taste, and beat until fluffy. I always like to add a pat of butter or two to the serving bowl before it is placed on the dining table. You may serve the potatoes "as is" or turn the mixture into a buttered casserole dish and bake at 350° until well heated (about 15 to 20 minutes).

– Castle Island Fresh Coleslaw –

John Rice: "By October, we remove any food left in the kitchen and seal up whatever stays. We take down the tackle and anything else of value from our little shop by the dining room. We store the watercraft and camp equipment, and all the shutters come down. It takes three to four weeks to open in the spring and one week to close up in the fall."

Rhonda Rice: "Here is a salad using fresh ingredients from the season."

> 3 cups mayonnaise, 3/4 cup apple cider vinegar, 1/4 cup brown
> sugar, 2 tsp. prepared horseradish, 1/2 tsp. poppy seeds
> (optional), 1/4 head purple cabbage, 1 head regular cabbage,
> 3 to 4 carrots

In a big bowl, mix first four ingredients together (and poppy seeds if desired). Shred the cabbage and carrots in a food processor (or chop/grate by hand) and add to bowl. Mix well and chill for several hours or overnight.

– Deer Run Potato Salad –

Darlene Berry: "The Italian salad dressing in this recipe acts as a marinade and adds the 'zing' to the salad."

2 pounds white potatoes (about 6 medium), 1/4 cup finely chopped onion, salt and pepper to taste, 1/4 cup creamy Italian salad dressing, 1/2 cup mayonnaise, 1/2 cup chopped celery, 2 hard-boiled eggs chopped

Cook unpeeled whole potatoes in boiling water approximately 30 to 35 minutes or until the skin starts to split and the potatoes are fork-tender. Drain, cool, and peel. Cut the potatoes into bite-sized pieces and combine with the onions. Sprinkle with salt and pepper and mix gently with the salad dressing. Cover and refrigerate at least 2 hours. Just before serving, add the mayonnaise and toss gently until the potatoes are well coated. Stir in the celery and eggs. Serves 4 to 6.

– Jalbert's Smashing Squash –

1 large (or 2 small) butternut squash, 2 large onions, 1 green pepper, 10 white mushrooms, 1/2 stick butter, 1 package stuffing mix

Cube the squash, steam until soft, and put through a food mill. If you don't have a food mill, peel the squash before cooking. When cooked, drain the squash (saving the cooking liquid). Mash the squash and set aside.

Slice the onions, green pepper, and mushrooms and sauté in the butter. Follow the directions on the stuffing mix, except use the reserved cooking liquid instead of (or in addition to) the amount of water called for. Combine everything in a large bowl and mix well. Place in a baking dish or casserole and bake at 350° for 30 minutes.

– Long Lake Vegetarian Italian Lasagna –

Sandra Smith: "This is a real Italian lasagna. I was married to an Italian, and my former mother-in-law, Eleanor, taught me how to cook lasagna her way. Try to get fresh farm eggs if you can. I set aside a small amount of the tomato sauce to serve with the lasagna."

1 package lasagna noodles, 1 pound ricotta cheese, 3/4 cup
grated Parmesan cheese, 2 T parsley flakes or fresh parsley
diced fine, 1/4 tsp. black pepper, 2 eggs slightly beaten, 2 to
3 quarts fresh or canned tomato sauce (spaghetti sauce),
10 hard-boiled eggs, 1 pound shredded mozzarella cheese

Cook noodles according to directions on the package. Drain. In a large
bowl, mix the next five ingredients together for filling. Ladle out enough
tomato sauce to cover the bottom of a 13 x 20 x 2-inch pan, or equivalent.
Lay down first layer of noodles (one-third of noodles). Spoon out a layer
of the filling. Arrange 3 sliced hard-boiled eggs over the filling. Sprinkle
on a layer of cheese. Repeat layers twice (with 4 sliced eggs covered with
cheese at the end). Bake in a 350° oven for 30 minutes or until bubbly.
Remove from the oven and set on a cooling rack for at least 10 minutes
before serving, so it holds together when sliced. Serves 9 to 12.

– Maynard's Broccoli-Cauliflower Casserole –

2 cups fresh or 1 package frozen broccoli florets, 2 cups fresh
or 1 package frozen cauliflower florets, 1 can cream of mushroom soup, 3/4 cup sharp cheddar cheese grated, 2 beaten
eggs, 1/2 cup mayonnaise, 1 sleeve Ritz crackers

Steam the broccoli and cauliflower until fork-tender. Drain, rinse under
cold water, and place in a bowl with all remaining ingredients except the
crackers. Mix gently and turn into a casserole dish. Crush the crackers on
the top. Bake in a 375° oven for 30 minutes, or until the mixture is bubbly.

– The Pines Fall Salad –

Nancy Norris: "We call this George's Salad because one of our guests loves it so much he
requests it specially. This keeps well in the fridge."

Salad:

1 head cauliflower, 1 head broccoli, 1 cup celery, 1/2 cup
walnuts chopped, 2 to 3 apples cut up with the skins on,
6 slices cooked crisp bacon chopped up, 1 cup cheddar or
Colby cheese grated or cubed

Chop up the cauliflower, broccoli, and celery. Combine everything in a big bowl and pour dressing over and combine well.

Creamy Dressing:

> 1 cup mayonnaise, $1/4$ cup cider vinegar, $1/4$ cup sugar, $1/4$ cup olive oil

Combine ingredients and mix well.

– Pleasant Point Sautéed Cauliflower –

Clif George: "I had a catering business at one point, and I enjoy doing a lot of cooking at camp. Give this a try; many cauliflower haters have been converted by this recipe."

> 1 head fresh cauliflower, 1 tsp. lemon juice, $1/2$ cup butter, $1/2$ cup oil, 2 cloves fresh garlic (chopped), pinch of garlic powder

Peel the leaves from the cauliflower and steam it in 1 inch of water with the lemon juice for 12 to 15 minutes or until just fork-tender. Remove from the heat. In a skillet, melt the butter and oil. Add the garlic. Place the cauliflower in the skillet and break up the florets with a spatula. Remove the core. Sauté cauliflower until lightly browned.

– Tim Pond Baked Beans –

> 2 pounds dry beans, $1/2$ pound salt pork, $1/4$ cup sugar, 1 cup molasses, 2 tsp. dry mustard, salt and pepper to taste (about $1/2$ tsp. each), 1 medium onion cut in half, $2/3$ cup brown sugar

In a pot, soak the beans overnight in plenty of water to cover (they will absorb a lot of water).

Next morning, parboil the beans, on medium-high heat, in the soaking water (add more to cover if necessary). Boil the beans until their skins crack. (Take a spoonful, blow onto the beans, and the skins will crack if they're done.) Do not boil them too long or the beans will be mushy.

Put the beans into a bean pot. Cut the salt pork in cubes and place on top of the beans along with the sugar, molasses, mustard, salt, and pepper. Poke the onion halves down a bit. Cover with water and bake in a 325° oven for $1/2$ hour. Add the brown sugar on top. Lower the heat to 300° and cook at least $4 1/2$ to 5 hours. Serves 10.

– Wapiti Red Cabbage –

Frank Ramelli: "Before we bought these camps, I spent twenty-three years traveling back and forth to Austria for work. This delicious recipe is a souvenir from there."

1 head red cabbage, 3 to 4 medium apples, $1/2$ cup white vinegar, 3 T water, a dash or two of paprika and/or ground cloves, $1/2$ tsp. cinnamon, 1 T cornstarch

Shred the cabbage. Core, peel, and chop the apples fine. Put in a frying pan (or saucepan) with a cover along with everything else except the cornstarch. Let simmer $1/2$ hour until the cabbage/apples are soft. Taste, and if not sweet enough, add a little sweetener of choice. Mix cornstarch with $1/4$ cup of water and add to the mixture to thicken it a bit.

– Weatherby's Teriyaki Stir-Fry –

1 cauliflower and 1 bunch of broccoli cut into bite-sized pieces, 4 stalks celery cut diagonally, 1 carrot totally peeled, 1 onion halved and cut in strips, 1 pound snow peas, 2 green peppers cut into slices

Blanch the vegetables in boiling water for 2 to 3 minutes. Set aside.

Teriyaki Sauce:

4 to 6 cloves chopped garlic, 4 ounces finely chopped ginger-root, 2 T oil, $1/2$ cup soy sauce, $1/2$ cup water, 1 cup brown sugar, 1 cup white sugar, 2 T oil, salt and pepper to taste, $1/2$ cup cornstarch

In a saucepan, sauté the garlic and ginger in the oil until slightly golden. Add the soy sauce, water, and sugars and bring to a boil, stirring. Boil gently for 4 to 5 minutes.

In a large skillet or wok, add the next 2 T oil; heat the oil over high until very hot but not smoking. Add the vegetables and sauté for 30 seconds. Season with the salt and pepper. Add the teriyaki sauce and stir well. Mix cornstarch with $1/2$ cup of water in a small bowl. Add to the stir-fry and stir until sauce is thickened (a minute or two).

Sauces

– The Birches Cranberry-Onion Salsa –

I mixed in a couple of cups of this salsa with our Meatless Chili ingredients (p. 33), cooked it all up, and it was delicious! You can use a food processor to chop up the onions and pepper.

> 3 cups finely chopped onion, 2 T sugar, 1 tsp. salt,
> 6 T fresh lime juice (2 limes), 4 T orange juice, 3 T red wine
> vinegar, 1 cup finely chopped red or green bell pepper,
> 4 T chopped fresh flat-leaf parsley, 2 cups canned whole-berry
> cranberry sauce

In a large bowl, mix the onion, sugar, and salt and let stand 15 minutes. Add the remaining ingredients and mix well. Cover and refrigerate until use.

– Chet's Fish Sauce –

Sue LaPlante: "One of our clients gave us this recipe to use primarily with whitefish. When I cook, I don't really measure much, just adjust seasonings and ingredients to taste, which is what I encourage people to do with this recipe. It's very quick and easy."

> $3/4$ cup olive oil, 2 cloves minced garlic, $1/2$ tsp. dill weed,
> $1/3$ of a small jar of capers, $1/4$ cup lemon or lime juice, paprika

Combine all ingredients except paprika in a bowl and mix well. Microwave sauce for 30 seconds to a minute until heated thoroughly (or combine ingredients in a saucepan and heat thoroughly). Place whatever fish fillets you're using in a baking pan and pour the heated sauce over the fillets. Bake in a 350° oven for 30 to 35 minutes. When serving, sprinkle on a few dashes of paprika for color.

– Harrison's Poppy Seed Salad Dressing –

Tim Harrison: "When Sterling's Camps opened in 1934, what are now our living quarters and the kitchen were the dining camp. The dining and recreation room were added on later. Back then, there were no logging roads into here."

Fran Harrison: "When you're cooking full-time for a sporting camp, you—ironically—

don't get to be outdoors very often, but you do get to be in the woods, and as an owner, it's nice to be your own boss. I wouldn't do this if I didn't like being here and enjoy cooking."

> **1 cup sugar, $1/2$ cup vegetable oil, $1/2$ cup vinegar, 1 tsp. paprika, 2 T poppy seed**

In a small saucepan, combine the sugar, oil, vinegar, and paprika. Bring to a boil, stirring constantly. Remove from the heat and add poppy seeds. Let cool to room temperature and then refrigerate. Let stand at room temperature before using, then shake well. This will keep for up to 2 weeks in the refrigerator.

– Jalbert's Fresh Tomato Sauce –

Nancy Thibodeau, camp cook: "This is delicious over linguini whenever you have ripe tomatoes and basil on hand."

> **2 T chopped fresh sweet basil, 2 T chopped fresh parsley, 3 cloves garlic finely chopped, 5 large ripe tomatoes seeded and diced, $1/4$ cup olive oil, $1/4$ cup freshly grated Parmesan cheese, $1/4$ cup grated mozzarella cheese, $1/4$ tsp. salt, $1/4$ tsp. pepper**

Combine the first four ingredients in a bowl and mix together. Add the remaining ingredients and mix well. Serve at room temperature.

– Rideout's Creamy Cheese Sauce –

Jami Lorigan: "If you've got someone who won't eat cauliflower, try this on them and see what happens! It is also our base for fettuccini Alfredo."

> **$1 1/2$ cups butter, $1 1/2$ cups Parmesan cheese, $3/4$ cup half-and-half _or_ heavy cream**

Melt the butter in a nonstick saucepan over low heat. Add the cheese and cream, keeping the temperature low. (If you want, you can use a double boiler to make the process easier.) Heat until the mixture is well combined. The sauce will thicken as it simmers.

Desserts

– Alden's Whoopie Pies –

Martha Minkel: "Whoopie Pies seem to be a Maine favorite. We certainly make a lot of them, as you can tell by the quantities in this recipe. The amounts are easily reduced."

Whoopie Pies:
> 4 cups sugar, 2 cups vegetable shortening, 8 egg yolks, 4 cups buttermilk, 8 cups flour, 4 tsp. baking powder, 2 tsp. salt, 4 tsp. baking soda, $1^1/4$ cups unsweetened cocoa

Preheat the oven to 350°. Mix together first four ingredients. In a separate bowl, sift together remaining ingredients. Add sifted dry ingredients to the wet mixture and stir until well combined. Drop onto cookie sheet(s) by $1/4$ cup (we use an ice-cream scoop) and bake for 10 to 15 minutes (test one in the middle with a toothpick). Allow to cool before adding filling.

Filling:
> 2 fresh eggs, 2 T vanilla, $1/4$ tsp. salt, 1 cup water, 6 cups confectioners' sugar, 3 cups vegetable shortening

In a large bowl, beat the eggs. Add the remaining ingredients and beat well. Cut the cakes through the middle lengthwise and fill with the filling mixture.

∙∙∙

GROWING APPLES IN MAINE

Growing apples is a generational effort. A sapling can easily grow up to outlive the man or woman who planted it. The apple industry is a way of life where grandchildren truly reap the fruits of their grandparents' labors. Trees are pruned yearly to produce a horizontal rather than vertical profile, for ease of picking and to allow enough sunlight through. Maine's climate and soil produce excellent Macintoshes and Cortlands (along with other varieties such as Macoun and Honey Crisp). The Maine wholesale apple industry has been eroding over the last twenty years, but there are still about two thousand acres of commercial trees, and about twenty-five families across the state who earn the bulk of their income from growing apples.

∙∙∙

– Attean's Apple Chocolate Chip Cake* –

Andrea Holden: "I came to Attean Lake Lodge to work as a waitress (I was hired by my husband, Brad), and have been here ever since. Jackman has a limited labor pool, but we've had luck getting good additional staff through programs that send us people from abroad. They stay through September and are great workers, and the guests love them."

From Judy Mason, former pastry chef.

> 1 cup sugar, 1 cup oil, 2 eggs slightly beaten, 2 tsp. vanilla,
> 2 cups flour, 1 tsp. baking soda, 1 tsp. cinnamon, 1/2 tsp. salt,
> 3 cups thinly diced apples, 1 cup chocolate chips, 1/2 cup
> chopped nuts

In a bowl, mix the first four (wet) ingredients. In another bowl, blend the next four (dry) ingredients. Combine wet and dry ingredients and mix well. Fold in the remaining ingredients and pour into a greased 9 x 13-inch baking pan (or 10-inch tube pan). Bake at 325° for 45 minutes to an hour, or until toothpick inserted in the cake comes out clean.

– Bear Spring Chocolate Pudding Cake –

Ron Churchill: "When you're the owner of a sporting camp, you end up having to do a little bit of everything. For example, I've even done a stint as the pastry chef."

Peg Churchill: "Ron made some peanut butter squares that were so flat, we joked we'd have to staple them to an index card so the guests could see them."

Ron: "Right! But I learned quite a bit from our chef, Ed Pearl. If we couldn't cover his day off, Peg would do the food part and I'd do the baking part. Lunch is our big meal; it's the old New England way of doing things. At night we'll have something light like soup, sandwich, quiche, and dessert."

> 3/4 cup white sugar, 1 cup flour, 2 tsp. baking powder, dash
> of salt, 1 ounce unsweetened chocolate (or 3 T unsweetened
> cocoa), 2 T melted butter, 1/2 cup milk, 1/2 tsp. vanilla

Sift sugar, flour, baking powder, and salt. Melt butter and chocolate (or cocoa) together. Add to flour mixture. Add milk and vanilla and pour into a 9 x 9-inch buttered pan.

Topping:

> 1/2 cup white sugar, 1/2 cup brown sugar, 4 T unsweetened
> cocoa, 1 1/2 cups cold coffee or water

Combine the sugars and cocoa and scatter over the batter. Next, pour the coffee or water over top. Bake at 350° for 40 minutes. Serve warm with ice cream or whipped cream.

– Bosebuck's Carrot Cake –

Heritage Recipe from Tom Rideout.

Cake:

> 1 cup cooking oil, 4 eggs, 2 cups sugar, 2 cups flour, 1 tsp.
> baking powder, 1 tsp. baking soda, 1 tsp. salt, 1 tsp. cinnamon,
> 3 cups shredded carrots, 1/2 cup drained crushed pineapple,
> 1/2 cup shredded coconut, 1/2 cup golden raisins, 1/2 cup
> chopped walnuts

Preheat oven to 325°. Grease and lightly flour a 9 x 13-inch pan. In a big bowl, beat together oil, eggs, and sugar. Add dry ingredients alternately with carrots and pineapple. Blend in the last three ingredients. Bake for 1 hour. Cool and dust with powdered sugar or use cream cheese frosting recipe.

Cream Cheese Frosting:

> 2 (8-ounce) packages cream cheese, 4 T margarine, 1 tsp. vanilla,
> 2 cups (or more if needed) powdered sugar, 1/4 cup lemon juice,
> 1/4 to 1/2 cup chopped walnuts (optional)

Combine everything but walnuts in a bowl, adding more powdered sugar if necessary to get a spreadable consistency. Spread on the cooled cake and sprinkle with walnuts if desired.

– Bradford's/Ma Dudley's Apple Cobbler –

Heritage Recipe from Dave and Nancy Youland.

I made this recipe when I was almost out of sugar. I used 1/2 cup of maple syrup instead of 1 cup of sugar at the beginning, and didn't use the final sugar-syrup topping. It turned out great!

Peel and slice 8 apples into a buttered 8 x 10-inch pan or casserole dish. Mix 1 cup sugar with 1 1/2 tsp. cinnamon and sprinkle over the apples. Pour

1/4 cup water over the apples. Set the pan in a preheated 350° oven for 15 minutes to let the apples start cooking.

While the apples are cooking, sift 1 1/2 cups flour, 3 tsp. baking powder, 1/2 tsp. salt, 1 tsp. nutmeg, and 1/3 cup sugar together into a mixing bowl. Add 1 1/3 cups milk and 2 T melted butter or margarine and mix well.

Take the apples out of the oven, spread the batter over the apples, and return to the oven; bake for 30 minutes or until the top is golden.

While apples are cooking the second time, make the sauce by cooking together until clear: 1 cup sugar, 1 tsp. cornstarch, 1 T butter, 1 cup hot water. Add 1 T vanilla.

Turn off the oven, pour the sauce over the baked cobbler, and return to oven for about 10 more minutes. Serve warm with whipped or ice cream.

– Enchanted Outfitters' Apple Crisp –

Gloria Hewey: "I was racking my brain as to what to make for snowmobile and hunting seasons (our biggest seasons) when this recipe came from my sister, Neddy (Annette). When someone orders this, invariably everyone at the table (and the nearby tables) wants it, too, so I always make a huge batch (which still is just enough sometimes!). We cook this in what is called a steam pan, which measures twelve by twenty inches. The recipe is easy to halve."

> 40 apples (2 bags), 1/2 cup water, 2 T lemon juice, 4 tsp. cinnamon, 1 tsp. nutmeg, 2 cups flour, 2 cups melted butter, 4 cups dry oatmeal, 4 cups brown sugar

Peel, core, and slice the apples into the bottom of the pan. Combine the water and lemon juice and pour over the apples. Sprinkle the cinnamon and nutmeg over the apples. In a bowl, combine the remaining ingredients for topping. Mix well, and spoon over the apples. Bake 1 hour in a 350° oven, or until top browns.

– Grant's Apple-Cranberry Pie Filling –

Joy Russell, pastry chef and breakfast cook at Grant's, not only uses this recipe for pie, but also saves aside 2 cups to make her Apple-Cranberry-Nut Coffee Cake (see p. 138). And it's confession time on my part—I was raised in a family that sometimes ate fruit pie for break-

fast. I passed that tradition on to my family with the following justification: "With the fruit, it's better for you than some other breakfast foods people eat regularly. And if you put a dairy product on top, it has even more nutritional value." (!) But think about it—a nice wedge of pie with a dollop of yogurt (or whatever) on top, a steaming mug of your favorite beverage— Morning, world!

This filling needs to be prepared several hours ahead.

> **12 apples peeled and sliced, 2 cups cranberries chopped, 3 tsp. cornstarch, $1/2$ cup brown sugar, 1 cup sugar, 1 tsp. cinnamon, $1/2$ tsp. nutmeg, 2 eggs**

In a large bowl, combine apples and cranberries. In a medium bowl, mix remaining ingredients except eggs and add to apples/cranberries. In the now-empty medium bowl, beat 2 eggs and stir this into the ingredients in the big bowl, mixing well. Refrigerate overnight before using for pie.

(In the morning, you can also use 2 cups of the mixture for the coffee cake, if desired. Try not to get too much of the juice from the pie filling, although a little is fine.)

Yields enough filling for two 9-inch pies.

– King and Bartlett's Cranberry-Butterscotch Bars –

Cathy Charles: "Jeff started here in 1996, working as head guide, and I joined him in 2001 when we became the managers. One of my early highlights was a weekend we had here with 'Casting for Recovery,' a national organization that works with women who are recovering from breast cancer. For us, that was a really powerful and great time. Each season has a different flavor to it."

> **$1^1/3$ cup raisins, $1/4$ cup rum (or water), 1 cup chopped cranberries, 1 pound dark brown sugar, 1 stick butter, 2 large eggs (beaten), 1 tsp. vanilla, $1^3/4$ cups flour, $1/2$ tsp. baking powder, $2/3$ cup toasted walnuts**

Boil the raisins and rum (water) together for 5 minutes, or until the liquid is absorbed. Let cool. Add 2 T sugar to the chopped cranberries and let sit until ready to use. In a saucepan, melt the butter and add the remaining sugar. Cook until bubbly. Let cool 15 minutes. Transfer to a bowl and add the remaining ingredients. Fold in the cranberries, walnuts, and raisins. Spread in a greased 9 x 13-inch pan. Bake at 350° for 35 to 45 minutes.

– Lakewood Apple Torte –

1 cup flour, dash of salt, $1/2$ tsp. baking powder, $1/2$ cup
softened butter, 1 egg yolk, $1/4$ cup sugar, 5 to 6 sweet apples,
2 to 3 T lemon juice, $1/4$ cup sugar, 1 cup flour, 1 cup brown
sugar, $1/4$ pound butter, $1/2$ tsp. salt, $1/2$ tsp. cinnamon,
confectioners' sugar

Sift the first three ingredients into a bowl. Add the butter, egg yolk, and
sugar, and mix together to form a firm dough. Chill several hours or
overnight.

Grease and flour a 10-inch springform pan; press dough in, easing to
within $1/2$ inch of the top. Prick dough with a fork. Peel and quarter apples,
then slice thinly and arrange slices in a circular pattern on the dough.
Sprinkle lemon juice and sugar on top of the apples.

In a bowl, mix together the next five ingredients and crumble the
mixture over the apples. Bake in a 375° oven for 1 hour. Cool, unmold, and
sprinkle with confectioners' sugar to serve.

– Libby's Pumpkin Pie Squares –

Crust Layer:

1 cup flour, $1/2$ cup quick-cooking oats, $1/2$ cup brown sugar,
$1/2$ cup margarine or softened butter

Combine until crumbly and press in a greased 9 x 13-inch pan. Bake at 350°
for 20 minutes.

Second Layer:

2 cans pumpkin, 2 cans (12 ounces each) evaporated milk,
4 eggs, $1 1/2$ cups sugar, 2 tsp. cinnamon, 1 tsp. ginger, $1/2$ tsp.
cloves, 1 tsp. salt

Beat filling ingredients until smooth, pour over the crust, and bake at 350°
for 45 minutes.

Top Layer:

$1/2$ cup brown sugar, $1/2$ cup chopped pecans, 2 T softened
butter

Combine and sprinkle over the filling. Bake for 15 to 20 minutes more or
until knife inserted in center tests clean.

– Long Lake Bottomless Cookie Jar Cookies –

Sandra Smith: "Years ago I came up with this idea that people should always be able to get cookies out of the cookie jar whenever they wanted some." Doug Clements: "The trouble was, we were having to make them about every day!" Sandra: "Now we don't do that, but these still seem to disappear as soon as we make them."

> 1 cup each butter, brown sugar, and white sugar, 2 tsp. vanilla,
> 2 T milk, 2 eggs, 2 cups flour, 1 tsp. each salt, baking soda,
> and baking powder; 2 1/2 cups old-fashioned oats, 1 1/2 cups
> chopped walnuts, 12 ounces chocolate chips

In a big saucepan, melt the butter. Take off the heat and add the sugars, stirring well. Add the vanilla, milk, and eggs and combine thoroughly. Sift the dry ingredients into the mixture and stir until combined. Stir in the oats, walnuts, and then the chocolate chips. Drop by spoonfuls 1 1/2 inches apart on greased cookie sheets. Bake at 350° for 5 to 8 minutes or until cookies are golden. Makes 5 dozen.

– Loon Lodge Chocolate Surprise Cake –

Mike Yencha: "We're in a lovely wilderness spot that supports a variety of wildlife, including muskie, a member of the pike family and the largest freshwater fish in Maine. We mail out three pages of directions for people driving into camp because we're three hours from any town."

Linda Yencha: "Because we're so remote, I rely on boxes and cans and bulk supplies."

> 12 ounces cream cheese softened, 1/4 cup sugar, 1 egg,
> 1/2 tsp. vanilla, 1 box devil's food cake mix

Heat oven to 350°. Grease and flour a bundt pan. In a small bowl, beat everything but the cake mix together until smooth. Set aside. Prepare the cake according to the directions. Pour the batter into the bundt pan and spoon the cream cheese mixture on top. Follow the baking time suggested on the box. Unmold from the pan and pour a can of prepared icing (whatever flavor you prefer) over the cake while it is still warm.

– Mount Chase Whoopie Pies –

Cookies:
> 6 T vegetable shortening or margarine, 1 cup sugar, 1 egg,
> 1 cup milk, 1 tsp. vanilla, 2 cups flour, 6 T unsweetened cocoa,
> 1 1/2 tsp. baking soda, 1 tsp. salt

In one bowl, cream shortening, sugar, egg, milk, and vanilla. In another bowl, sift dry ingredients together and combine with creamed mixture. Drop onto cookie sheet by tablespoonfuls (making an even number). Bake at 350° for 10 to 13 minutes. Cool.

Filling:
> 3/4 cup vegetable shortening, 1 1/2 cups powdered sugar,
> 7 T marshmallow fluff, 1 tsp. vanilla, 3 T milk

Beat all ingredients together until fluffy and well blended. Spread a layer between 2 cooled cookies and serve. Makes about a dozen.

– Pleasant Point Oatmeal Cake –

Cake:
> 1 1/2 cups boiling water, 1 cup quick rolled oats, 1 stick butter,
> 1 1/2 cups flour, 1 cup sugar, 1 cup brown sugar, 1 tsp. each
> baking soda, cinnamon, and salt, 2 eggs, 1 tsp. vanilla

In a bowl, combine the first three ingredients and set aside for 20 minutes. Mix together all the dry ingredients, beat the egg with the vanilla, and add to dry ingredients along with the oatmeal mixture. Bake in a greased and floured 9 x 13-inch baking pan in a 350° oven for 45 minutes, or until a toothpick inserted in the center of the cake comes out clean.

Topping:
> 1 cup brown sugar, 3 T soft butter, 1 cup coconut, 1/2 cup
> canned evaporated milk

Mix everything together in a bowl and spread on top of the cake. Turn on the broiler and broil frosting until it turns brown (watching to be sure it doesn't burn).

– Red River "What Happened to the Chocolate Chips?" Cookies –

Mike Brophy: "One morning I was making a regular batch of chocolate chip cookies. I had just put all the ingredients into the bowl of a Kitchen Aid mixer and turned it on when the phone rang. The call required me to jump into my owner's role and paddle a canoe out to my island camp to deliver an important message to my guests there. On my return, a half hour later, I realized what I had done when I walked in and heard the mixer still running.

"I shut off the mixer, and when I looked in the bowl, the dough was now a very dark brown, with no chips to be found! I stuck in my finger and gave it the taste test. It was delicious, but I had used the last of the chocolate chips for this batch. While looking for a bag of walnuts to doctor up the dough a bit, I found a large bag of peanut butter chips. I dumped them in, mixed lightly, baked the cookies, and the result was some of the best cookies ever produced in this kitchen (and that's saying a lot!). So go ahead, mix up your favorite chocolate chip cookies in a mixer, forget about them for a while, add some peanut butter chips, bake them off, and you'll be pleasantly surprised."

– Tim Pond Quick Whoopie Pies –

Betty Calden: "The quality of some baked goods is affected by heat and/or humidity. (For example, forget about making cream puffs on a hot, muggy day.) *This* recipe will work fine whatever the weather."

You can use any flavor cake mix and any filling. For the cake, you simply follow the directions on the box, but add an extra cup of flour. Drop by tablespoonfuls onto a cookie sheet and cook at 325° for about 15 to 20 minutes. Cool, and cut each little cake in half like an English muffin.

Then cook up a box of any flavor pudding, adding an envelope of plain gelatin to make it thicker. (You can also add 1/4 to 1/2 cup smooth peanut butter for a change.) Cool, and fill the whoopie pies.

– West Branch Pond Apple Crisp –

Carol Kealiher: "When my son, Nathan, was ten years old, he discovered and made this recipe one day when I was off lobbying. It's deceptively simple and is supposed to serve six—but you'll be lucky if it serves three!"

4 cups sliced apples, 1 tsp. cinnamon, $3/4$ cup flour, $1/3$ cup dry
milk (this is what makes it brown up so nicely), 1 cup sugar,
$1/3$ cup butter

Peel, core, and cut the apples into a buttered 9 x 9-inch baking pan or a
casserole dish, and sprinkle with the cinnamon. In a bowl, combine the
flour, dry milk, and sugar. Slice the butter into the mixture and combine
ingredients with a pastry blender. Spoon the topping over the apples to
cover. Bake in a 350° oven for 40 minutes.

– West Branch Pond Election Day Pie –

Carol Kealiher: "I used this recipe as part of my handout when I ran for state represen-
tative in 1992. I encouraged people to have it on hand for an after-voting reward. Vote,
and enjoy!"

$3/4$ cup quick oatmeal (uncooked), $3/4$ cup dark corn syrup,
1 cup sugar, 1 stick butter melted, $3/4$ cup milk, 2 eggs beaten,
pinch of salt, $1/2$ tsp. vanilla

In a bowl, combine all the ingredients and stir well. Pour into a 9-inch
unbaked pie crust. Bake the pie at 350° for 40 minutes. Place the pie on
a rack to cool. If you wish, serve with a dollop of real whipped cream.

– Wheaton's Zucchini Chocolate Cake –

$1/2$ cup margarine or butter, $1/2$ cup vegetable oil, $1 1/4$ cups
sugar, 2 eggs, 1 tsp. vanilla, $1/2$ cup buttermilk, $2 1/2$ cups
unsifted flour, 4 T unsweetened cocoa, $1/2$ tsp. baking powder,
1 tsp. baking soda, $1/2$ tsp. each cinnamon and cloves, 2 cups
grated zucchini (with skin), $1/2$ cup chocolate chips

Preheat oven to 325°. In a big bowl, cream together butter, oil, and sugar.
Add eggs and vanilla and beat until well blended. Combine dry ingredients
and add to bowl alternately with buttermilk. Fold in zucchini. Spoon into
a greased and floured 9 x 13-inch baking pan and sprinkle with the chocolate chips. Bake for 35 to 40 minutes or until toothpick inserted in the
center comes out clean.

Miscellaneous

– Cobb's Mincemeat –

Betty Cobb: "In November, we have three weeks of deer hunting, and then we're done for another season. We've already closed up some of the cabins by that time; most of our staff is gone, and we're down to two meals a day in the dining room because I make up packed lunches for the hunters to take with them. This recipe is from Gary's grandmother—kind of a ritual during deer season—and really a two-day project."

Day One:
Boil enough deer meat for at least 4 cups ground meat in a big pot of water with a little salt. (We put it on our big woodstove and let it boil gently until it's tender.) Take the meat out of the pot to cool. (I save the broth and put it in a cool/cold place; I skim off the fat next morning and use the broth for soup.)

Day Two:
Grind cooked meat in a meat grinder to make 4 cups. Grind enough peeled, cored, chunked apples to make 12 cups. Place in a big pot and add: 1 pound margarine, 2 packages golden raisins, 1 package currants, 2 cups cider, 2 tsp. each cinnamon, cloves, and nutmeg, 1 1/2 cups brown sugar, 1/2 cup molasses, 2 tsp. salt, 1 cup leftover applesauce, grated rind and juice of 1 lemon and 1 orange (optional).

Boil gently for at least 1 hour, stirring occasionally with a wooden spoon. Pack into jars and process for about an hour in a hot-water bath to seal lids.

– Loon Lodge Cranberry Relish –

Linda Yencha: "This is not too sweet and very easy—great at Thanksgiving."

1 can whole cranberries, 1 jar orange marmalade
Combine ingredients in a saucepan and bring to a boil so the flavors blend. Serve warm or cool over turkey or pork roast.

– The Pines Black Ant Solution –

Nancy Norris: "Put this in places where ants are seen: areas with moisture, grease, or food. The ants eat it and bring it back to their nest. It takes a little time to kill the nest, but it does work. The solution will dry up on the jar lid after a while. Simply rinse and add some more. Keep caution in mind with small children."

3 cups water, 1 cup sugar, 4 tsp. boric acid powder
Dissolve the ingredients and pour into jar lids to distribute around problem areas.

– South Branch Lake Fall Banking –

Russ Aldridge: "When it's time to rake and prepare the driveway for winter, I create our cabin insulation at the same time: I take thirty-gallon trash bags and fill them with the pine needles and leaves I've raked from the driveway. Then I tuck them in around the outside sills of each cabin. As snow arrives, I'll shovel it up against the bags so no wind can creep in around the sills. But that's not all: When spring rolls around, you can use that same mixture as a bedding for dogs, because it repels fleas."

Winter Season
December through March

Winter for some sporting-camp owners is their busiest season. The year-round camps in this book are: The Birches Resort, Bosebuck Mountain Camps, Bowlin Camps, Eagle Lake Camps, Enchanted Outfitters and Lodge, Jalbert Camps, Katahdin Lake Wilderness Camps, McNally's and Nugent's Camps, Mount Chase Lodge, Nicatous Lodge, Pleasant Point Camps, Ross Lake Camps, and South Branch Lake Camps. (This list is subject to change and lengthens considerably if you include the year-round housekeeping camps.) With the cold weather, owners are hard at work: Wood needs to be chopped, woodbins kept full, woodstoves in uninsulated cabins kept going. Guests who are not coming in on their own, via snowmobile, cross-country skis, or ski plane, need to be picked up where the plowed road ends. Supplies still need to be lugged in, despite drifting snow, freezing winds, and periodic mechanical breakdowns.

For sporting-camp owners with school-age children, winter means continuing home schooling or battling long, treacherous miles of snowy, icy back roads to the nearest school bus. Or it may mean occasionally visiting the children they have had to board out because the school is too far away or the road is too long.

For the seasonal camps, it is a time for owners to connect with past and current guests and market to prospective visitors. It is a time to reorder inventory and perhaps make a few major purchases for the upcoming season. Many owners attend various sporting shows throughout the East.

Maine has a vast network of snowmobile trails, and some of the camps are on or very near a marked ITS (International Trail System). For guests into nonmotorized winter fun, some camps are cross-country-ski and snowshoe-only access, or they provide separate snowmobile and cross-country trails. There is a bit of ice fishing. And, as always, the camps provide a place to get away and experience a simple, quiet time and space. There's time to follow tracks in the snow, to hear the snap/boom sound of freezing trees or ice in the forest or lake, to gaze at the dark night sky, or to read a good book by glowing oil lamps, feet stretched out toward a crackling fire. Whatever the facilities and utilities, when the wind howls and a blanket of sparkling snow covers the land, sporting camps are real oases for the winter wanderer. They provide a welcome respite from the cold. They offer cozy warmth, friendly hospitality, and good, hot food.

Breakfast Fare

– Eagle Lodge Breakfast Sausage Bread –

This is a portable meal when you're out in the field (wherever your field might be!).

1 large onion cut or chopped, 1 large green pepper cut or chopped, 1 package bulk sausage, 2 packages bread dough, 1 package grated mozzarella or cheddar cheese,

In a skillet, sauté the onion and pepper with a couple of drops of water to soften. Add the sausage and cook until browned through. Roll out the dough. Cover with the sausage mixture, sprinkle the cheese over that, and roll up. Place in a greased loaf pan and bake at 350° for 20 minutes. Let cool. Slice and eat.

– King and Bartlett's Fat-Free Muffins –

Karen Bishop: "This batter keeps for weeks, covered and refrigerated. It is my adaptation of an old 'six-week muffin' classic. The original was very high in fat, though. I use this basic recipe for anything from tea-sized up to Texas-sized muffins. And I have used every berry available, plus diced apples, pears, and ginger (ground or diced candied), peaches, well-drained canned crushed pineapple, canned pumpkin and spices—even a fresh orange chopped whole in the food processor. The variations are endless. This recipe is a godsend because, no matter how many guests you have or how busy you are with other food prep, you know you're covered—you have something good. Simply pull it out of the fridge, stir it up well, and bake at will."

5 1/2 cups flake cereal (bran, corn, oats, and/or wheat), 3 cups sugar, 5 cups all-purpose flour, 1 heaping T baking soda, 2 tsp. salt, 1 quart skim buttermilk, 6 beaten egg whites

Combine the dry ingredients in a big bowl. Add wet ingredients and mix until the dry ingredients are thoroughly incorporated. Stir or fold in your fruit(s) of choice. Bake in a 400° oven for 15 to 20 minutes (depending on muffin size—the larger the muffin, the longer the baking time). Yield: 24 Texas-sized, 48 regular-sized, or 96 tea-sized muffins.

– Long Lake Sausage Gravy –

Sandra Smith: "Serve this over halved freshly baked biscuits for a stick-to-your-ribs North Woods breakfast."

> **3 pounds bulk sausage, 3 T cornstarch, 1 3/4 cups milk, 1 (12-ounce) can evaporated milk, 1/2 tsp. salt, 1/4 tsp. white pepper, 4 T butter**

Fry up the sausage and drain in a colander, rinsing away the grease with very hot water. In a saucepan, whisk together the milks, salt and pepper, and cornstarch until smooth. Place over medium heat and continue to whisk frequently until mixture thickens and begins to boil. Add butter and sausage and stir over low heat until sausage is heated. Serves 6 to 8.

– Long Lake Sourdough Pancakes –

Sandra Smith: "In the winter of 1990, the local game warden welcomed me to the camp on Penobscot Lake. Shortly after, he gave me a camp-warming gift of sourdough starter. I have kept it going ever since, and it's part of the menu here at Long Lake Camps. Not only is the starter that game warden's recipe, but so are the following pancakes. Personally, I never used to like pancakes for breakfast because they seemed heavy and hard to digest; these, however, are light and delicious."

Sourdough Starter:

> **2 cups unbleached flour, 3 T sugar, 1 T dry yeast, 2 cups warm water**

Mix all of the ingredients together in a bowl and let set at room temperature for 2 to 3 days. Stir several times a day. Then store in the refrigerator, in a nonmetallic, nonairtight container (I use an old bean pot).

Whenever you take out a cup of starter, replenish with 1/2 cup of water and 1/2 cup of flour. You should also "feed" the starter every week or two if you have not been using it for recipes. Just a tablespoon each of flour and water is usually enough to keep it fed for another week.

Sourdough Pancakes:
> **1 egg, 1 cup sourdough starter, 3 T oil, 1 cup milk, 1 cup flour,**
> **2 tsp. baking powder, 1/4 tsp. baking soda, 1 T sugar**

Sift the dry ingredients into a mixing bowl. Add the liquid ingredients and stir just until the mixture is moistened (batter will be lumpy). Adjust the amounts of flour and milk according to personal taste on thickness of pancakes. Cook on a hot greased griddle or fry pan until golden brown on both sides.

....

WAFFLES FOR DINNER

I loved the waffle dinners I had as a kid. We'd start out with a quarter piece and put my father's homemade applesauce on that as a sort of appetizer. Next round, we'd have a whole or half waffle with the creamed mixture topping (salmon/chicken/tuna and peas) my mother made up. For dessert, we'd have a quarter piece with ice cream and chocolate or fruit sauce. Dinner had a cozy pacing because of the at-the-table cooking. There was even suspense: How would the next waffle turn out? Eventually, my own family was enjoying the occasional waffle dinner. The same procedure could be done with any of the good pancake recipes found in this book.

....

– South Branch Lake Hearty Breakfast Sandwich –

Cindy Aldridge: "I make this for Russ to take with him hunting in the fall and pack it for his winter caribou-hunting trips in Canada. I wrap it in aluminum foil. I use homemade bread for this (we make about two thousand loaves a season, so there's always some on hand). The amounts depend on how many days and people you're making this for."

Russ Aldridge: "When I head outside I'll put it in an inside breast pocket. My body heat helps keep it from freezing, and I've got a delicious powerhouse of nutrition right there."

Cut homemade bread into 3/4-inch slices. Make them up into French toast, putting a spoonful or two of sugar in with the beaten egg(s) and milk. Fry up some good-quality sausage patties. Place a patty between two pieces of French toast. Wrap to go.

– Weatherby's Fried Puffins –

Steve Clark, chef: "This recipe involves deep-frying eggs. I can give you the amount of fat or shortening you will need to make the recipe, but the quantity of eggs, and so forth, will depend on the number of people you are serving."

> **2 cups melted bacon fat or shortening, eggs, English muffins,**
> **chunky tomato sauce, Swiss cheese**

In a small saucepan, bring the fat/shortening to approximately 325°. Crack the eggs into the hot fat very carefully so the yolk remains whole. Let the eggs poach/deep-fry until the desired doneness. Put a split, toasted English muffin on a microwavable plate and place an egg on each muffin. Spoon some tomato sauce over the eggs and top each with a slice of Swiss cheese. Place in a microwave for approximately 30 seconds or until the cheese is melted.

– West Branch Pond Graham Muffins –

Carol Kealiher: "This is a recipe from my grandmother's old cookbook. They're basic, but everyone loves them."

> **1 cup graham (or whole wheat) flour, 1 cup all-purpose white**
> **flour, 1/3 cup sugar, pinch of salt, 1 T baking powder, 1 beaten**
> **egg, 1 cup milk, 2 T melted butter or oil**

Sift the dry ingredients together into a bowl. Make a well in the dry ingredients and add the egg, milk, and butter/oil. Stir until just moistened (if you mix it too much, the muffins will be tough). Pour into greased muffin tins, and fill about two-thirds full. Bake at 400° for 20 to 25 minutes. Makes 8 to 12 muffins (depending on size of muffin cups).

Breads

••

PARKER HOUSE ROLLS

The Parker House has been a Boston landmark since 1855. I called and learned the following: To shape rolls, cut with a round cutter dipped in flour, take a knife, dip it in the flour, and make a crease through the middle of each piece of cut dough. Brush half of each dough piece with melted butter, fold over, and press the edges together. As the rolls rise, they will part slightly to create the distinctive Parker House shape.

••

– Bowlin's Raised Cornmeal Rolls –

Betty Smallwood: "This was a favorite of my husband Jon's family before we were married. I've made these almost once a week for thirty-plus years, so you could say it's tried and true! You can also shape the dough into two loaves and make elegant toast. Steamed leftover rolls are almost as good as fresh."

2 cups milk, 1/2 cup cornmeal, 1/2 cup margarine, 1 1/2 tsp. salt, 1/2 cup sugar, 1 T dry yeast, 1/4 cup warm water, 2 eggs, approximately 5 1/2 cups all-purpose flour

Pour 1 1/2 cups of the milk into a medium-sized saucepan over medium heat. Mix the cornmeal with the remaining milk and stir into the warm milk in the saucepan. Cook and stir until the mixture is slightly thickened.

Remove from the heat and add the margarine, salt, and all but 1 T of the sugar. Stir together until the margarine is melted and the salt and sugar are dissolved. Pour into a large mixing bowl.

While cornmeal mixture is cooling, mix yeast and the 1 T sugar with the warm water. When cornmeal is lukewarm, add yeast mixture. Beat the 2 eggs and stir into the mixture thoroughly.

Gradually add the flour, beating after each addition, until dough is stiff enough to knead. Turn out on a floured board and knead until smooth and not sticky. Place in a greased bowl and let rise until double in bulk.

Punch down and turn out onto floured board. Roll or pat to about 1/4 inch thick. Using a 2- or 3-inch cookie or biscuit cutter (or glass), cut, then shape into Parker House rolls (see sidebar). Place into a greased baking dish, about 1 inch apart, and let rise until at least double in size. Bake in a 350° oven for about 30 minutes, or until pale golden brown.

– Cobb's Anadama Bread –

Betty Cobb: "Each week during our season, I usually use one hundred pounds of flour, thirty dozen eggs, and gallons and gallons of milk. This recipe makes up into four loaves."

Cook, stirring until thickened: 4 cups cold water and 1 cup cornmeal. Pour into a large bowl and add 1/4 cup margarine, 1 cup molasses, 1 T salt.

In a small bowl, combine 4 dry yeast packets with 1 1/2 cups warm water. After 5 minutes, add yeast mixture to ingredients in big bowl and stir in 10 or so cups of white flour.

Knead on a well-floured board. Let rise in a greased bowl away from drafts. Punch down. Turn out onto board and divide in four. Make loaves and place in greased bread pans. Let rise until dough is even with tops of pans. Bake at 350° for about 40 minutes or until bread sounds hollow when tapped lightly on top. Remove from oven, coat tops with butter, remove from bread pans, and let cool on rack.

– Long Lake Sweet Coffee Braids –

Sandra Smith: "When I started in the sporting-camp business in 1987, I knew absolutely nothing about making bread. After I'd made four or five disastrous attempts, a friend came into camp and showed me the basics that most cookbooks fail to mention. Then I began experimenting with sweet breads. This recipe not only tastes great, but it looks good too. I use this for Christmas as well as for camp."

1/2 cup lukewarm water, 2 T dry yeast, 2 cups milk, 1 cup sugar, 1/2 cup butter, 1 tsp. salt, 2 eggs, 1/4 tsp. ground cloves, 8 to 9 cups flour

Pour the water into a small bowl, sprinkle the yeast over it, and set aside to begin to bubble. Meanwhile, scald the milk. (Tip: When scalding milk, use a wet pan and you prevent the milk from sticking.) Pour milk into a large bowl, stir in the sugar, butter, and salt, and cool to lukewarm.

Stir in bubbling yeast mixture, eggs, and cloves. Add 2 cups of the flour and mix well. Gradually add enough of the remaining flour to make a soft dough that pulls away from the sides of the bowl. Turn the dough onto a floured surface and knead until smooth and satiny (about 8 to 10 minutes). Place in a lightly oiled bowl and turn the dough over to expose the greased top. Cover with plastic wrap and let rise until doubled.

Turn the dough onto a floured surface once again and divide into fourths. Then divide each of those fourths into thirds. Roll each third into a 10-inch strip. Braid 3 strips together for each loaf. Place the 4 loaves on 2 greased baking sheets and let rise until doubled. Bake at 375° until golden (about 30 minutes).

While the breads are still warm, drizzle with almond glaze and decorate with nuts and cherries if desired.

Almond Glaze:

2 cups confectioners' sugar, 1/2 tsp. almond flavoring, 3 T milk
Combine ingredients in a bowl and blend until smooth.

– McNally's/Nugent's Dinner Rolls –

John Richardson: "January through March is our busiest season at camp (along with May and June). We get a lot of people cross-country skiing, snowshoeing, and snowmobiling."

Regina Webster: "These seem to be everybody's favorite rolls."

1 cup milk, 1/4 cup vegetable shortening, 2 packages dry yeast,
2 eggs, 1/4 cup sugar, 1 tsp. salt, 3 to 4 cups flour
Heat the milk to scalding and pour it into a large bowl. Add the shortening to melt it. Let the mixture cool until it is warm to the touch. Add yeast and let it dissolve. Beat in the eggs, sugar, and salt. Gradually add 1 cup flour and stir well. Stir in the remaining flour, a cup at a time, until the dough is stiff and not sticking to the sides of the bowl. Turn dough out onto a floured surface and knead until smooth and elastic (5 minutes or so). Wash and grease the bowl. Place dough in the bowl, turn over to expose grease, cover with a clean towel, and let rise until double in a warm place (about 1 hour).

Punch the dough down and then shape into rolls. What I do is squeeze a bit of dough up through my index finger and thumb and then tear it off. Knead slightly into a ball and place in a greased and floured glass baking dish. Leave about 1/2 inch of space between rolls. The rolls should set at least 15 minutes, covered, to rise. Bake in a 350° oven for 25 to 30 minutes or until golden brown. Makes 18 rolls.

– South Branch Lake Zucchini Winter Bread –

Russ Aldridge: "Each year I take a limited number of clients way up north into Canada for a caribou hunt. From camp it's about a twenty-seven-hour drive to the east side of James Bay. It's beautiful wild country. We go the second or third week in December, so it's also very *cold* country. Over the years, we've learned a couple of tricks for feeding people out in the bush in the middle of winter. Cindy makes up this bread, and each hunter carries a couple of big pieces for a massive energy boost."

> 3 cups flour, 1 1/2 cups white sugar, 2 T brown sugar, 1 tsp. cinnamon, 1 tsp. salt, 1 tsp. baking powder, 3/4 tsp. baking soda, 2 cups grated unpeeled zucchini, 1 cup chopped walnuts, 1 cup raisins, 3 eggs, 1 cup vegetable oil, 1 tsp. vanilla

Preheat oven to 350°. In a large bowl, stir together all the ingredients except the eggs, oil, and vanilla. In another bowl, beat the eggs, oil, and vanilla. Pour the wet mixture over the dry mixture and stir until combined. Turn into 2 greased and floured glass loaf pans (8 1/2 x 4 1/2 x 2 1/2 inches) and bake about 50 minutes, or until the middle, when tested with a cake tester, comes out clean.

– Whisperwood's Banana Bread –

Candee McCafferty: "It was the dream of my parents that they'd live to see all three of their kids owning their own businesses. Being the youngest, I was lucky—we bought the place in April 2000, and my mother passed away in June. It was a busy, busy time. To be a sporting-camp owner, you have to be a jack-of-all-trades. Doug and I use all the skills and experience we have between us."

> 2/3 cup sugar, 1/2 cup butter, 2 eggs beaten, 3 bananas, 2 cups flour, 1 tsp. baking soda, 1 tsp. salt, 1/2 cup nuts (optional)

In a bowl, cream sugar and butter. Add eggs and mashed bananas and mix well. Sift dry ingredients into the bowl and combine everything until well blended. Fold in nuts (if desired). Pour into a greased loaf pan and bake at 325° for 1 hour. Cool slightly before turning out of pan.

Appetizers

– Cobb's Crabmeat Spread –

Betty Cobb: "Winter's the time we send out Christmas cards and put together our newsletter. In January, I do my ordering for things we need at camp. We try to replace the bedspread, rugs, and linens for one cabin each year."

Gary Cobb: "We also go in to camp and cut ten to twelve tons (almost two hundred blocks) of ice to be packed in sawdust and stored in our icehouse. During the camp season, we'll use that in lunch coolers, and it helps with the refrigeration."

> 1 can crabmeat, 1 tsp. minced onion, 2 T hot horseradish,
> 1/2 tsp. salt, 1/2 cup mayonnaise, 1 T lemon juice

Combine all ingredients in a bowl until thoroughly mixed. Refrigerate until use. Spread on toasted French baguette slices or cracker/toast of choice.

– Cobb's Kielbasa Bites with Sweet-Tangy Dipping Sauce –

> 1 package ("round") of kielbasa, 3/4 cup chili (tomato) sauce,
> 3/4 cup grape jelly, 1/2 tsp. each cinnamon, nutmeg, and ginger,
> 4 tsp. red wine, 2 tsp. sweet (or hot, according to taste)
> prepared mustard, 1 1/2 tsp. soy sauce

Slice kielbasa into bite-sized pieces. Place on cookie sheet and cook in 350° oven until heated through. Combine remaining ingredients in a bowl and mix well. Place the bowl in the middle of a large plate. Arrange the kielbasa around it and stick toothpicks in the kielbasa.

– Eagle Lodge Italian Meatballs –

Tami Rogers gave me this recipe from Loraine Guardino Morse. It is from Loraine's grand-mother. Loraine and her husband, Justin, are the new owners of Eagle Lodge.

1 to 1 1/2 pounds ground meat (beef, venison, moose, bear), 1 cup unseasoned breadcrumbs, 1 tsp. each fresh minced parsley, salt, and pepper, 1/2 cup freshly grated Parmesan cheese (use more to taste), 2 lightly beaten eggs, vegetable oil

In a medium bowl, mix everything together well. Roll into balls in the palm of your hand. Cover the bottom of a frying pan with oil and fry the meatballs, turning gently to cook on all sides, until well browned. Use with your favorite dipping sauce for an appetizer (or add to tomato sauce for spaghetti).

– King and Bartlett's Smoked Trout Pâté –

Former camp cook Karen Bishop: "At King and Bartlett, we once had a gatekeeper who loved to smoke lake trout, or togue. They're the bane of our existing natural trout and salmon populations, so catch-and-release was never an issue. The best fish to smoke are those, like togue, with a high fat content. It's a delicious way to extend the life of your catch."

1 pound cream cheese, 1 cup chopped fresh chives (or 1/2 cup dried), one 12- to 14-ounce smoked trout broken into pieces

Whip the cream cheese in a food processor for a few seconds until slightly fluffy. Add remaining ingredients and pulse to mix, leaving small lumps of fish for texture. Serve at room temperature with your favorite crackers.

– Moose Point Roasted Garlic and Goat Cheese Appetizer –

Kathy McGough, camp cook: "We get the last of our hunters in for black-powder season at the end of the first week in December. They'll come in and gather around the fireplace to relax and talk over their day, and I'll give them something like this."

> 1 whole head garlic, 1 can chicken broth, 1 bag sun-dried
> tomatoes, 1 log plain goat cheese, 1 long loaf crusty
> French bread

Preheat the oven to 350°. Take the garlic head and rub off the loose outer-most papery skin (but don't separate or peel the cloves). Place the garlic head in the middle of a glass pie plate and pour the chicken broth around it and put in the oven to bake.

While the garlic is cooking, put the tomatoes in a small dish and cover with hot water to soften them. After 10 minutes, drain the tomatoes and add them to the chicken broth around the garlic. Continue cooking.

Chop the goat cheese and slice the French bread while the garlic and tomato cook for another 10 minutes. Then sprinkle the goat cheese around with the tomatoes and bake everything another 10 minutes. (Total cooking time is now 30 minutes.) Test the garlic with a fork to see if it is tender, and bake a few minutes more if necessary.

Remove from the oven, separate the cloves, and squeeze out the garlic pieces into a small bowl or plate. (Do this with a fork and/or knife since garlic will be hot.) Spread the garlic on the slices of bread and top with tomatoes and goat cheese. Arrange on a platter.

– The Pines French Bread Cheese Puffs –

Steve Norris: "It's hard enough these days for couples like us, with a young family, to buy a house. But to go in and buy a sporting camp and operate with limited revenue, especially seasonally, is really a hard ticket."

Nancy Norris: "A lot of people find seasonal jobs in the summer. We rely on winter jobs to allow us to do our business in the summer.

"This recipe is really easy. If I don't have French bread, I use English muffin halves. Five minutes, and you've got something really tasty."

> 1 T dry ranch dressing, 2 cups grated favorite sharp cheese,
> 3/4 cup mayonnaise

Mix everything together and spread on the bread. Broil 2 to 3 minutes or until puffed.

Soups

– The Birches Clam Chowder –

John Willard: "When I first came up here, I attended the University of Maine and studied forestry. Then I lived here in a trailer and in one of the smaller cabins for two or three winters, with no running water; I dug holes in the ice just to get my water out. Some people look around and say, 'Wow, you've got it made.' And I tell them, 'With a little luck, if you stick with the same job, 24/7, for thirty years, you'll have it made, too!' This is the accumulation of a lot of plain old hard work."

> **2 (3-pound) cans chopped clams with juice, 6 potatoes chopped to bite sized, 1 1/2 packages bacon, 4 stalks celery chopped, 1 large onion chopped, 3 T granulated garlic, 3 T fresh-ground white (or black) pepper, 1/2 to 1 cup dry vermouth, 1 cup white wine, 1 T clam base, 3 quarts cream (*or* half-and-half)**

Drain clam juice into a large pot. Add the potatoes and heat slowly, stirring, so the mixture does not burn. In a large skillet, fry the bacon until very crisp but not burned. Set aside. Drain all but a tablespoon or two of fat from the pan. Add the chopped onion and celery. Crumble bacon into the skillet and sauté until the onion is translucent. Add to the pot. Add garlic, pepper, vermouth, wine, and clam base to the pot. Cook over medium heat until the potatoes are done. Add the clams and cream and stir while cooking until the chowder is hot but not boiling.

– The Birches French Onion Soup –

This can be prepared a day ahead, refrigerated, and returned to a simmer before serving.

> **1/2 stick butter, 12 onions sliced, 6 garlic cloves sliced (or 3 T granulated garlic), 2 cups red wine, 3 cups canned beef broth (or 5 T beef base and water), salt and pepper to taste (we go heavy on the pepper)**

Melt the butter in a large saucepan over medium heat. Add the onions and garlic and sauté until very tender and brown, about 45 minutes. Add the wine and simmer until reduced to a glaze, about 3 minutes. Stir in the beef broth. Simmer 20 minutes. Season to taste with salt and pepper.

If you like bread and cheese on top: Ladle soup into broiler-proof bowls. Top each with a few croutons (or a slice of toast), then top that with a slice of provolone cheese (or use some grated cheese of your choice—Gruyère and Parmesan work well together). Broil until the cheese melts and bubbles.

– Bowlin's Clam Chowder –

4 slices uncooked smoked bacon diced, 3 large onions diced, 8 pounds diced potatoes, 6 quarts chopped canned clams (and broth), 3 (12-ounce) cans condensed milk, 1/2 stick butter, salt and pepper to taste, cheddar cheese (optional)

In a large stockpot, fry the bacon and onion until the onion is transparent and the bacon browned. Add potatoes and enough broth from the cans (and additional water if necessary) to just cover the potatoes. Cook until the potatoes are just fork-tender.

Add the clams, stir, and continue to cook. After 3 to 5 minutes, add the milk, butter, and salt and pepper. Simmer for 10 to 15 minutes and serve hot with biscuits or homemade bread. Grated cheese may be tossed into the bowls just prior to serving. Yields 40 one-cup portions.

– Castle Island Black Bean Soup –

John Rice: "Although the camps are closed in winter, we live nearby in what was once Rhonda's grandmother's house." Rhonda Rice: "Our daughters, Lydia and Elizabeth, are in the room my father grew up in."

John: "We use the winter season for camp bookkeeping and marketing. We also send out around six hundred Christmas cards and plan next season's remodeling project. We try to fix one cabin a year, and may start around March to get a head start on the season."

Rhonda: "Here is a family favorite. We serve this hearty soup with a dollop of sour cream and blue corn chips on the side."

> 3 T olive oil, 1 small onion diced, 3 tsp. cumin, 2 cans black
> beans drained but not rinsed, 1 can diced tomatoes (seasoned
> if desired), 1 can chicken broth

In a 2-quart saucepan, heat the olive oil and sauté the onion with the
cumin until the onion is soft. Add the remaining ingredients and simmer
15 minutes. Use a blender or food processor to puree the soup. Adjust
consistency with a little boiling water if desired.

– Chet's Kale Stew –

Sue LaPlante: "I like recipes that can easily be expanded and are adaptable as far as ingredients go—like this one. The linguia mentioned is a Portuguese sausage similar to kielbasa,
only spicier. You can substitute something else of your choosing, or leave it out. I serve
this with homemade bread for a hot, satisfying meal."

> 2- to 3-pound pot roast, 2 to 3 diced onions, 2 cans kidney
> beans, 6 cups fresh kale cooked and chopped (or 3 packages
> frozen chopped kale), 2 to 3 large potatoes diced, 5 to 6
> carrots sliced, 1 to 2 pounds sliced linguia, salt and pepper
> to taste

Place the pot roast and onions in a heavy saucepan or soup pot and cover
with water. Simmer until the meat is fork-tender (approximately 2 hours).
Cool and skim off the fat. Remove the meat.

To the stock in the pan, add the remaining ingredients and simmer
until the vegetables are tender. While vegetables are cooking, cut up the
pot roast, and when the vegetables are done, add the cut-up beef to the
rest of the stew. Adjust seasonings to taste.

– Deer Run Stormy Day Soup –

Darlene Berry: "After baking a ham, there is always a bone left behind. Before all the meat
is cut off from it, consider trying this soup. It's great for taking the chill off a cold day."

> 1 ham bone with some meat, 1 pound dry navy beans, 7 cups
> water, 2 cups cubed cooked smoked ham, 1/4 cup minced
> onion, 1/2 tsp. salt, 1 bay leaf, pepper to taste

In a soup pot, place ham bone in just enough water to cover. Bring to a boil and then simmer until the meat falls from the bone. Remove the bone, keep the water to use for the beans, and set the bone meat aside to add back later.

Rinse the beans. In the soup pot, pour ham water and enough additional water to make 7 cups liquid. Add the beans and heat to boiling, then boil gently for 2 minutes. Remove from the heat and let stand 1 hour.

Add the remaining ingredients to the pot and heat to boiling again. Reduce heat, cover, and simmer about 1 1/4 hours, or until the beans are soft. Skim off the foam occasionally and add more water if necessary. Remove the bay leaf and season to taste. Serves 4 to 6.

– Enchanted Outfitters' Fish Chowder –

Gloria Hewey: "I serve this chowder to our snowmobiling and hunting groups. This is our busiest season, and I make a huge pot every weekend in winter. You can use canned clams with this, too."

> **piece of salt pork about the size of a medium onion, medium onion, 2 T butter, 4 medium potatoes cubed, 2 pounds of your preferred fish (i.e., haddock, hake), 2 cans evaporated milk, salt and pepper to taste**

Cut up the salt pork and the onion into little chunks. Put 1 T butter in the bottom of a medium saucepan. Sauté together. (The secret is to let them sauté together until the salt pork browns; the onion will get good and brown, too.)

Add around a cup of water to the saucepan and scrape up the brown from the bottom. Add 4 potatoes, cubed, and enough water to cover. Cook potatoes until they are almost soft.

Chunk up fish and lay it on top of the potatoes. Cover saucepan and reduce heat to low so fish can steam. Cook until the fish is done, about 15 minutes. Then pour in the milk and salt and pepper to taste. Put another T of butter on top. Serves 6 to 8.

– Harrison's Clam Chowder –

Fran Harrison: "I like my chowder thick. If you don't, just add more half-and-half or water."

**5 strips uncooked bacon diced, 1 diced onion, 1 stick butter,
2 T sherry, 1 tsp. each dried tarragon, Old Bay Seasoning, garlic
salt, and turmeric (if desired), 5 medium potatoes chopped
small, 1/2 cup flour, 2 cans each chopped and whole clams with
juice, 1 quart half-and-half**

In a heavy soup pot, fry up bacon until cooked but not too crisp. Add onion
and butter and cook until butter is melted. Add sherry and desired seasonings and simmer until the onion is clear. Add potatoes and sprinkle in the
flour, stirring until potatoes are well covered. Add juice from the cans of
clams and enough water, if necessary, to just cover the potatoes.

Slowly cook, adding more liquid if necessary, until the potatoes are
just tender. Add the clams and half-and-half until desired consistency is
reached. Add more seasonings to taste. Serves 8 to 10.

– Indian Rock Creamy Split Pea Soup –

Ken Cannell: "We save the ham and bone from a boiled dinner, plus two quarts of the cooking liquid from that dinner. We put whole cloves in our ham, so this soup has a slight clove
taste, which is delicious."

**ham bone, 1 to 3 cups ham diced fine, 1 onion diced fine,
2 quarts boiled-dinner liquid (or water with a cube or two of
chicken bouillon), 2 bags dry green split peas, 1 to 2 cans
condensed milk**

In a large soup pot, place the ham bone, ham, onion, liquid, and split peas,
and simmer the mixture at least 4 hours. If you cook the soup slowly, the
peas will soak up the juice, and there will be no saltiness left, just a thick,
creamy, rich soup. Stir it toward the end so it doesn't stick to the bottom
of the pot.

When it's almost the consistency of mashed potatoes, add the milk
(not more water). Taste and adjust seasonings if desired.

– Lakewood Hearty Beef and Vegetable Soup –

Robin Carter: "Even though we're not open in the winter, we do get cold days throughout our season. That's when our guests love this rich soup. We serve prime rib, and this is how we use the leftovers."

> rib roast leftovers, $1/2$ cabbage chopped, 5 carrots sliced,
> 1 large onion chopped, $11/2$ tsp. Worcestershire sauce,
> 1 quart tomato juice, 1 (28-ounce) can diced or crushed
> tomatoes, 1 pint au jus or beef broth, $1/2$ bag frozen
> uncooked corn, $1/2$ bag frozen uncooked green beans

Take all the bones and any meat available from prime rib leftovers and put into a large kettle. Cover with water and boil gently for 2 hours. Drain the liquid through a strainer back into the pot. Pick the bones for meat and return all meat back to the pot. Add cabbage, carrots, and onion to the pot and cook everything for 15 to 20 minutes. Add everything else to the pot and stop cooking. Let soup sit to allow the flavors to combine. Reheat when it's time to serve.

– Leen's Kielbasa Soup –

Charles Driza: "Our cook, Tammy Ward, is well known for her soups; this is one of her most highly acclaimed recipes. It works well for the cold weather because of its hearty and spicy nature."

> 2 onions, 2 stalks celery, 1 green and 1 red bell pepper, 2 to 3 T
> butter, 1 pound smoked kielbasa, 2 cans undrained red kidney
> beans, 3 cans seasoned diced tomatoes, 2 cans chicken broth,
> 1 quart V8 or tomato juice, 1-pound package frozen mixed
> vegetables, 2 T Italian seasoning, 2 T dried minced garlic,
> salt and pepper to taste

Dice the onions, celery, and peppers and sauté with butter in a skillet until they are tender. Transfer them to a large soup pot. Slice the kielbasa into bite-sized pieces and brown in the same skillet. Use a slotted spoon to drain and move the kielbasa to the soup pot. Add all remaining ingredients and simmer on medium heat for 2 hours before serving.

– Libby's Cheddar Chowder –

Ellen Libby: "This is a good chowder recipe. At least, we really like it."

2 cups chicken broth (homemade or canned), 2 cups diced potatoes, 1/2 cup diced carrots, 1/2 cup diced celery, 1/4 cup chopped onions, 1 tsp. salt, 1/4 tsp. pepper, 1 cup cubed cooked ham

In a large soup kettle, combine all the ingredients except ham and bring to a boil. Boil for 10 to 12 minutes. Meanwhile make the white sauce.

White Sauce:

1/4 cup butter, 1/4 cup flour, 2 cups milk, 2 cups grated cheddar cheese

In a saucepan, melt the butter. Add flour and stir until smooth (a minute or two). Slowly add the milk, and stir well until sauce is thickened. Add cheese and stir until it melts. Add white sauce and ham to chowder. Stir gently and do not boil again. Serves 6.

– Loon Lodge French Onion Soup –

Linda Yencha: "It can get brisk in here toward the end of the season. When our hunters come in, they're ready for a good, hot meal. This is a quick and easy recipe for those days when you need something hot fast."

4 large onions sliced thin, 1/2 stick butter or margarine, 6 cups water, 4 beef bouillon cubes, 1 T Worcestershire sauce, 1 box onion soup mix, mozzarella cheese (optional)

Fry the onions in the butter until they are translucent. Put the rest of the ingredients in a heavy soup pot. Add the onions and bring to a boil. Simmer for 30 minutes and ladle into soup bowls. You can sprinkle each portion with mozzarella cheese if you wish. Serves 4 to 6.

– South Branch Lake Seafood "Chowdah" –

Russ Aldridge: "For me, hunting and fishing are not so much for the kill of the animal, but for harvesting food for the future, and just being out there. Every time I go into the woods, I become completely attuned to all the signs and changes there. We both left full-time jobs and sold our farm to run these camps, and we feel it's one of the best decisions we've ever made. It's hard work, but there's a real satisfaction at the end of the day."

Cindy Aldridge: "This is one of Russ's specialties. It's really nourishing and delicious anytime, but we love it on a cold winter's night."

5 strips bacon halved, 2 to 3 T bacon fat, 1 medium onion diced, 1 celery stalk diced, 2 cups milk, 2 large potatoes cut in small chunks, 2 cans evaporated milk, 1 can baby clams with broth, 1 T butter, 2 whole haddock fillets, 1/2 pound sea scallops halved, 15 to 20 medium shrimp, 1 T finely chopped fresh parsley (or 1/2 tsp. dried), 1 tsp. freshly ground black pepper

In a frying pan over medium heat, cook the bacon until it is crisp. Remove from pan. In a large Dutch oven, add 2 to 3 T of the bacon fat and sauté onion and celery until tender. Add the milk, potatoes, juice from the clams, and 1 can evaporated milk, and simmer for 12 minutes. In the bacon frying pan, add butter and haddock, and cook until the fish flakes. Remove from pan and add scallops and shrimp; cook until they are about half done (2 to 3 minutes). Add all the fish to the Dutch oven. Pour in the second can of evaporated milk and parsley. Simmer 20 to 30 minutes. Pepper (and salt) to taste. Serve in deep bowls with the bacon strips for garnish. Serves 4 to 6.

Fish

– Alden's Thai Shrimp Stir-Fry –

Joe Plumstead was Alden's chef for fifteen years. (He now owns his own restaurant in nearby Waterville.) During the camp's off-season months, Joe would spend time in Thailand learning about their cuisine; then he would bring back his new knowledge and recipes and try some out on the lucky guests. Several of Alden's current kitchen staff were trained by Joe.

Sauce:

> 1 cup water, 3 T brown sugar, 3 T molasses, 1 1/2 T soy sauce,
> 1/2 cup frozen orange juice concentrate

Slowly bring sauce to a boil. Reduce heat and allow to simmer until contents have reduced by half. Set aside.

Stir-Fry:

> 1 (8-ounce) package rice noodles/rice sticks *or* cellophane
> noodles, 1/4 cup vegetable oil, 1 pound raw shrimp (peeled
> and deveined), 4 large shallots (sliced), 1/4 pound firm tofu
> (crumbled), 4 large eggs (beaten), 1/3 cup chicken stock or
> bouillon, 1/2 cup unsalted peanuts (chopped), 1/2 pound
> mung bean sprouts

Garnish:

> 6 scallions (chopped), 3 limes (cut into wedges), 1/2 cup whole
> unsalted peanuts, 1/2 pound mung bean sprouts

Soak noodles in warm water for 5 to 10 minutes or until soft. Drain.

Prepare shrimp, tofu, and vegetables as noted above before you begin to stir-fry.

Heat vegetable oil in a wok or deep-sided skillet. Add shrimp and stir-fry until pink, about 3 to 4 minutes. Add shallots. Stir-fry 1 minute. Add tofu, stir-fry 1 minute. Add eggs and stir until well scrambled.

Add chicken stock, chopped peanuts, noodles, and half of the bean sprouts. Stir-fry until the noodles have absorbed the chicken stock. Add sauce and continue to stir-fry until all or most of the sauce is absorbed by the noodles.

Serve on a large platter, garnished with the whole peanuts, chopped scallions, remaining bean sprouts, and lime wedges (the limes are great to squeeze over individual servings). Serves 4 to 6.

– Leen's Shrimp in Vodka Sauce –

Charles Driza: "My mother, Rita, and sister, Cecilia, inspired the following recipe, which is part of our menu at the lodge. Having grown up in an Italian household, delicious food was part of my life. We are happy to pass on some of these treats to our guests."

**2 pounds penne pasta, 2 sticks salted butter, 1 clove garlic,
12 ounces tomato paste, 2 cups chicken broth, 6 ounces vodka,
2 pounds cleaned raw shrimp, 1 cup heavy cream, cayenne
pepper to taste, parsley for garnish**

Cook penne according to directions on package until al dente. Meanwhile, melt the butter in a large skillet, press the garlic, and sauté it in the butter for a minute. Add tomato paste, chicken broth, and vodka and stir well. After mixture is heated, add shrimp and cook until just done (shrimp is whitish and firm). Blend in cream and season to taste. Spoon shrimp mixture over drained pasta and garnish with parsley.

– McNally's/Nugent's Whitefish Casserole –

John Richardson: "We're on Ross Stream, originally called *Chemquassabamticook*, or 'place of many fish.' And it is good fishing. Will McNally, often called the father of north Maine woods sporting camps, had a son, Dana, who built McNally's in 1951. We bought the camps from Mycki, Dana's wife, who offers this winter tip: 'Do you know the only sandwich that won't freeze? Peanut butter and bacon.'"

Regina Webster: "You can use fresh or frozen fillet of haddock, pollack, or hake for this meal. When we're over at Nugent's, I use whitefish from Chamberlain Lake—when they're biting!"

**2 pounds fish fillets, 1 can frozen cream of shrimp soup, 1 T
sherry *or* lemon juice, $1/2$ cup melted butter or margarine,
$1/2$ tsp. minced onions, garlic salt to taste, $1/2$ tsp. Worcestershire sauce, 30 Ritz crackers**

Place the fish in a casserole dish and sprinkle with salt to taste. Combine the soup and lemon juice/sherry and pour over fish. Bake uncovered in a 375° oven for 20 minutes.

While the fish is baking, stir onions, garlic salt, and Worcestershire sauce into the melted butter and blend into the crumbled crackers. Sprinkle the crumb mixture over the fish and bake an additional 10 minutes, or until top is brown and bubbly.

Poultry/Small Game

– Bald Mountain Roasted Cornish Game Hens –

Stephen Philbrick: "My wife, Fernlyn, our two boys, and I live at the camps year-round. I've considered winterizing because snowmobiling is such a big thing around here, but it would cost sixty-five thousand dollars per cabin. So, I opened up the BMC Diner in town instead. Another thing we do in winter is cut ice for the buckets of springwater that we provide for our guests every day in the summer.

"When the ice gets to be eighteen inches thick on the lake [Mooselookmeguntic], we clear off a section with a truck plow. We hand-shovel whatever's left so we're down to the ice. We score it into eighteen-inch squares and chainsaw down ten inches, using a hand saw for the last eight inches. Then we'll get that block onto the conveyor belt I have feeding into the truck. The ice blocks get hauled off to our icehouse where they're layered with sawdust to keep them cold through the summer. We'll take out as many as twenty-eight hundred blocks of ice each winter."

Meg Godaire: "Since the camps are seasonal, we all do different things in the winter. I have a place called The Farmhouse Inn, and my busiest time there is in the winter, so it works out perfectly for me to cook here from spring to fall, and cook at my inn for the winter."

4 Cornish game hens, 4 T fresh thyme, salt and pepper to taste
Place the hens in a roasting pan and rub with salt and pepper and thyme. Roast for 1/2 hour at 350°. While the hens are cooking, make the glaze.

Glaze:
2 shallots, 1 T butter, 1 jar apricot jam, 1/2 cup orange juice
Chop the shallots fine and sauté them with the butter in a small saucepan. Add the jam and orange juice and stir well. Set aside.

After the hens have cooked for 1/2 hour, take them out of the oven, spoon the glaze over them, return to the oven, and roast another 10 minutes. Serve with pan glaze if desired. Serves 4.

– Grant's Almond-Crusted Rabbit or Hare –

Although hunting for cottontail rabbits and snowshoe hares begins in October, the major season for most Maine hunters is in the winter months.

Joy Russell: "I created this recipe one day when some hunters brought back a rabbit and asked me to cook it. I told them I'd never cooked rabbit, but I did know how to fry poultry/game so it would be tender (helpful for rabbit, which has a reputation for being stringy and/or tough). I prepared it this way for them. A couple of days later they brought in another rabbit, this time an older one, and I fixed it the same way. It was also melt-in-your-mouth tender, so I guess it works! They all liked it so much, they begged me to call and see if I could get it into this cookbook at the last minute."

We're lucky—one day later, and it would've been too late.

First, you cut the belly open and clean out the insides. Then you pull the skin right off (similar to skinning a deer), cut off the head, and cut into pieces at the joints. Then you coat the pieces with the following mixture:

    1 cup flour, ¹/₈ tsp. cayenne pepper, 1 T onion powder, 1 tsp. garlic powder

Place the coated pieces in a plastic bag and leave in the refrigerator for at least 4 hours (and if you don't have eager hunters breathing down your neck, overnight is even better).

Remove from the plastic bag and fry the rabbit pieces in 4 to 5 T of butter until both sides are golden brown. Cool the pieces for about 30 minutes. Then, with your hand, rub off any of the coating that's left, along with the thin, transparent skin coating that may be there. (It's on most meat; chicken pieces will have it sometimes.) Continue with the next step.

    3 eggs, ¹/₂ cup cream, 1 sleeve crackers (any brand or combination of plain or buttery-type crackers is fine), 1 cup toasted almonds, cooking oil

In a bowl, beat the eggs with the cream. Crush the crackers with a rolling pin. Grind the almonds in a food processor and combine with the cracker crumbs on a plate.

Heat about 2 inches of oil in a skillet. Dip the rabbit pieces first in the egg wash, then in the crumb mixture. Place in the skillet and fry for about 20 minutes or until deep golden brown on both sides. Drain on paper towels and serve.

– Katahdin Lake Rabbit in Gravy –

Al Cooper: "December through March is rabbit-hunting season. People often use beagles for the hunt."

Suzan Cooper: "Rabbit meat is fat-free, but it is also somewhat stringy. The vinegar we use in this recipe tenderizes it nicely."

> 1 rabbit (approximately 5 pounds), 2 T salt, $^1/4$ cup cider vine-
> gar, $^1/4$ cup oil, 1 large onion chopped, 3 cloves minced garlic,
> 2 stalks celery chopped, $^1/4$ cup flour, $^3/4$ cup cold water, 1 tsp.
> paprika, salt and pepper to taste

Place the rabbit in water to cover. Add the salt and cider vinegar and soak the rabbit in the brine overnight.

Next day, cut the rabbit into bite-sized pieces. Heat the oil in a heavy, cast-iron skillet or Dutch oven, and sauté the rabbit, onion, garlic, and celery until rabbit is lightly browned and vegetables are soft. Add hot water to cover and cook, covered, until tender, about 45 minutes to an hour. Check and add more water if necessary.

In a small bowl, mix the flour with $^3/4$ cup cold water and stir until smooth. Add to the rabbit mixture to thicken the gravy. Add the paprika and season to taste.

WILDERNESS WOMEN

A number of sporting camps owe their longevity to stalwart women—legends in their own time. Patty Nugent (Nugent's), Mycki McNally (McNally's), Alys Parsons (Lakewood), Violette Holden (Attean Lake), Elise Libby (Libby's), and Margie McBurnie (Tomhegan) all kept their camps running long after their husbands had died.

It takes a special person, male or female, to live at and run a wilderness outpost. One needs stamina, patience, determination, and a certain sensibility to be a long-term sporting-camp owner. A good many of the owners featured in this book belong in the "Legends in Their Own Time" category.

– Long Lake Sweet and Sour Rabbit –

Sandra Smith: "It seems like a hundred years ago that I was a 4-H Club member with a primary focus on raising rabbits. I put together a cookbook of rabbit recipes, never thinking that I would someday be living in the woods. Domestic rabbit is all white meat, very high in protein, low in fat, and very good. In the Midwest and California, they sell it fresh over the counter. Here you can only get rabbit meat frozen, unless you know a hunter or a rabbit breeder."

> 1 rabbit boned and cut into small pieces, peanut oil, 1/4 cup
> water, 1 regular-sized can pineapple chunks with juice, 1/4 cup
> brown sugar, 2 T cornstarch, 1/2 tsp. salt, 1/4 cup cider vinegar,
> 1 T soy sauce, 3/4 cup green pepper sliced into strips, 1/4 cup
> onion sliced thin

In a large fry pan or skillet, place the rabbit in about 1/4 inch of peanut oil and brown slowly. Then add the water and simmer until tender (domestic rabbit for 20 minutes, wild rabbit closer to 40 minutes).

Drain the pineapple and save the juice. In a large saucepan, mix the brown sugar, cornstarch, and salt. Stir in pineapple juice, vinegar, and soy sauce. Cook the mixture over low heat, stirring, until thick. Add the cooked rabbit, pineapple chunks, pepper, and onion and cook an additional 3 to 5 minutes. Serve on rice. Serves 2 to 4.

– McNally's/Nugent's Fried Rabbit and Partridge –

Regina Webster: "I serve rabbit and partridge with mashed potatoes, gravy, and peas. The amounts depend on what and who you have on hand."

Rabbit:

> 1 to 2 rabbits, 1 to 2 cups water, 1 onion quartered, 1 tsp. each
> salt and pepper, 1/4 cup flour, olive or vegetable oil

Cut the rabbit into serving pieces and place in a pressure cooker. Pour in just enough water to come to the top but not cover the rabbit. Add the onion and salt and pepper. Cook for about 20 to 25 minutes.

Remove the meat from the cooker and save the broth for gravy. Roll the rabbit pieces in the flour. Heat the oil in a large skillet and brown the rabbit pieces quickly. Remove from skillet and keep warm.

Partridge:

2 to 3 partridges, olive oil, 1 to 2 onions diced

Fillet the partridge breasts off the bone and sauté, along with the diced onion, in the same skillet you used for the rabbit, adding more oil if necessary. Sauté until golden brown (1 to 2 minutes).

Gravy:

Pour the broth remaining in the pressure cooker into a small saucepan and add 1 to 2 T flour, and salt, pepper, and garlic powder to taste. Cook over medium-low heat, stirring, until gravy is smooth and of desired consistency (adding more flour if necessary).

– The Pines Chicken Pie –

Nancy Norris: "You can top this pie with either biscuits or a pie crust. I generally use a pie crust, so I'll give you that recipe as well. The recipe makes extra. I freeze what I don't need so I have it available for other pies."

When I tried this, I did two versions: one with the top crust, and another with a bottom crust and a breadcrumb/Parmesan cheese topping ($1/2$ cup of each). For both, I poured the sauce over the meat/veggies in the pie pan.

2 T butter, 2 T flour, 1 tsp. salt, pinch of pepper or to taste, $1/4$ tsp. dried thyme, $1/2$ to $3/4$ cup chicken broth, $1/2$ cup light cream (2 percent milk works fine), 2 cups each (cooked) diced chicken, peas/carrots/celery, and boiled onions/diced potatoes

Melt the butter and add flour, stirring well. Add spices, chicken broth, and cream. Heat to boiling. Boil and stir 1 minute and stir in chicken/vegetables. Place in pie pan and cover with pie crust.

Pie Crust (makes 5 shells):

5 cups flour (unsifted), 1 pound lard, 1 T salt, 1 egg, 3 T white vinegar, water

Mix together first three ingredients with a pastry blender until crumbly. Add enough water to the egg and vinegar to make 1 cup. Mix well and stir into the flour mixture. Work together gently and briefly. Divide in 5 portions. Slightly flatten 4 pieces and wrap and freeze for later use. Roll out remaining piece for chicken pie.

Bake pie in a 350° oven for 35 to 45 minutes, or until the crust is brown and the filling is bubbling.

– Wheaton's Crunchy Chicken Casserole –

Dale Wheaton: "We established a land trust to protect our region; if we had not done so, our beautiful environment would have slipped away very quickly. If you're going to be a successful sporting-camp operator, you have to commit yourself for a lifetime; it's a way of life. To all the folks who think they can earn a small fortune in the sporting-camp business, we say, sure, but you've got to start with a *large* fortune . . ."

> **1 cup chopped celery, 2 T chopped onion, 1 T margarine or
> butter, 2 cups cooked diced chicken, 1 can condensed cream
> of chicken soup, 1 1/2 cups cooked rice, 1 can sliced water
> chestnuts, 3/4 cup mayonnaise, salt and pepper to taste,
> 1 cup dry breadcrumbs, 3 T butter**

Sauté celery and onion in margarine/butter until tender. In a bowl, combine ingredients up to breadcrumbs. Add the celery/onions and stir well. Sauté breadcrumbs in butter. Pour veggie/chicken mixture in a 9 x 13-inch baking pan, and top with buttered breadcrumbs. Bake in a 350° oven for 25 to 30 minutes or until crumbs are golden brown. Serves 6 to 8.

Meat/Big Game

– Attean's Grilled Flank Steaks –

Recipe from former chef Daryl Goslant.

**10 pounds flank steaks, 2 cups cider vinegar, 2 T each salt and
dry mustard, 2 tsp. sugar, 1 tsp. white pepper, 3 pints salad oil,
2 cups ketchup, 1/2 cup grated onion (or 1/4 cup onion flakes)**

Place the steaks in a large pan. In a big bowl, combine the remaining ingredients and mix well. Pour over the steaks and marinate at least 3 hours.
Grill the steaks, brushing with the marinade. Serves 40 to 45. Marinade
makes up into 2 1/2 quarts.

– The Birches Beef Stew with Wine and Herbs –

John Willard: "I get different types of people each season. In the winter it's probably seventy percent Maine residents, whereas during fall hunting season it's about the same percentage from out of state. We groom a forty-kilometer cross-country-ski trail system. We
have three yurts in the woods where people can stay, and they can ski to the lodge for the
hot tub or meals. We also have rooms in the lodge and are busy with snowmobilers and
maybe a few ice fishermen."

**4 T bacon drippings or other fat, 4 pounds stewing beef cut
into 2-inch cubes, 2 cups red wine, 2 (16-ounce) cans peeled
tomatoes, 2 bay leaves, 3 cloves garlic crushed, 2 cups beef
stock, 3 stalks celery with leaves chopped, 2 medium onions
slivered, 1/2 tsp. thyme, 10 whole cloves**

Heat the bacon drippings in a large skillet over medium heat. Add the
meat and brown it to a deep color on all sides. When the meat is done,
drain the remaining drippings from the pan and add 1 cup of the wine.
Simmer the meat in the wine for a couple of minutes. Transfer the meat/
wine to a large pot. Add the remaining ingredients and simmer until the
beef is tender (45 minutes or so). Remove the bay leaves before serving.
Serves 12 to 14.

– Cobb's Venison Tenderloin Strips –

Betty Cobb: "We eat this ourselves during hunting season or in the winter. It's a very simple, old-fashioned meal. I'll just give you the gist of it.

"We'll slice up some venison into thin strips and fry them quickly in a little hot bacon fat. You take the meat out and put some boiling water in the skillet and stir that up to make a little gravy. I have a pan of biscuits ready in the oven, and we'll eat the meat and biscuits with the juice from the skillet, and we put some molasses on our plates too—nothing fancy, just good hearty food."

– Cobb's Wild Game Meat Loaf –

Betty Cobb: "We don't serve wild game to our guests. But this is good with ground venison or moose meat, or any combination of ground meat you can get at the grocer's."

> 1 green pepper, 1 large onion, 3 to 4 pounds ground venison
> or combination of meats, 1 can mushroom soup, 2 eggs,
> 1 sleeve saltine crackers (crushed), 2 tsp. Worcestershire sauce,
> 1 T Italian seasonings, 1 tsp. poultry seasoning, $1/2$ tsp. each
> salt and pepper

In a meat grinder or food processor, grind together the green pepper and onion and spoon into a large bowl. Add the remaining ingredients and mix until thoroughly combined. Place the mixture into 2 loaf pans and bake at 350° for 45 minutes.

– Dad's Pâté –

Therese Thibodeau: "I make up this pâté for Christmas and other holidays as our main meat. People are so eager to get some, they'll have a bowl of it in the morning before our big lunch. I get pork, either boneless or with bone, it doesn't matter; it *is* important that the pork is on the fatty side."

> 10 pounds pork, salt and pepper and onion powder to taste,
> $1/4$ tsp. each ground cinnamon and allspice, 10 cups flour

Dice the pork meat and layer half of it in the bottom of a big baking pan. Season the meat.

In a big bowl, combine the flour with enough water to make a stiff dough (bread consistency). On a floured surface, roll out half the dough the same size as the baking pan and about 2 inches thick and place on top of the meat. Repeat both layers and pour cold water over everything 2 inches above the top of the dough. Bake in a 300° oven overnight. In the morning, remove the pan and stir the meat and dough together. Eat with potatoes and coleslaw.

– Grant's Oriental Beef Stir-Fry –

Recipe from lunch/dinner cook Richard Outcalt. He suggests using leftover rib eye or New York sirloin steak, gauging the amount you'll need by the number you'll be serving.

Take leftover rib eye or New York sirloin steak and cut into strips. Then take whatever vegetables you have on hand (such as mushrooms, onions, peppers, carrots, celery, and broccoli) and chop those up. Cook a package of egg noodles per directions, and prepare the sauce.

Stir-Fry Sauce:

1 cup soy sauce, 1 cup either orange juice or pineapple juice, 1 cup melted butter, 2 tsp. grated ginger (I use fresh if possible; if not, ground will do), 2 cloves garlic mashed, 4 T cornstarch

In a saucepan, combine all sauce ingredients except cornstarch. Heat and add cornstarch to thicken to gravy consistency. Set aside.

In a large fry pan, heat 3 T oil. Add 1 mashed clove of garlic, the meat, and 3 T sauce. Cook 2 minutes, stirring, to heat beef slightly. Add vegetables and cook, stirring, for 2 minutes. Add 3 T more sauce, then noodles, 3 T more sauce, and cook for 2 more minutes, stirring. Transfer to a serving bowl and enjoy.

– Harrison's Yankee Pot Roast –

Fran Harrison: "At the beginning and end of the school year, when we're at camp, we home-school our children. Otherwise, they go to school during the winter when we live and work in New Hampshire. It involves a lot of work to close up camp. For instance, one thing we need to do is put up strong support beams in the dining room so the roof doesn't fall in from the weight of the snow."

2 T butter, 1 diced onion, a 5-pound shoulder roast, 1 small jar horseradish (around 3 ounces), 1/4 to 1/2 cup flour, 2 cans dark beer, 2 T Gravy Master (or similar product)

Melt butter in a heavy, cast-iron, stovetop pan. Add onion and sauté over medium heat. Meanwhile, coat one side of the roast with half the horseradish, then cover with half the flour. Place in pan with floured side down to sear.

While the first side is searing, coat the other side the same way and then flip meat over. Once the meat is seared on both sides, pour the beer over it and drizzle on the Gravy Master. Cover the pan and cook on very low heat for about 4 hours, flipping meat about once every hour. If you cook it slowly enough, you shouldn't have to add water, and you should have a nice gravy when it's done.

If desired, cook some potatoes and vegetables in with the meat during the last half hour or so (or you can remove some of the pan juices to a saucepan and cook the vegetables in it). Serves 8.

– Jalbert's Beef-Cabbage Rolls –

Phyllis Jalbert: "I got this recipe from my friend Mary Marquis."

1 large white cabbage, 1 egg, 1 large onion chopped fine, 1 tsp. Worcestershire sauce, 3/4 tsp. salt, dash of pepper, 1 pound ground beef, 1/2 to 3/4 cup uncooked rice, 1 small can tomato soup, 2 to 3 cans tomatoes (14 1/2 ounces each), 1 can or bottle tomato juice, 1 T brown sugar, 1 T lemon juice

In a large pot, immerse cabbage in boiling water. Boil until the cabbage is blanched enough to remove the now-flexible large leaves (approximately 5 to 10 minutes depending upon the size of the cabbage). Drain cabbage and set it aside to cool slightly.

In a large mixing bowl, beat the egg with the seasonings. Add the meat and rice and mix thoroughly. Remove a cabbage leaf and place 1/4 to 1/2 cup of meat mixture in the middle of the leaf. Fold in the sides and roll up, making sure the folded sides are included in the roll. Repeat until all the filling mixture is used.

Mix together the remaining ingredients for sauce. Lay the leftover cabbage leaves in the bottom of a large pot and arrange the filled rolls on top of them. Pour the sauce over the rolls. (You can lay any extra leaves on top of the rolls first, if desired.) Cover the pot and cook slowly on top of the stove for at least 1 1/2 to 2 hours, checking to make sure tomato juice has not all evaporated and adding more, if necessary.

– Long Lake Elk Stew –

Sandra Smith: "I like to make this recipe in a Crock-Pot, so that when you come in after a cold day of skiing or working in the woods, it's all hot and ready to eat. It works well with any meat you have on hand. If using a Crock-Pot, mix everything together and cook. Do the cornstarch thickening when you get ready to eat."

2 pounds elk (or any meat) cut in chunks, 1 T shortening, 4 cups boiling water, 1 T Worcestershire sauce, 1 medium onion sliced, 1 to 2 bay leaves, 2 tsp. salt, 1 tsp. sugar, 1/2 tsp. pepper, 1/2 tsp. paprika, dash of ground cloves, 6 carrots, 6 potatoes, 1 to 2 T cornstarch, 1/4 cup water

Melt the shortening in a deep soup pot. On medium high, brown meat on all sides. Reduce heat to medium and add the rest of the ingredients up to the carrots and potatoes. Cover and simmer for 2 hours.

Slice the carrots, cut the potatoes into chunks and add them to the soup, and cook 30 minutes more.

In a small bowl, mix cornstarch with water and add to stew. Stir and cook an additional 5 minutes. For thicker stew, add more cornstarch mixed with a little of the stew juice.

– Maynard's Venison Goulash –

Gail Maynard: "I can't serve game to the guests, but we use it for ourselves when we get our deer."

2 T butter, 2 pounds Bermuda onions sliced, 2 T bacon fat, 2 pounds venison or chuck cut into 1 1/2-inch cubes, 2 T sweet paprika, 1 tsp. cayenne pepper, 1 cup ketchup, 1 tsp. salt

Sauté the onions in the butter until they are clear. Brown the meat in the bacon fat and combine all the ingredients. Simmer for 1 1/2 hours. Serve over wide noodles. Serves 4 to 6.

– Rideout's American Chop Suey –

Jami Lorigan: "I think people generally call this goulash, but around here we say chop suey. We make gallons and gallons of this, and no matter how much we make, people seem to eat it all. I came into the kitchen the other day, and there was the cook shaking her head and scraping the bottom of the pot. She'd made so much that she was sure there'd be some left over, but no!"

1 onion chopped, 2 T oil or butter (or combination), 2 1/2 pounds ground beef, 3 tsp. dried oregano, 2 tsp. each dried basil and garlic, 2 T sugar, 4 cups spaghetti sauce, 10 cups uncooked macaroni shells

In a large frying pan, sauté the onion in the oil/butter until transparent. Add the meat and cook until brown all through. Add spices and mix well. Add sugar and spaghetti sauce. Stir and simmer 30 minutes.

Meanwhile, cook macaroni according to directions on the package (being careful not to overcook). Drain and gently mix with the meat sauce. Serve in a small casserole dish or chili bowl. Serves 10 to 12 (maybe!).

– Ross Lake No-Peek Beef Stew –

Andrea Foley and Don Lavoie: "The trick on this recipe is to *not* lift the lid at any time while it's baking."

> **2 pounds cubed beef, 3 large potatoes cubed, 1 large onion diced, 4 to 5 carrots diced, 1 green pepper diced, 1 T sugar, 3 T minute tapioca, salt and pepper to taste, 12 ounces V8 vegetable juice**

Combine all ingredients in a large baking casserole and stir until blended. Cover and bake 250° for 5 hours. Remember, no peeking!

– West Branch Pond Ham Bake –

Carol Kealiher: "My family always raised pigs. We butchered them in fall and had hams hanging from the larder ceiling for winter-to-spring eating. I still raise a pig at camp. The man who delivered our pig in May for the 2003 season said he got him from a French-speaking part of Canada, so I thought, *'Francois!'* We kept him in the barn to protect him from the bears. One Thursday, Francois got loose and started rooting up the plumbing system. Thursday is prime rib day, a busy cooking day. Fortunately the pie was done, the bread rising, and I had time to try to get the pig back in the barn. I'd always been told to grab them by the ear(s). Well, I caught hold and pulled, but Francois pulled harder."

Charles Furbush: "I looked out, and here's Carol being dragged through the mud holding on to one of the pig's ears. I came out, looked that pig in the eye, grunted to him, and he followed right along."

Carol: "Must've been a guy thing. But we almost had pork chops à la hoof that day—mostly because of me. I almost scared Francois to death! *[Carol and Charles laugh uproariously.]* I decided early on, when I started running the place, that I would try to laugh when things went wrong or were just crazy—and the way things go around here, we're laughing all the time!

"This recipe isn't fancy, but it's a flavorful meal, preferred by some to prime rib."

> **4 thick slices ham, 1 cup milk, 4 tsp. prepared mustard, 1/2 cup brown sugar**

Preheat oven to 350°. Arrange the ham slices in a baking dish. Pour the milk into the dish. Spread a tsp. of mustard on each slice. Sprinkle each slice with about 2 T brown sugar. Bake for 40 minutes. Serves 4.

– Wheaton's Meat Loaf with Special Tomato Sauce –

Jana Wheaton: "Once the ingredients are combined, I knead this meat loaf with my hands for a good five minutes, patting it into a submarine shape. That way, when you slice it, it will hold together."

> **2 pounds 75 percent lean hamburger, 2 cups fine breadcrumbs, 1 small can stewed tomatoes, 1 T garlic powder, 1 T chili powder, 1 tsp. each dried thyme and marjoram, 2 T Worcestershire sauce, 3/4 cup brown sugar, 1 to 2 tsp. Tabasco sauce (or to taste), 3/4 cup finely chopped onion, 2 T dried parsley, 2 eggs**

Combine all ingredients in a large bowl and mix thoroughly. Place tinfoil on a cookie sheet and spray the foil with cooking spray. Start kneading the meat loaf with your hands. If the mixture seems crumbly or dry and does not hold together well, add a little milk. Place the meat loaf on the cookie sheet and form into a submarine shape. Pat it into shape until it gets to the point where it's going to hold together (you should be able to tell by "feel"). Then pour enough ketchup over the meat to cover it (my "special tomato sauce"!). Bake at 350° for 50 minutes to an hour.

Salads/Side Dishes/Vegetarian

– Bear Spring Caribbean Coleslaw –

Ron Churchill: "At the end of the season, we do an inventory of everything and wash, sort, and store all the linens. I will also do any necessary remodeling and repairing, with the help of two of the kitchen staff. Peggy works on taxes—all the W2s for the staff—and we send out our advertising and winter newsletter. We enjoy time together with our son and daughter and Peg's mother, Marguerite, who lives here and ran the camps for years. After the holidays, we work on the bookings and interview new staff members. We'll buy a few new linens, and I try to buy either a new boat or a new motor, or both, every year. And then, it starts all over again!"

Peg Churchill: "We use this recipe for our buffet if we do a tropical theme."

> 1 head green or purple cabbage (or both), 1 cup mayonnaise,
> 1 can whole-kernel corn, 1/4 cup each sliced green and black
> olives, 1 to 2 T fresh diced chives, salt and pepper to taste

Shred the cabbage and mix all the ingredients together in a bowl. Taste and adjust seasonings or proportions of other ingredients if desired.

– Cobb's Stuffed Acorn Squash –

Betty Cobb: "My friend Tess (from North New Portland, where we live in the winter) gave me this recipe."

> 1 acorn squash, 2 T melted butter, 3 T chopped onion, 2 T
> bacon fat, 1/2 cup soft breadcrumbs, 1/4 cup water, 1 egg, salt
> and pepper to taste, 1/2 cup dry breadcrumbs, 3 T butter

Cut the squash in half. Remove the seeds and stringy pulp and wipe dry. Brush with the melted butter. Place cut side down on cookie sheet and bake in a 325° oven for 1 1/4 hours. Remove squash from the oven, scoop out cooked pulp (being careful not to destroy the shells), and mash it.

In a saucepan or skillet, brown onion in the fat. Soak soft bread-crumbs (pulse day-old bread in the food processor) in the water. Mash the watered crumbs and add to the onions. Add the mashed squash and cook about 15 minutes, stirring occasionally.

In a small bowl, beat the egg, and add to the squash mixture, stirring well. Season to taste with salt and pepper. Place the mixture back in the original shells. Sprinkle with dry breadcrumbs and dot with butter. Bake in a 375° oven for 20 minutes. Serves 2.

– Eagle Lodge Black Beans and Rice –

Tami Rogers: "I rarely measure my spices or seasonings. I go by smell and then taste. These beans can last in your refrigerator for a couple of weeks, and they are best when made ahead."

> 1 1/2 T olive oil, 1 cup chopped onion, 3 to 4 diced garlic cloves, 2 (16-ounce) cans black beans (undrained, or use homemade cooked black beans), 1 T ground cumin, Eagle Lodge "river spice" to taste, juice of 1 lemon or lime

To make a batch of "river spice," mix:
> 1 T garlic salt, 1/2 to 1 T cayenne pepper (or more, to taste), 1 T dried oregano, 1/2 T celery salt, 1 T dried basil, 1 T crushed black pepper

In a food processor, chop onion and garlic very fine. In a frying pan, heat olive oil and cook onion/garlic until tender. Add the undrained beans and cumin (use more than a tablespoonful if you like). Then add the "river spice" to taste, and lemon or lime juice, and stir well.

Cook over medium heat until boiling, then reduce heat and simmer for 30 to 45 minutes. When ready to use, cook up your favorite rice, reheat the bean mixture, and serve together.

– Lakewood Barbecued Beans –

> 4 large cans baked beans or about 8 cups homemade, 1/3 to 1/2 cup barbecue sauce, 2 medium onions chopped fine, 1 apple cut up, 2 T brown sugar, 3/4 cup golden raisins, 4 slices uncooked bacon cut up

In a bowl, combine all ingredients, except the bacon, and pour into a casserole or bean pot. Top with the bacon and bake at 350° for 1 1/2 hours.

– Long Lake Bourbon-Glazed Carrots –

**2 pounds carrots, 3 T butter, 2 tsp. sugar, 1 tsp. salt, 2 ounces
bourbon**

Use baby carrots or cut large carrots into thick julienne strips. Combine all
the remaining ingredients except the bourbon in a skillet and bring to a
boil. Cover and cook over medium heat for 7 to 12 minutes, or until carrots
are slightly underdone. (Do not overcook!) Uncover skillet, raise heat, and
boil liquid down until it becomes a syrupy glaze that coats the carrots. Stir
often to keep carrots from burning. Add bourbon all at once and keep
stirring until it evaporates. Remove from the heat and serve at once.

– Long Lake Saturday Night Baked Beans –

Sandra Smith: "Ever since I've been in the sporting-camp business, I've baked beans for
Saturday dinner. It is the only night I have a set menu.

"Here's a tip for measuring molasses: Grease the measuring cup, and the molasses
will slide right out without sticking."

**2 pounds dry pea beans, 1 medium-sized onion, 1/2 pound salt
pork, 1/2 cup molasses, 1/2 cup brown sugar, 1 1/2 tsp. dry
mustard, 1/2 tsp. pepper, 1 cup hot water, 1/2 cup maple syrup**

Put the beans in a large, deep pot. Cover the beans with water and soak
overnight. Drain.

(If you forget to the soak the beans, or want a quicker method, cover
the beans with hot water, bring the mixture to a boil over medium heat,
and simmer for 1/2 hour. Drain.)

Place the peeled onion and the salt pork (scored) in the bottom of
a large crockery bean pot. Add the beans.

I use a 4-cup glass measuring container to mix the molasses, brown
sugar, mustard, pepper, and hot water. Stir the molasses mixture and pour
it over the beans. Add enough additional hot water to cover the beans,
cover the pot, and bake at 400° until the beans boil.

Reduce the temperature to 325° and bake for 3 hours with the cover
on. Remove the cover and bake for 2 more hours. Throughout the baking
process, keep adding water to cover the beans so they don't dry out.

Last, add the maple syrup and cook 1 more hour.

– Loon Lodge Pot Potatoes –

Linda Yencha: "This makes for an easy potato dish which goes well with meat loaf. I'm sorry that I can't be more exact with the amounts: Just keep layering as you go, and be stingy with the butter—keep it to half a stick—because the mixture will thicken as it cooks. Depending on how many you have to feed, you can add more potatoes and onions—just keep the butter amount the same."

5 or 6 potatoes, 3 or 4 onions, $^1/_2$ stick butter, salt and pepper to taste

Peel and slice the potatoes and the onions. In a heavy pot, on low heat, melt the butter and put a layer of potatoes on the bottom. Then put a layer of onions, and season the mixture generously with salt and pepper. Continue layering until your pot is three-quarters full.

Now put some water in the pot (you want the water to go only half-way up the sides because the potatoes have water in them). Bring to a boil, and then turn heat down to low, cover, and simmer until the potatoes are fork-tender.

Peek at the mixture every now and then—you don't want it to burn. You may need to add a little more water before they're cooked through.

– Mount Chase Baked Bean Quintet –

Sara Hill: "People always say how lucky we are. Well, we've never gotten rich in here, but then, it's all in your definition of wealth. We feel enriched by our surroundings and by our guests. We've had a number of people come here saying they just wanted to return one more time before they die to show their whole family where they've had so many happy adventures. We joke that this doesn't do much for return business! But seriously, it does show us we're doing something right.

"For this recipe, I like the small baked beans, like B & M baked beans (made in Maine), but you can use whatever you prefer."

1 chopped medium onion, 6 slices uncooked bacon cut up, 1 clove minced garlic, 1 (16-ounce) can lima beans (drained), 2 (16-ounce) cans baked beans, 1 (15-ounce) can red kidney beans (drained), 1 (15-ounce) can butter beans (undrained), 1 (15-ounce) can garbanzo beans (undrained), 1 cup ketchup, $^1/_2$ cup molasses, $^1/_4$ cup brown sugar, 1 T mustard, 1 T Worcestershire sauce

In a skillet, fry onions, bacon, and garlic until bacon is done. Put with remaining ingredients in a 4-quart casserole or bean pot. Bake at 325° for
1 hour. Serves 12 to 16.

– Maynard's Red Cabbage –

4 cups shredded red cabbage, $1/3$ cup white vinegar, $1/3$ cup
cider vinegar, 1 apple peeled and diced, 1 T sugar, 1 tsp. salt,
$1/2$ tsp. caraway seeds

Mix everything together well in a glass casserole dish. Cover and microwave on high for 8 to 10 minutes, stirring twice during the cooking, until
the cabbage is tender. Let stand, covered, for 10 minutes before serving.

– The Pines Wooden Spoon Potatoes –

Nancy Norris: "This is a fun-looking potato to serve. People always want to know how I do
it. I think baking potatoes are the best to use."

Wash desired amount of potatoes. Lay 2 wooden spoons down, side by
side, with the handles about 2 inches apart, on a cutting surface. Place a
potato between the handles and pull the handles close to the potato. Using
a sharp knife, slice down through the potato until the knife hits the spoon
handles (not allowing the knife to go all the way through the potato).
Make thin slices. Repeat with the other potatoes.

Place potatoes cut side up on a greased cookie sheet and brush the
tops with olive oil. Sprinkle with garlic powder or garlic salt, and some
oregano, basil, or any other spices you like. Bake in a 350° oven for about
an hour. Remove and serve.

– West Branch Pond Harvard Beets –

$1/4$ cup sugar, 1 T cornstarch, $1/3$ cup cider vinegar, 1 T melted
butter/margarine, 1 small onion finely diced, 1 quart cooked
sliced beets (two 16-ounce cans, or preserved/fresh)

In a saucepan, combine the sugar and cornstarch. Slowly stir in the vinegar,
whisking until the mixture is smooth. Add the melted butter/margarine

and onion and stir. Turn the heat to medium and cook, stirring constantly, until thickened. Reduce the heat to low. Drain the beets and add them to the saucepan. Stir gently and cook until heated through. Serves 6.

– Wilderness Island Braised Cabbage –

Mike LaRosa: "I have what I call 'the seven-minute challenge' to cooking. I think the last seven minutes before serving a meal are the most important, because you're doing a lot of things at once. I've solved this problem by cooking with a lot of timers; they all have different sounds, and I can identify each one.

"This recipe takes about eight minutes to cook and serves about four people; it's a good dish for the winter when there may not be a lot of fresh vegetables around."

Sauce:

> 2 T soy sauce, 2 tsp. sugar, a pinch of Accent or similar season-
> ing, 1/3 cup water, 2 T white vinegar, several shakes of
> Worcestershire sauce

Combine in a small bowl and set aside.

Vegetables:

> 1 pound cabbage, 1/2 Bermuda (or any kind) onion, 1 red or
> green pepper, 1 cup canned drained mushrooms

Slice the cabbage very thin—no more than 1/4 inch—and set aside in a bowl. Slice the onions very thin and add to the cabbage. Cut the pepper into thin strips and put in a small bowl. Add the mushrooms, and set aside.

Preheat a large frying skillet. Add 2 T oil to coat the pan. Heat on medium heat until the oil sizzles a bit. Add the cabbage/onion and stir-fry for 2 minutes. Stir in the pepper/mushrooms and stir-fry 1 minute. Add the soy sauce mixture. Reduce heat to medium low. Cover the pan and cook about 5 minutes. Shake the pan occasionally to keep the mixture moving. Serve immediately.

Sauces

– Alden's Brandy Sauce –

Former camp chef Joe Plumstead: "This is great for bread pudding, fruit salad, or pancakes."

**2 1/2 cups sour cream, 1/4 cup honey, 1/4 cup brandy, juice of 2
lemons, 1/2 cup brown sugar**
In a bowl, mix thoroughly. Serve warm or at room temperature.

– The Birches Honey Poppy Seed Dressing –

**1 1/2 cups olive oil, 1 cup honey, 1/2 cup white wine vinegar,
3 large tsp. poppy seeds, 3 large tsp. grated onion, 1 tsp. salt**
Mix everything together in a bowl or shake together in a bottle with a lid.

– Cobb's Sweet and Sour Sauce –

Gary Cobb: "There's just something about the experience of being here at Pierce Pond
Camps that occupies a special place in the hearts of people who keep coming back. Even
with our older guests, it's amazing how much better they look physically after they've been
at camp a few days. I think a lot of it comes from the fact that there's been very little
change over the years. We had a fellow in recently who had been a regular for thirty years,
wasn't here for thirty years, and then came back. The view was the same, there was nothing
radically changed—and he was so pleased. That's what's really at the heart of this place."

**1 1/2 cups vegetable oil, 4 cans pineapple chunks (with juice),
1 1/2 cups soy sauce, 1 1/2 cups cider vinegar, 1 T Worcestershire
sauce, 1 cup sugar, salt and pepper to taste, 2 green peppers
chopped, 2 cans water chestnuts, 1/4 cup chili sauce, 1 tsp.
ginger, 1/4 cup orange juice**
In a saucepan, combine all ingredients and cook gently until warmed
through. You can add chunks of poultry or pork to the sauce, or serve
meat/poultry whole and pour sauce over it. Serve with rice.

– West Branch Pond Chocolate Sauce –

Carol Kealiher: "Use the best chocolate chips you can find for this. It's so good, you may want to double it right off."

1 cup semisweet chocolate chips, $^1/_2$ cup light corn syrup,
$^1/_4$ cup half-and-half (*or* canned or whole milk)

In a small saucepan, melt the chips with the corn syrup over low heat. Stir in the half-and-half (or milk) and mix well. Serve warm. Makes 1$^1/_3$ cups.

Desserts

– Alice's Apricot-Almond Cookies –

This recipe came about because, ages ago, I had a bag of apricots and some almond paste and decided to create a cookie using both. The result was so successful it's been a Christmas cookie regular ever since. This is definitely a fun, social, hands-on project. I have always used a Kitchen-Aid–type mixer, but a food processor might work too. These cookies also keep and ship well if you're sending off a care package.

> **6 T butter softened, 1 "log" almond paste, 1/2 cup brown sugar, 1 1/4 cups flour, 1/2 tsp. baking soda, 1/2 tsp. vanilla, 36 to 40 good-quality dried apricot halves**

Combine all ingredients except apricots in a mixer and blend together well. Turn the dough out onto a piece of wax paper, form into a ball, flatten slightly, wrap up, and refrigerate overnight.

Remove the dough from the refrigerator (if doing this on your own, start with half the dough and keep the rest chilled). Pinch off a chunk about the size of a large marble and gently squeeze it flat until it's a bit larger than a silver dollar. Place an apricot in the middle of the dough and fold the dough around it, squeezing the "seams" together so you have a smooth little dough packet with an apricot inside. You want an even enclosure of the apricot—pinch off excess dough or add more if necessary. (Hint: Work quickly with the tips of your fingers. If the dough gets sticky, dip fingertips in a bit of flour and proceed.)

Place cookies on cookie sheet (they can be 3 to 4 across because they don't expand much) and bake at 350° for 8 to 10 minutes. Makes about 3 dozen cookies.

Happy holidays!

– Bear Spring Eggless Chocolate Cake with Peanut Butter Frosting –

Cook Edward Pearl Sr.: "This is a popular flavor combination most folks enjoy."

Cake:
>1 2/3 cups flour, 1 cup sugar, 1/2 cup unsweetened cocoa, 1 tsp. baking soda, 1/2 tsp. salt, 1 cup buttermilk or sour milk, 1/2 cup melted margarine or butter, 1 1/2 tsp. vanilla

Sift the first five ingredients together into a bowl. Beat in the wet ingredients until the batter is smooth. Spread in a 9 x 13-inch buttered and floured baking pan. Bake at 375° for 30 minutes. Cool and frost with Peanut Butter Frosting.

Peanut Butter Frosting:
>1 pound confectioners' sugar, 2 cups smooth or chunky peanut butter, 1 tsp. vanilla, 1 1/4 to 1 1/2 cups milk

Mix all ingredients together in a bowl until the frosting is of spreadable consistency. The amount of milk you use will depend on the weather; the more moisture in the air, the less milk you'll have to use. Spread the frosting on the cooled cake and serve.

– Bosebuck's Nut and Raisin Cake –

Diane Schyberg: "A guide named Perley Flint and his business partner built Bosebuck Camps in 1910. Mina was Perley's wife, and this is her recipe. Their daughter Gete (short for Marguerite) owned the camps from the forties through the early sixties. There's so much tradition and history at these places. We wanted to hear some of the old stories, and we were lucky to meet Gete the year before she died. She even gave us a real taste of the old days by passing along this recipe, which she said was Mina's favorite cake. It's wonderful anytime, of course, but is really helpful in the winter if you're far from a store and fresh produce, because you can use dried fruit."

>1 cup sugar, 1 cup shortening, 1 egg, 2 cups flour, 1 tsp. baking soda, 1 tsp. salt, 1 cup sour milk, 1 tsp. vanilla, 1 cup chopped walnuts, 1 cup raisins (or any favorite dried fruit or dried fruit mixture)

(If you don't have sour milk, mix 1 cup regular milk with 1/2 tsp. lemon juice and set aside for 5 minutes.)

Cream the sugar and shortening together until fluffy. Add the egg and beat until mixed. Sift together the flour, baking soda, and salt. Add a third of the flour mixture to the egg mixture along with a third of the sour milk, and beat until mixed together. Add additional flour and milk, a third at a time, beating well after each addition. Beating in vanilla with last flour/milk addition. Fold in nuts and dried fruit.

Pour into a 9 x 9-inch (or 7 x 10 $1/2$-inch or 8 x 11 $1/2$-inch) greased pan. Bake at 350° for about 35 minutes, until top is nicely browned and cake starts to pull away slightly from the sides. Yields 9 to 12 pieces.

– Bradford's Dark Star Cupcakes –

Preheat oven to 375°. Line muffin tins with cupcake papers.

Filling:

8 ounces cream cheese (room temperature), 1 egg, $1/3$ cup sugar, $1/8$ tsp. salt, 1 cup semisweet chocolate chips

Blend the first four ingredients with a wooden spoon. Fold in the chocolate chips and set aside.

Batter:

1 $1/2$ cups flour, 1 cup sugar, $1/4$ cup unsweetened cocoa, 1 tsp. baking soda, $1/2$ tsp. salt, 1 cup water, $1/3$ cup vegetable oil, 1 T white vinegar, 1 tsp. vanilla

In another bowl, combine the dry ingredients and mix well. Add the remaining ingredients and blend thoroughly. Fill the cupcake papers three quarters full with batter. Drop 1 heaping T of filling into the center of each cupcake. Bake 35 to 40 minutes.

– Cobb's Rob Roy Cookies –

Betty Cobb: "Gary's mother, Maud, always made these, and they're delicious."

$1/4$ cup milk, 1 tsp. white vinegar (or lemon), $3/4$ tsp. baking soda, 1 cup margarine, $1/2$ tsp. each cinnamon and cloves, 1 $1/2$ cups brown sugar, 2 beaten eggs, 1 $1/2$ cups dry oatmeal, 2 cups flour, $1/2$ cup raisins, 1 cup nuts

In a small bowl, sour the milk by mixing in the vinegar (or lemon). Add the baking soda.

In a large bowl, cream margarine, spices, and sugar together. Add eggs and stir until well blended. Stir in oatmeal and flour and sour milk and mix thoroughly. Stir in raisins and nuts.

Drop by spoonfuls onto greased cookie sheets and bake at 325° for 10 to 12 minutes or until golden.

– Cobb's Sunday Brownies –

Betty Cobb: "We serve these brownies with ice cream and chocolate sauce every Sunday night during the season."

Brownies:

10 eggs, 6 cups granulated sugar, 3 cups melted margarine or butter, 2 tsp. vanilla, 2 cups unsweetened cocoa, 4 cups flour, 3 tsp. baking powder, 2 cups walnuts

Beat the eggs in a large bowl. Add the sugar, margarine/butter, vanilla, and cocoa. Sift in the flour and baking powder. Fold in the walnuts and pour into two 11 1/2 x 17-inch pans. Bake at 350° for approximately 25 minutes. Serve with Cobb's Chocolate Sauce.

Cobb's Chocolate Sauce:

4 squares unsweetened chocolate, 2 sticks butter or margarine, 1 1/3 cups evaporated canned milk, 4 cups confectioners' sugar, 1/4 tsp. salt, 2 tsp. vanilla

Melt chocolate and butter/margarine in a double boiler. Add the milk, sugar, and salt. Stir thoroughly with whisk and add the vanilla when sauce is thickened. Makes 4 cups.

– Grant's Boston Cream Pie –

Joy Russell, pastry cook: "I've experimented with this. The cake itself was originally a chocolate cake recipe I liked because it is moist. What I serve doesn't look like the typical Boston cream pie with the filling in the middle and a chocolate frosting on top. I have one layer of cake on the bottom, spread the filling on top of that, and when I'm ready to serve, I'll slice the cake, put a spoonful of the chocolate frosting on top of each slice, and it sort of spreads out down the sides."

The cake portion of the recipe makes 3 layers, so you will have 2 extras, if you follow Joy's example and use just 1 cake layer—or 1 extra, if you prefer your Boston Cream Pie with 2 layers of cake. You can either save the extra cake for another use, or make more of the filling and frosting. (The quantities given below will fill/frost 1 cake layer.)

Cake:

4 cups sugar, 1 1/3 cups oil, 4 tsp. baking powder, 2 tsp. salt, 6 cups flour, 1/2 cup cider vinegar, 4 cups water, 4 tsp. vanilla

Simply mix all the ingredients together in a big bowl until well blended. Pour into three 10-inch-round greased and floured cake pans and bake at 350° for 25 to 30 minutes, or until a toothpick inserted in the center of the cakes comes out clean. Cool on rack and invert.

Cream Filling:

1 (3 1/2-ounce) package of instant French vanilla pudding, 1 cup milk, 2 cups heavy cream

In a bowl, mix pudding and milk. Whip the cream and add to the pudding. Smooth on top of the cake and refrigerate.

Frosting:

1/2 cup canned condensed milk, 1 cup chocolate chips, 1 cup confectioners' sugar

In a saucepan, heat the milk and add the chocolate. Stir until melted and stir in the sugar until the mixture is smooth. Set aside until mixture thickens. Spoon on top of the filling.

– Katahdin Lake Spicy Hermits –

Al Cooper: "We've been so lucky to raise our family and live out our dream here at Katahdin Lake." Suzan Cooper: "As time marches on, sporting camps have a sense of timelessness about them. Quiet and secluded wilderness camps ought to be preserved; they are living, working reminders of the way life used to be."

3/4 cup shortening, 1/2 cup dark brown sugar, 1/2 cup white sugar, 1 cup molasses, 2 eggs, 1 tsp. vanilla, 3 1/2 cups flour, 1 tsp. baking soda, 1/2 tsp. salt, 1 tsp. each ground cinnamon, nutmeg, ginger, cloves

Cream together the shortening, sugars, and molasses. Add beaten eggs and vanilla. Sift remaining ingredients together and add to the creamed mixture. The batter will be stiff. Spoon and flatten into a greased 9 x 13 x 2-inch pan. Bake in a 350° oven for 20 to 30 minutes. Slice into squares when slightly cooled.

– King and Bartlett's Poached Dried Fruit –

Former camp cook Karen Bishop: "Winter in the deep woods leaves us with little access to fresh berries. This is a wonderful alternative. I serve it with pound cake and good-quality vanilla ice cream. For the four dried fruits, I usually use cranberries, blueberries, cherries, and pears, if I have them."

> 2 cups (plus) white wine (either Chardonnay or Riesling is good), $1/4$ cup sugar, 2 tsp. anise seed, zest of 1 lemon (in strips, with pith removed), $1/2$ pound each of 4 favorite dried fruits

In a large saucepan, combine 2 cups wine with all the other ingredients and simmer, covered, for 20 minutes. Check and stir often, adding more wine if mixture becomes too thick. Pour into a bowl, remove strips of lemon zest, and refrigerate. Serves 12 easily.

– Lakewood's Trailside Cookies –

Robin Carter: "Lakewood Camps turned 150 in 2003, and our family is only the sixth owner in all that time. That's one of the main things that appealed to us. My husband, Bill, came up here to the Rangeley Lakes with his parents when he was a boy. He and I got a cabin and started coming up to the area years ago, so we were able to share the experience with our two daughters and son, Whitney, who helps us run the place with his wife, Maureen.

"Bill retired from the ministry after thirty-five years, and we started looking into running this place as we turned sixty. People told us we were crazy, but all those earlier strands weave together, and suddenly you find yourself in a place that feels like home. We looked at Lakewood two days before September 11; it was nice to know there are still places where people can feel safe and things stay the same."

> $1 3/4$ cups flour, 1 tsp. baking soda, $1/2$ tsp. salt, $1/2$ cup margarine, $1/2$ cup chunky peanut butter, 1 cup sugar, 1 cup brown sugar, 2 eggs, $1/4$ cup milk, 1 tsp. vanilla, $2 1/2$ cups rolled oats, 1 cup chocolate chips, 1 cup raisins

Sift together the first three ingredients. In a bowl, cream together the next four ingredients. Beat the next three ingredients into the creamed mixture and then add the flour mixture, stirring well to combine. Add the last three ingredients and stir well. Drop by spoonful onto greased cookie sheets and bake in a 350° oven for 8 to 10 minutes or until light golden.

– Maynard's Gingersnaps –

Gail Maynard: "Every winter we hope for a good snowfall. My husband, Bill, plows driveways to help tide us over during the off-season.

"This recipe was given to me by one of our guests. I think it's Bill's favorite cookie. It's quick and easy, and it can be refrigerated so it's always on hand—which helps!"

> $3/4$ cup vegetable shortening or margarine, 1 cup dark brown sugar, $1/4$ cup molasses, 1 egg, $2 1/4$ cups flour, 2 tsp. baking soda, $1/2$ tsp. salt, 1 tsp. ground ginger, 1 tsp. ground cinnamon, $1/2$ tsp. ground cloves

Cream the first four ingredients until fluffy. Sift the dry ingredients together and stir into the molasses mixture. Form into small balls (big marble sized). Roll in granulated sugar. Place 2 inches apart on a greased cookie sheet and bake in a 375° oven for approximately 10 minutes. Makes about 4 dozen.

– Moose Point Sugar and Spice Cookies –

Kathy McGough, camp cook: "These are so popular, I make them once a week."

> $3/4$ cup margarine, 1 cup sugar, 1 egg, $1/4$ cup molasses, 2 cups flour, 2 tsp. baking soda, $1/4$ tsp. salt, 1 tsp. cinnamon, $3/4$ tsp. ginger, confectioners' sugar

Mix together the first four ingredients. Sift together everything else except the confectioners' sugar. Mix the dry and wet ingredients together and drop by teaspoonfuls onto a greased baking sheet (I make the cookies small, about 2 inches wide when baked). Bake at 375° for about 8 minutes.

In a 9 x 13-inch pan, sprinkle enough confectioners' sugar to cover the bottom well. As you remove the cookies from the oven, use a spatula to place them, still hot, in the confectioners' sugar, coating both sides. Place on cookie racks to cool.

– Nicatous Lodge Peanut Butter Pie –

A Heritage Recipe from Chris Norris.

> 8 ounces cream cheese, 2 cups confectioners' sugar, 2/3 cup
> creamy peanut butter, 1/2 cup milk, 9 ounces dairy whip,
> 9-inch prepared graham-cracker crust, crushed peanuts,
> chocolate syrup

In a bowl, whip cream cheese until soft and fluffy; add the sugar and peanut butter. Gradually add the milk and fold in the dairy whip. Pour into a
9-inch pie pan with a prepared graham-cracker crust. Freeze the pie.

When ready to serve, let it sit out of the freezer briefly and cut into
6 pieces. Sprinkle each piece with crushed peanuts, if desired, and the
desired amount of chocolate syrup. Serves 6.

– The Pines Peanut Butter Fudge –

Nancy Norris: "If you use an eighteen-ounce jar of peanut butter and double the rest of the
ingredients, it will make up into an amount that will fit in a nine-by-thirteen-inch pan."

> 3 cups white sugar, 1 cup canned evaporated milk, 1/2 cup
> marshmallow fluff, 1 cup smooth peanut butter, 2 tsp. vanilla,
> 1/2 cup chopped walnuts (if desired)

In a large saucepan, boil sugar and milk together to soft-ball stage. (Take a
bit and drop it in a glass of cold water. If it forms a soft ball, it's ready. This
takes approximately 7 minutes of boiling time.) Remove from the heat and
add remaining ingredients. Beat with a wooden spoon until mixture starts
to thicken. Pour into a 9 x 9-inch pan that has been lined with aluminum
foil. Allow to cool slightly; lift out onto a cutting board and cut into
squares. Yields 16 squares.

– Pleasant Point Steamed Chocolate Pudding –

Mardi George: "This is Clif's favorite, and I like to make it for him on those lazy winter
afternoons when the wind is howling down Fourth Debsconeag Lake."

*Because the sauce contains raw egg, you may want to make it immediately before serv-
ing. Keep any leftover sauce in the refrigerator.*

> 3 T butter, 2/3 cup sugar, 1 beaten egg, 2 squares unsweetened
> chocolate melted, 1 3/4 cups flour, 1/4 tsp. salt, 3 tsp. baking
> powder, 1 cup milk

In a bowl, cream the butter and sugar. Add the egg and beat vigorously. Add the melted chocolate and mix well. Sift the dry ingredients together and add alternately with the milk, mixing thoroughly after each addition. Fill a greased mold two-thirds full. Top with a piece of wax paper and cover. (Or use a 1-pound coffee can, covering the top with wax paper and then aluminum foil held on with a rubber band.)

Place in a pan (with a cover) slightly larger than mold/can, and pour in boiling water to come two-thirds of the way up the side of the mold/can. Cover and steam over low heat for 2 hours (checking the water level). Remove from water bath, unmold, and top with Sunshine Sauce.

Sunshine Sauce:

> 1 egg yolk, 1/4 cup sugar, 1 egg white, 1/4 cup sugar,
> 1 tsp. vanilla, 1 cup heavy cream

Beat the egg yolk and add 1/4 cup sugar slowly, beating all the time. In another bowl, beat the egg white until soft peaks form. Add 1/4 cup sugar and continue beating until stiff peaks form. Fold the egg yolk mixture into the egg white mixture. Stir in the vanilla. Just before you are ready to serve, whip the cream and fold it into the topping.

– Red River Extraordinary Cookies –

Mike Brophy: "After the bear, bird, and deer seasons, I may stay in and do a little trapping. I used to trap for pine marten and fisher. Now that the state has bought up this township, they've made it easier to get in and out of here. We used to come in by way of a road near the Canadian border (only twenty miles away). To give you an idea, that was a twenty-two-mile road and it took us two hours to get in here. . . .

"When I want a change of pace from our delicious peanut butter cookies, I'll add some chocolate chips and salted nuts to the basic recipe. Definitely not your ordinary cookie!"

> 1 1/2 cups creamy peanut butter, 1 cup vegetable shortening or
> margarine, 2 1/2 cups brown sugar, 6 T milk, 2 T vanilla, 2 eggs,
> 3 1/2 cups flour, 3/4 tsp. salt, 1 1/2 tsp. baking soda, 3/4 cup choco-
> late chips, 3/4 cup salted skinless peanuts coarsely chopped

In a big bowl, cream peanut butter, shortening, and sugar together. Add remaining ingredients and stir well. The dough should be the consistency of Play-Doh. If it isn't, add a bit more flour (otherwise the cookie will be flat). Drop by tablespoonfuls on ungreased cookie sheets, flatten with a fork, and bake at 375° for 7 to 8 minutes.

– Rideout's Graham-Cracker Pie Crusts –

Jami Lorigan: "We use this as an easy reference guide. It helps when fifty things are going on at the same time and your mind is on overload."

# pies	crumbs	sugar	butter or margarine
1	1 1/2 cups	2 T	3/4 stick (6 T)
2	3 cups	1/4 cup	1 1/2 sticks (3/4 cup)
3	4 1/2 cups	6 T	2 1/4 sticks (1 cup plus 2 T)
4	6 cups	1/2 cup	3 sticks (1 1/2 cups)
6	9 cups	3/4 cup	4 1/2 sticks (1 pound plus 1/2 stick)
8	12 cups	1 cup	6 sticks (1 1/2 pounds)

– Rideout's Peanut Butter Pie –

8 ounces cream cheese softened, 1 cup powdered sugar, 1/2 cup smooth peanut butter, 1/2 cup milk, 8 ounces dairy whip, 1/4 cup nuts, 1/4 cup chocolate chips

In a bowl or mixer, beat the cream cheese until it's fluffy. Mix in the sugar and peanut butter. Slowly add cold milk and mix well. Fold in the dairy whip and pour into a prepared graham-cracker crust. Sprinkle with nuts or chocolate chips if desired, and place in the freezer. Freeze until firm. Let sit a moment or two at room temperature when ready to eat.

– Tim Pond Pecan Pie –

1 cup dark Karo syrup, 1/2 cup sugar, 3 T butter, 3 eggs, 1 tsp.
vanilla, pinch of salt, 1 cup cut-up pecans, 1 T flour, 1 T sugar,
unbaked 8-inch pie crust

In a medium saucepan, combine Karo syrup and sugar and bring to a boil.
Remove from the heat and add the butter. Add the eggs and beat well.
Add the vanilla, salt, and pecans and stir together. Mix together the flour
and sugar and sprinkle it into the bottom of the prepared pie crust. Pour
the pecan mixture into the pie shell and bake at 350° for 45 minutes.

– Wilderness Island Hawaiian Delight –

Mike LaRosa: "We do a lot of dinner business during our season. For several years we
offered an international buffet every Sunday: Mexican, Spanish, Hawaiian—which someone told me was crazy. 'How can you have a Hawaiian buffet in the middle of the north
Maine woods?!' But we did it. And it worked. We dressed in Hawaiian shirts and pants, had
straw hats on. We decorated the whole main lodge with Hawaiian paraphernalia. We just
had a ball with it! We'll cook Chinese, Italian, Arabic—whatever you want. If we don't know
how to cook it now, we'll know by the time you get here!"

1 box vanilla wafers, 1 large (or 2 regular) size boxes coconut
cream pudding, 1/2 pint heavy cream, 1 can crushed pineapple,
1 jar cherries, 1/2 cup chopped walnuts, 1/2 cup shredded
coconut

Crumble half the vanilla wafer cookies in the bottom of a 10 x 13-inch
pan. Press down, and pour cooked and cooled pudding over the crumbs.
Refrigerate until set.

Beat the cream, sweetened to taste, and add drained crushed
pineapple, drained and chopped cherries, nuts, and coconut, and spread
over the cold pudding. Sprinkle with the remaining crushed cookies and
refrigerate.

Miscellaneous

– Eagle Lodge Hot Ginger Tea –

Tami Rogers: "Ginger tea and trimming the tree at Christmas is a nice tradition. Ginger has a heartwarming quality that goes with the loving environment of family and friends gathered during the holiday season."

1 large knob fresh ginger, 1 lemon, 8 to 10 whole cloves, 4 cups water, 1 stick cinnamon, 3/4 cup firmly packed brown sugar or 1/2 cup honey

Slice the ginger and the lemon and stick the cloves into 6 pieces of lemon. In a saucepan, combine ginger, lemon, cloves, water, and cinnamon, and bring to a boil. Decrease heat and simmer for 15 to 20 minutes. Sweeten with brown sugar/honey (and add more water if it's too strong for your taste). Strain and serve hot.

– Harrison's Winter Critter Protection –

Fran Harrison: "Every year when we leave camp, we put each set of bedding into a bag with a sheet of fabric softener, which prevents it from being chewed at in the winter. To deal with some of the mice, we take five-gallon buckets and put a little peanut butter halfway down the side and water with bleach a third of the way up. The water/bleach combination kills the mice as quickly and humanely as possible."

– Jalbert's Snow Cave –

Phyllis Jalbert: "We began our winter camping in 1988. In 1992, we started the next phase, which was taking off from the camps on foot—no snow machine backups, no dogs—using only human-powered toboggans specially created by our longtime Maine Guide, Dana Shaw. We pull the sleds four miles along the Allagash River to our tent site. The next day, we go four miles above that and stay in our outback cabin. Then we'll go two more miles and swing back and stay at the tent site again; the last day, we return to the camps.

"We have a cook tent set up at the tent site, and we have made-to-order cotton sleeping tents (which help prevent freezing condensation inside). The trick is to layer up so you don't get too overheated and perspire, because that moisture will freeze—and so will you. It's so beautiful here in winter, but you have to have respect for the elements. Here's a life-saving outdoor winter 'recipe.'"

First, this assumes there's snow! Using a snowshoe or a shovel, heap up an elongated mound of snow about 10 x 7 feet long and about 4 to 5 feet high. As you heap the snow on, really pack it down with your shovel/snowshoe. The weight of the snow will keep pushing it down and the snow will settle. When it's set, in about 2 hours, you can just dig out your snow cave. Be careful not to dig too close to the outside, or it will collapse. Keep about a foot of snow all the way around. You do this by taking some foot-long twigs and sticking them into the top and sides. That way, when you come to the twig inside, you know to stop digging.

The secret is to make the opening very small, just enough to crawl down into. And make the inside just big enough so you can turn over and move around some, but not so large that your body heat can escape. When you're in there, it actually warms up to a little below freezing. Even if the temperature outside is ten to twenty below, it doesn't matter—you should be able to make it safely through the night.

– Katahdin Lake Spiced Cider –

Suzan Cooper: "In winter, Baxter Park's loop road is closed, which means people cross-country ski (or hire a ski plane) to get in here."

Al Cooper: "We find sweets are a big thing here in fall and winter, because, boy, you're working like crazy: hunting; cutting, hauling, splitting wood; feeding the mules and horses; trying to stay warm." Suzan: "So this spiced cider is wonderful. It warms you, even more than tea, because it has more calories and is sweeter."

Al: "We buy honey in five-gallon pails and go through forty to fifty pounds of it a year. (We don't have hives, since we'd have to put them up on telescoping poles or something to keep them out of reach of the bears.) We get the raw, unprocessed kind. Honey crystallizes rapidly, and you can cut it up with a knife."

Suzan: "I make gallons and gallons of spiced cider for a fall/winter energy boost."

1 quart apple cider, 1 quart cranberry juice, juice of 1 lemon,
1 T whole cloves, 2 cinnamon sticks, 1 T whole allspice,
1/3 cup honey (or brown sugar)

Put the spices in a square of cheesecloth and tie with a loop for ease of removal. Combine all the ingredients in a large pot or kettle and bring to a boil. Lower the heat and simmer for 15 minutes. Remove the spices and serve. Serves 8.

– Mount Chase Lodge Burnt-Pan Cleaner –

Sara Hill: "I think every cook has had to deal with a burnt pan. When you do, just take a fabric softener sheet, put it in the pan, and soak that overnight. It's gross because the burnt stuff attaches to the sheet, but it works! Just wipe it off."

– The Pines Homemade Sweetened Condensed Milk –

Nancy Norris: "When you're miles away from the nearest store (which goes for most of us in the sporting-camp business), it's always helpful to have a 'fallback' recipe for some basic item."

1/2 cup boiling water, 3 T butter, 1/2 cup granulated sugar,
1 1/3 cups instant dried milk powder

Place all the ingredients in a blender. Blend briefly and scrape down sides. Blend until completely smooth (about 30 seconds to a minute).

Resources

Several Maine-made products are featured in this book. Big chains (including health-food stores) may not be helpful in ordering these items, but I've found that smaller provisioners are very accommodating, or you can simply contact the manufacturers yourself:

Bakewell Cream (a leavening agent for baking), Apple Ledge Company, RFD 2, Box 6640, East Holden, ME 04429

Mos-Ness (French dressing), Schlotterbeck and Foss Co., 117 Preble Street, Portland, ME 04101; (207) 772–4666

Ployes (French Acadian buckwheat pancake/flat bread mix), Bouchard Family Farm, RR 2, Box 2690, Fort Kent, ME 04743; (207) 834–3237

OTHER CONTACTS

Maine Sporting Camp Association: www.mainesportingcamps.com
Maine Dept. of Inland Fisheries and Wildlife: www.mefishwildlife.com

FOR FURTHER READING

If you are interested in learning more about sporting camps, and perhaps visiting one, I have written the only sporting-camp guide on the market for your reference and enjoyment. *Maine Sporting Camps* (Third Edition, Countryman Press, 2003) includes the American Plan camps featured in this book, in addition to Housekeeping Plan camps (for a total of 96 sporting camps).

Maine Sporting Camps also includes maps, travel directions, interviews with sporting-camp owners, and an extensive selection of further reading suggestions. It's a wonderful companion to the cookbook!

Also, my biography of wilderness writer Louise Dickinson Rich—*She Took to the Woods*—takes an in-depth look at what it was like to live deep in the woods during the 1930s and '40s. Louise wrote her beloved classic, *We Took to the Woods,* while living just two miles away from Lakewood Camps, featured in this book.

All three of these books are available at bookstores or from Down East Books (www.downeastbooks.com or 1-800-766-1670).

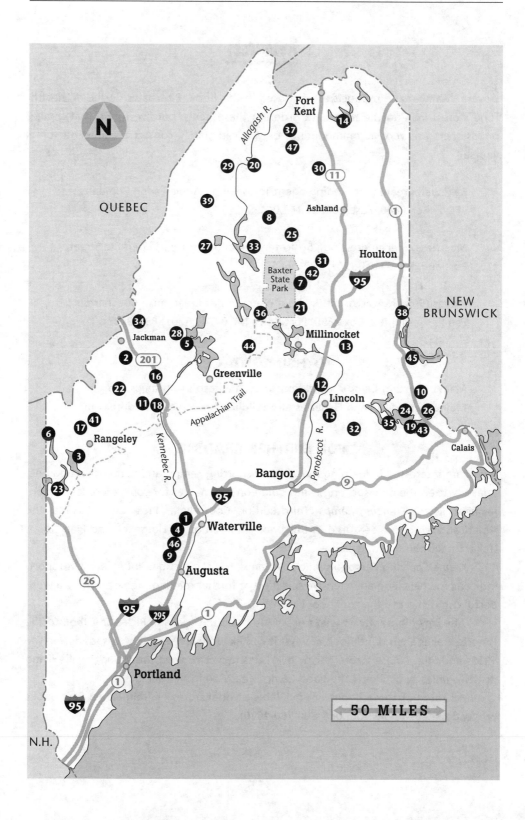

Camps Featured

Here are the contacts for the sporting camps as of the time I did my research. Every year people retire and camps get sold, however, so some camps may be in new ownership by the time you read this. You can verify any information at the Maine Sporting Camp Association's Web site at www.mainesportingcamps.com.

1. Alden Camps: Martha and Carter Minkel, RFD 2, Box 1140, Oakland, ME 04963; (207) 465–7703; info@aldencamps.com, www.aldencamps.com

2. Attean Lake Lodge: Andrea and Brad Holden, P.O. Box 457, Jackman, ME 04945; (207) 668–3792; info@atteanlodge.com, www.atteanlodge.com

3. Bald Mountain Camps: Ferlyn and Stephen Philbrick, P.O. Box 332, Oquossoc, ME 04964; (207) 864–3671; baldmtcamp@aol.com, www.baldmountaincamps.com

4. Bear Spring Camps: Peg and Ron Churchill, RR 3, Box 9900, Oakland, ME 04963; (207) 397–2341; church@tdstelme.net

5. The Birches Resort: John Willard, Box 81–SC, Rockwood, ME 04478; (207) 534–7305 or (800) 825–9453; wwld@aol.com, www.birches.com

6. Bosebuck Mountain Camps: Diane and Bob Schyberg, P.O. Box 1213, Rangeley, ME 04970; (207) 446–2825; bosebuck@aol.com, www.bosebuck.com

7. Bowlin Camps: Ken Conaster, P.O. Box 251, Patten, ME 04765; (207) 528–2022; bowlincamps@ainop.com, www.bowlincamps.com

8. Bradford Camps: Karen and Igor Sikorsky, Box 729, Ashland, ME 04732; (207) 746–7777, winter: (207) 439–6364; maine@bradfordcamps.com, www.bradfordcamps.com

9. Castle Island Camps: Rhonda and John Rice, P.O. Box 251, Belgrade Lakes, ME 04918; (207) 495–3312; www.castleisland.com

10. Chet's Camps: Sue and Al LaPlante, HCR 78, Box 5, Princeton, ME 04668; (207) 796–5557; al_laplante@msn.com, www.chetscamps.com

11. Cobb's Pierce Pond Camps: Betty and Gary Cobb, P.O. Box 124–SC, North New Portland, ME 04961; (207) 628–2819, winter: (207) 628–3612; gbcobb@tdstelme.net

12. Dad's Camps: Therese Thibodeau, P.O. Box 142, West Enfield, ME 04493; (207) 732–5309; dadscamps@hotmail.com, www.dadscamps.com

13. Deer Run Sporting Camps: Edith McGovern, Darlene and Robert Berry, 385 Aroostook Road, Molunkus, ME 04459; (207) 765–3900, fax: (207) 765–2400; deerruncamps@gwi.net

14. Eagle Lake Camps: Paula and Ed Clark, P.O. Box 377, Eagle Lake, ME 04739; (207) 752–0556; EdwEClark@aol.com, www.eaglelakesportingcamps.com

15. Eagle Lodge and Camps: Justin and Loraine Guardino Morse (former owners: Tami and John Rogers), P.O. Box 686, Lincoln, ME 04457; (207) 794–2181; www.eaglelodgemaine.com

16. Enchanted Outfitters and Lodge: Gloria Hewey and Craig Hallock, HCR 63, Box 134, West Forks, ME 04985; (207) 663–2238; enchantedoutfitters@prexar.com, www.enchantedoutfitters.com

17. Grant's Kennebago Camps: Carolyn and John Blunt, P.O. Box 786, Rangeley, ME 04970; (800) 633–4815; grants@rangeley.org; winter: grantscamps@midmaine.com, www.grantscamps.com

18. Harrison's Pierce Pond Camps: Fran and Tim Harrison, P.O. Box 315, Bingham, ME 04920; (207) 672–3625, winter: (603) 524–5060

19. Indian Rock Camps: JoAnne and Ken Cannell, P.O. Box 117, Grand Lake Stream, ME 04637; (800) 498–2821 or (207) 796–2822; indianrockcamp@nemaine.com, www.indianrockcamps.com

20. (Willard) Jalbert Camps: Box 312–SC, State Street, Brooklyn, NY 11201; (718) 858–4496, riverat@rcn.com

21. Katahdin Lake Wilderness Camps: Suzan and Al Cooper, Box 398, Millinocket, ME 04462; (207) 723–4050, winter: (207) 723–9867; t3r8lake@ime.net, www.katahdinlakecamps.com

22. King and Bartlett Camps: Cathy and Jeff Charles, P.O. Box 4, Eustis, ME 04936; (207) 243–2956; info@kingandbartlett.com, www.kingandbartlett.com

23. Lakewood Camps: Whit, Maureen, Bill, and Robin Carter, P.O. Box 1275, Rangeley, ME 04970; (207) 243–2959, winter: (207) 864–2082; lakewoodcamps@yahoo.com, www.lakewoodcamps.com

24. Leen's Lodge: Charles Driza, P.O. Box 40, Grand Lake Stream, ME 04637; (800) 99LEENS or (207) 796–2929; info@leenslodge.com, www.leenslodge.com

25. Libby Camps: Ellen and Matt Libby, P.O. Box 810, Ashland, ME 04732; (207) 435–8274; matt@libbycamps.com, www.libbycamps.com

26. Long Lake Camps: Sandra Smith and Doug Clements, P.O. Box 817, Princeton, ME 04668; (207) 796–2051; longlake@downeast.net, www.longlakecamps.com

27. Loon Lodge: Linda and Mike Yencha, P.O. Box 480, Millinocket, ME 04462; (207) 745–8168; relax@loonlodgemaine.com

28. Maynard's in Maine: Gail and Bill Maynard, P.O. Box 220, Rockwood, ME 04478; (207) 534–7703; gmaynards@hotmail.com, www.maynardsinmaine.com

29. McNally's Ross Stream Camps: Regina Webster and John Richardson, HC 76, Box 632, Greenville, ME 04441; (207) 944–5991; Richardson@starband.net, www.nugent-mcnallycamps.com

30. Moose Point Camps: Patricia Eltman and John Martin, P.O. Box 170, Portage, ME 04768; (207) 435–6156, winter: (207) 444–5556; www.moosepointcamps.com

31. Mount Chase Lodge: Sara and Rick Hill, RR 1, Box 281, Patten, ME 04765; (207) 528–2183; mtchaselodge@ainop.com, www.mtchaselodge.com

32. Nicatous Lodge: Linda and Ronald Sheldon, Box 100, Burlington, ME 04417; (207) 732–4771; nicatouslodge@starband.net, www.nicatouslodge.com

33. Nugent's Chamberlain Lakes Camp: Regina Webster and John Richardson, HC 76, Box 632, Greenville, ME 04441; (207) 944–5991; Richardson@starband.net, www.nugent-mcnallycamps.com

34. Penobscot Lake Lodge: Paul Fichtner, P.O. Box 359, Greenville Junction, ME 04442; penobscotlake@aol.com

35. The Pines: Nancy and Steve Norris, P.O. Box 158, Grand Lake Stream, ME 04637; (207) 557–7463, winter: (207) 825–4431; info@thepineslodge.com, www.thepineslodge.com

36. Pleasant Point Camps: Mardi and Clif George, P.O. Box 1505, Greenville, ME 04441; (207) 422–6826; Mardi@pleasantpointcamps.com, www.pleasantpointcamps.com

37. Red River Camps: Mike Brophy, P.O. Box 320, Portage, ME 04768; (207) 435–6000, winter: (207) 528–2259; redriver@intergate.com, www.redrivercamps.com

38. Rideout's Lakeside Lodge: Jami and Bob Lorigan Jr., RR 1, P.O. Box 64, East Grand Lake, Danforth, ME 04424; (800) 594–5391, info@rideouts.com, www.rideouts.com

39. Ross Lake Camps: Andrea Foley and Don Lavoie, P.O. Box 606, Clayton Lake, ME 04737; (207) 695–2821 (radio phone); www.rosslakecamps.com

40. South Branch Lake Camps: Cindy and Russ Aldridge, 1174 Cove Road, Seboeis, ME 04448; (207) 732–3446 or (800) 248–0554; sobranch@midmaine.com, www.southbranchlakecamps.com

41. Tim Pond Wilderness Camps: Betty and Harvey Calden, Box 22–SC, Eustis, ME 04936; (207) 243–2947, winter: (207) 897–4056; info@timpondcamps.com, www.timpondcamps.com

42. Wapiti Camps: Frank Ramelli, P.O. Box 340, Patten, ME 04765; (207) 528–2485; ifly@ainop.com

43. Weatherby's: Jeff McEvoy and Beth Rankin, P.O. Box 69, Grand Lake Steam, ME 04637; (207) 796–5558; info@weatherbys.com, www.weatherbys.com

44. West Branch Pond Camps: Carol Kealiher, P.O. Box 1153, Kokadjo, ME 04441; (207) 695–2561; info@westbranchpondcamps.com, www.westbranchpondcamps.com

45. Wheaton's Lodge and Camps: Jana and Dale Wheaton, HC 81, Box 120, Brookton, ME 04413; (207) 448–7723; wheatons1@hotmail.com, www.wheatonslodge.com

46. Whisperwood Lodge and Cottages: Candee and Doug McCafferty, Taylor Woods Road, Belgrade, ME 04917; (207) 465–3938; info@whisperwoodlodge.com, www.whisperwoodlodge.com

47. Wilderness Island Camps: Carol and Mike LaRosa, P.O. Box 220, Portage, ME 04768; (207) 435–6825; islandadventure@themainelink.com, www.islandadventureinmaine.com

Index